DATE DUE			
W MAY 5 1967			
FEB 1974			
GAYLORD 234			PRINTED IN U.S.A.

A Gift of Laughter

THE AUTOBIOGRAPHY OF

Allan Sherman

A Gift of Laughter

ATHENEUM PUBLISHERS

NEW YORK   1965

To Dee and Robbie and Nancy,
who came into my life one by one
with gifts of love and laughter

The things that happen in this book are true, as I remember them.

However, I have changed a few names where I felt I might hurt people's feelings or they might sue me.

Contents

1. A Yo-Yo on a Roller Coaster   3
2. The Drapes of Roth, and Other Things My Grandfather Pressed   16
3. Puberty Revisited, or Sex and the Single Me   52
4. Chug-a-Lugging, and Other Things I Learned in College   63
5. In Which I Go to New York to Seek Fame and Fortune and I Marry the Girl I Love and I Declare War on the Lincoln Hotel and If I Tell You Any More You Won't Need to Read This Chapter Altogether   81
6. Seven Years with the Wrong Income   95
7. Not So Nicely-Nicely   119
8. The Disorganization Man, or Up Madison Avenue with Goodson and Todman   123
9. The Four Faces of Freud   153
10. The Compleat Fun Person: Funny Songs, Cocktail Parties, Suburbia, and Other Noisy Symptoms of Desperation   168
11. And Now, As I Sink Slowly in the West . . .   191
12. One Fire and One Flood, and Go Easy on the Pestilence   214
13. You Can't Be Sure If It's Westinghouse   221

Contents

14. *Pluck and Luck, or Welcome Home, Horatio Alger* 243

15. *Allan in Wonderland* 250

16. *Now He Belongs to the Agents* 264

17. *I'll Never Forget What's-His-Name, or How It Feels to Be a Thrilling Celebrity* 270

18. *A Gift of Laughter* 306

  Index 325

A Gift of Laughter

CHAPTER 1

A Yo-Yo on a Roller Coaster

M Y LIFE has been a wild ride, up-and-down, up-and-down. I have always been a yo-yo on a roller coaster, and if I never quite fell off—if I've been able to hang on and enjoy the ride this far—it is because God gave me one shining thing, a gift of laughter. A sense of humor with which to laugh at myself and at trouble and at miscellaneous foolishness, and now and then to laugh at God himself, just to see if I still believe in him. It always turns out that I do.

So this is a funny book.

It is funny because *life* is funny, the human predicament is preposterous, and ridiculous things keep happening, and people act pompous and crazy sometimes, and Big Organizations are insane, and Great Institutions are nutty, and I learned to laugh very young because I *had* to. And in this book I have put down the things that made me laugh.

I say this is a funny book, and it is, and yet when I add up the things that happen in it—all of which are true—there are two divorces, four natural deaths, one accidental death, one suicide and a World War. In this true, funny book, I get expelled from college, arrested, fired from four jobs; I am raised during a world depression and later have seven years of total personal poverty during a world prosperity; I get rejected by both my parents and lie down beside four psychoanalysts; I live through a fire and a flood, and I get humiliated by girls and relatives and friends and executives more times than I can count.

A yo-yo on a roller coaster.

Up-and-down, up-and-down.

I guess the day I reached both the lowest low and the highest high was Monday, August 6, 1962.

That morning I picked up my weekly $55 unemployment check.

That night I recorded an album of crazy songs called *My Son, the Folk Singer,* and it became the fastest-selling record album of all time, and all of a sudden I was a Celebrity.

That's what this book is about. How I Became an Overnight Success in Only 38 Years.

Monday, August 6, 1962. I got up around ten o'clock that morning and stumbled sleepily into the lanai and plugged in the automatic coffee-maker and drank six or seven cups of automatic coffee. When I finally felt alive, I said good-bye to my wife and children and dog and I took the silver-gray Thunderbird and I drove out of Bel Air, down the beautiful curving mountain roads until I came to Sunset Boulevard, and through the UCLA campus in Westwood, and from Wilshire Boulevard to Santa Monica Boulevard, and there I parked the car in the parking space of the California Unemployment Bureau. In the parking lot there were Lincoln Continentals, Ferraris, Jaguars and Mercedes Benzes. I walked into the building and went into the main room and there was a long line of people and I got on the end of the line. You would be surprised at some of the famous people who were standing in line.

In Hollywood, we have some of the richest unemployed people in the world. They have sun tans. Some of them have chauffeurs in Rolls-Royces waiting outside. They have their golf clubs ready in the car. There is no law that says you can't play golf while being unemployed. Unfortunately, there *is* a law that says you can't send your chauffeur in to pick up the unemployment check. So you have to stand in line yourself and sign the receipt while your chauffeur is waiting in the car.

Let me tell you a lovely true story about my friend Harpo Marx. (Excuse me for name-dropping, but I am very impressed with the fact that Harpo Marx was my friend.)

At the time this happened, a few years ago, Harpo was semi-retired, working only four or five weeks a year, playing a few concerts and television guest appearances. He was living in Cathedral City, near Palm Springs, right on the Tamarisk Golf Course. In the summer when it got too hot in Palm Springs, Harpo would rent a house in Los Angeles. Mostly he would go to the Hillcrest Country Club and play golf, and then have lunch at the famous Round Table, where every day there gathered Jack Benny, George Burns, George Jessel, Eddie Cantor—the elder statesmen of comedy.

One day they were talking about unemployment payments, and it turned out that Harpo had never taken unemployment benefits, and they all jumped on him and said he was crazy.

Harpo said, "But I'm rich. I don't need the lousy money."

And they said, "Listen, idiot, you paid in a lot of money for so many years—there's no reason you shouldn't get that little

5

check every week. You're entitled. Besides, it's *tax-free* money."

This argument impressed Harpo, because in his bracket $55 tax free was like $500, but he still wasn't convinced. The members of the Round Table worked on him for weeks, and finally they persuaded him to be smart and take his unemployment payments, because, strictly speaking, he *was* out of work eleven months of the year. So he said, "All right. When I get back home to Cathedral City, I'll see about it."

So one morning Harpo got dressed up and got in *his* Thunderbird and drove to his nearest State Employment Office, which was in Indio, California.

Indio is a date-picking town. I mean the basic employment there is going around and picking dates off palm trees. The Indio Unemployment Office is not fancy, like the Hollywood Unemployment Office.

Harpo parked his Thunderbird among broken-down 1948 Chevrolets and Plymouth jalopies and Henry J's, and he walked into the room and it was full of grimy men in torn T-shirts and dungarees; Harpo was wearing a white suit made of Italian raw silk. He felt terrible. (You must realize that when you saw him without the Harpo costume and the Harpo makeup, what you saw was a sweet little bald-headed man; a very dignified gentleman with young, pixie eyes.)

So there he was, standing in line, and everybody was staring at him in his Italian suit and custom-made shoes and his beautiful tie and shirt. He was embarrassed, but he was determined to go through with it. When he got to the counter, he filled out the card and put down his real name, Adolph H. Marx. He gave them all the facts and said he was currently unemployed and showed that he was qualified for payments. They told him to come back in three weeks and his check would be ready. (During this period they process your data and also make sure you have looked for work.)

*   *   *

Three weeks passed, and Harpo drove to Indio again. But this time, to make sure he would not look out of place, he put on an old pair of blue jeans and a sport shirt, and he drove not *his* car, but his wife Susan's old Ford station wagon. He took his place in line, and he looked as much like a date-picker as everybody else. Finally he got to the counter and the lady took out his card and checked it as he gave his name, Adolph H. Marx, address: 7117 La Paz Avenue, Cathedral City, California.

The lady asked, "Have you had any work during the last three weeks?"

"Yes," he replied.

"How long did you work?"

"One day, ma'am."

"Just one day . . . *tsk, tsk, tsk* . . . and how much did you earn?"

Harpo said, "Eleven thousand, five hundred dollars."

The woman looked at him and said, "*Hmmm?*"

"I said, eleven thousand, five hundred dollars, ma'am."

She gave him a suspicious look and called out, "Gertrude, GERTRUDE . . . come here!"

And another lady came over and the first lady, Ethel, whispered something to Gertrude. Now Gertrude came to the window and said "Adolph H. Marx?"

"That's me," said Adolph H. Marx.

And Gertrude said, "Now. For your day's work, you received eleven dollars and fifty cents, isn't that right?"

And he said, "No, ma'am."

"How much, then?"

"Eleven thousand, five hundred dollars," he said.

"Just wait right here," she said. And she went away and came back with a third lady, Mildred. Mildred, who was the Head Lady, came cautiously to the window and started the whole interview over from the beginning; name, address, the whole thing, except she decided to humor him. Mildred said, "You say you worked *one da*y in the last three weeks and you made eleven thousand, five hundred dollars?" She smiled in a friendly way.

"That's right, ma'am," Harpo said, smiling back at her.

"I see. And *where did you work* that you made eleven thousand, five hundred dollars in one day?"

"Canada," Harpo said.

You've got to realize that saying "Canada" to a woman in that Godforsaken town of Indio, where the date-pickers never even get to Palm Springs, was like telling her he'd been to the moon.

She repeated it word for word, looking at him suspiciously.

"You say . . . you went to *Canada* . . . and you earned . . . eleven thousand, five hundred dollars in one day?"

"That's right," Harpo said.

"And *what did you do* in Canada to earn eleven thousand dollars in one day?"

At this Harpo could not resist showing her:

He flubbed his lips. He rolled his eyes. He whistled through his fingers. He made the Harpo face.

"That's what I did in Canada," Harpo said. "Then I shook some knives and forks out of my sleeve, and I cut off a girl's dress, and I held up a brassiere with three pockets."

Simultaneously, like three puppets yanked by one cord, Mildred, Gertrude and Ethel leaped back in horror.

Now they *knew* they had a madman on their hands.

Just then a date-picker strolled over, looked at Harpo, and said, "Hey, mister. I know you."

"Thank goodness," Harpo said, "*somebody* around here recognizes me."

The man said, "Sure—you're one of the Three Stooges!"

Harpo groaned.

Mildred asked him, "*Are* you in show business?"

Harpo said, "Yes, ma'am."

Mildred said, "I never heard of any Adolph H. Marx. Should I know you?"

Harpo said, "Well, the H stands for Harpo."

"*Oooh!*" shrieked Mildred. "Now I *know* you're a liar! *Harpo Marx can't talk!*"

Harpo jumped into his car and raced back home. He put on his Harpo costume—the trench coat, the blond, curly wig, the broken opera hat, the baggy pants, and he picked up his klaxon horn, and he raced back to Indio and dashed into the Employment Office.

As he stormed in, Harpo shot Gertrude a lascivious glance; then he honked madly three times on the klaxon horn; then he took Gertrude's arm and bent it and rested his right leg on it. Then he looked at her lasciviously again and whistled and stuck out his tongue, and by God, Gertrude was convinced, and she handed him his $55 check.

I had no such trouble getting *my* check. I cashed it. Fifty-five dollars was exactly what we were paying our maid per week, and I went right home and handed the money over to Maxine. You may ask how an unemployed man could have a full-time maid. The answer is I have always lived beyond my means. It is only in the last two years that my means have begun to catch up with me.

I don't want to give the impression that we were really paupers, Dee and I and the kids, on that miraculous Monday. But I *was* out of work, and I *was* on relief for the first and only time in my life. (I had always been ashamed to apply before.) And we *did* have an immense mortgage, and there was almost nothing left of what money I had been able to save in eighteen years in this crazy business.

In Hollywood, if you are not working, you are a leper. True, you are probably living in the most expensive leper colony in the world, inhabiting your own private unlisted leprosarium in Bel Air or Beverly Hills or Holmby Hills. But that makes no difference, because when you become an unemployed leper in Hollywood, nobody calls you up or comes to your house, and that includes the same people who were your good friends last week, or last year in New York. All of a sudden they don't invite you to their barbecues and pool parties, and if they see you walking up Wilshire Boulevard, they look over their shoulders into the nearest store window, so as not to notice you and be compelled to say hello.

Around five o'clock I drove over onto the freeway and got off at the Highland Avenue exit, which is in Hollywood proper, and then I drove to 1441 North McCadden, where there is a recording studio by the name of Radio Recorders. There were six musicians and six singers rehearsing, and the whole thing was being conducted by a lovely man named Lou Busch, and for three hours we rehearsed the nutty songs I was going to record that night.

At eight o'clock we opened the doors and started to let in the people. I wanted it to be like a party because all my life I had been singing my crazy songs at parties, so we had a bar set up in the back of the studio and we served hors d'oeuvres and J&B and I suppose other drinks, and there were about a hundred people there. Some of them were my friends, but most of them were total strangers invited by Warner Brothers. My favorite people in the world are songwriters, and some of the best were there: Leo Robin, who wrote "My Ideal" and "Prisoner of Love" and "Beyond the Blue Horizon"; and Harry Ruby, who wrote "Three Little Words" and all the crazy Marx Brothers songs; and Johnny Mercer, who wrote "Moon River" and "Laura" and "Accentuate the Positive"; and Harry Warren, who wrote "Lullaby of Broadway" and has three Academy Awards and is classified by ASCAP higher than any songwriter except Richard Rodgers and Irving Berlin. Harpo was there with his family, and Theodore Bikel, the folk singer. Pat Carroll, the comedienne, was there, and I knew I was going over very big with her because she laughed very hard, but, more important, during the time I was making the album she had to go to the ladies' room four times.

Louis Quinn, an old friend of mine who played Roscoe on *77 Sunset Strip*, introduced me to the audience, and the first number I did was my version of "The Streets of Laredo," which I called "The Streets of Miami," and when the audience heard the chorus repeating the last line of each stanza, they began screaming with laughter because this was an outrageous idea—to have a beautiful chorus singing the background material straight; we had done it in very good musical taste, with fine arrangements by Lou Busch.

The reason we did it this way is that I am indeed the worst singer in the world. (Dick Gehman, a writer and critic who *loves* me, searched his soul for the nicest thing he could say about my voice, and the highest compliment he could find was: *"Allan Sherman has a voice like a strangling mynah bird."*) But there seems to be some quality, or lack of quality, in my voice with which the average person can identify. I sing like anyone singing in a bathtub—not good, but with genuine enthusiasm, and that's why it is so important that the musical background and the chorus behind me should sound beautiful and legitimate and lush. The music is never funny. So the effect is something like this: You're looking into Tiffany's most elegant show window, and in the window is a black velvet pillow, and right in the middle of the pillow is an onion. That's me.

Well, it was one of those nights. I sang twelve songs including "Oh, Boy!" and "Seltzer Boy" and "Jump Down, Spin Around, Pick a Dress o' Cotton" and "Glory, Glory Harry Lewis." And I sang a duet with Mrs. Louis Quinn, whose stage name is Christine Nelson; the song we sang together was my version of "Frère Jacques"—"Sarah Jackman."

The excitement in the audience began with the first number, and it kept building all night. I wasn't aware of it, but the audience was. When it was over, people came up to me and said they had the feeling of being present at an event, that something electric had happened; that they had witnessed something completely new and fresh and different. They said this was a night they would remember.

I thanked them for their nice remarks. I knew I had done a good job and that the recording had come off well, and I also knew that these were nice, polite people giving me extravagant compliments, but I didn't really share their excitement about The Album.

I remember thinking, *Well, that came out nice, tomorrow I'd better start looking for work again.*

In my wildest imagining, I had no way of knowing or dreaming or predicting that that Monday night was going to turn my life upside down and hurl me into a whole new career and convert me into a Great American Success Story and make me a real-life Walter Mitty.

Two months later *My Son, the Folk Singer* was released. Two months and one week later everybody in the United States was singing "Sarah Jackman." Rock-'n'-roll stations all over the country changed their broadcast policies so they could play the record, and teen-agers were singing "Sarah Jackman" to each other in hot rods parked on Mulholland Drive. Milton Berle wrote a British version and sang it on the *Andy Williams Show*; Ed Sullivan hired two comics to lip-sync "Sarah Jackman" along with the record. (He called me first at home and asked me to come on his show and sing it, but I told him I was not a performer and was scared out of my wits and didn't want to make an ass of myself in front of 30 million people, which was the God's truth.) Lou Levy, head of Leeds Music, came back from Europe, where he had seen a little twelve-year-old French girl, and when her parents wanted to show her off, they had her sing the only words of English she knew: the lyrics of "Sarah Jackman." President John F. Kennedy walked through the lobby of the Carlyle Hotel in New York and out into his limousine, all the while softly singing "Sarah Jackman, Sarah Jackman, how's by you?" and he was heard by everyone in the lobby.

My Son, the Folk Singer sold 65,000 copies in the first week, and a half million in the first month, and it became the fastest-selling record album in history.

I felt like an Alice in Wonderland character who has gone through a looking glass and finds himself in a strange new country where money is growing on trees, where, as they told my grandfather to convince him to go to America, the streets are paved with gold; only mine was a weird, wild country where you suddenly have seventeen different agents and three sets of publicity people and business managers and personal managers, and you're being interviewed by the newspapers and the disc jockeys, and all of a sudden if you get a sore throat it's treated like a national catastrophe, and everybody wants to give you unlimited credit, and you're singing in Carnegie Hall and then you're starring at the Sands Hotel in Las Vegas and they're giving you $15,000 a week to sing the same songs you used to sing in people's living rooms all your life for free.

I had finally got hold of the Success I dreamed about all my life. I had it by the tail, and it all happened so fast that I only got a blurred look at it and at where it was taking me. I wasn't even sure I liked it; I only knew I mustn't let go. I might never get another chance. I had to hold on for dear life.

The record company flew me to Chicago and to San Francisco to make what they call personal appearances.

I went from seven A.M. every morning till three the next

morning, talking with disc jockeys, autographing The Album at record stores, having cocktails with columnists, posing for pictures.

Every experience of my life up to then had led me to prepare for the exact opposite of what was happening to me. Rejection I had learned to take; for eighteen years I had accustomed myself to not being sure where next month's mortgage payment was coming from. Now I knew the mortgage would be paid—not just next month's installment, but for the next ten or fifteen years.

Then why was I running? Why was I flying to Chicago? Why was I belting the double J&B's? If this was what I'd wanted all the time, why didn't I just lie back and enjoy it?

I couldn't sleep and I couldn't relax, and the double Scotches didn't help, and when I got back home from Chicago I collapsed. My doctor said the closest thing he had seen to my symptoms was during World War II when he treated combat fatigue. He gave me an electrocardiogram, and he said I had developed right bundle branch block of the heart. It's not a heart attack. He said there's nothing really *bad* about it. *But what's good about it? Who needs it?*

He put me to bed and I wasn't allowed to answer the telephone, and he gave me a red medicine, Elixir of Alurate, six times the normal dosage, which kept me alive, but barely.

After lying there for two weeks contemplating my thrilling success, I got an idea. I said to myself, *I have to get in practice for being rich; I have to buy something tangible to prove to myself that I'm really wealthy and famous and successful.* Deep down inside, I didn't believe the whole thing was happening to me. Success is like winning the sweepstakes or getting killed in an automobile crash. It always happens to somebody else.

So I said, *What the hell, I'll buy myself a tangible Lincoln Continental.* I called up Beverly Hills Lincoln-Mercury and I said, "Please send me a Lincoln Continental with air conditioning and AM-FM radio and Dual-90 tires and power ashtrays and . . ."

"Yes, sir. We'll be delighted to give you a demonstration, and—"

"I don't need a demonstration. I'll take it. Send it over."

"But, sir, this is quite extraordinary. It is our custom to demonstrate the many splendid features—"

"Send a gold one if you have it. If not, pick out a nice cheerful color. I'm not feeling well."

"Very well, sir, if you say so, sir."

It pained this man to have to do business with a person of my obvious low breeding; it hurt his feelings that I had deprived him of the chance to make the little speech where he shows you where the keyhole is and which pedal is the accelerator. In fact, he didn't like my whole big rush. But I had to touch that Lincoln and feel it and sit in it *right away*.

So now there it stood, gleaming in my driveway. I touched it. It was still unreal. I thought about my beautiful wife, my two lovely, bright children, my pure-blooded beagle whose paternal grandfather has his picture in the *Encyclopaedia Britannica*. From one corner of my eye I saw my gardener snipping away at the tree in our backyard which spews forth inedible bananas, and from the other I saw my full-time maid roasting a haunch of something or other. I could hear the soft swishings of my swimming-pool man purifying the water lest I contaminate my toesies, and again I surveyed my $85,000 Bel Air estate, which is worth $45,000 including the palm trees, and the gorgeous sliding glass in my lanai, and the swimming pool shaped like a human kidney. And after I looked at all this magnificent splendor, I went back inside and went to bed because I was still feeling rotten.

Lying in bed, I asked myself a profound question:

Allan Sherman, you stupid son-of-a-bitch, how the hell did you ever get yourself into such a jam?

CHAPTER 2

The Drapes of Roth,
AND Other Things My Grandfather Pressed

EVERYBODY IN MY FAMILY was crazy. Not *crazy*-crazy. *Nice*-crazy. *Sweet*-crazy.

All they ever had was trouble, trouble. When the great history of trouble is written, my family will stand extremely high in the table of contents. But the sound I remember best from my relatives is the sound of laughter. They were noisy people: they screamed and yelled at each other; they slammed doors and threw things. But afterward they all knew you were supposed to "make nice." That's how my grandmother put it. You can make nice on a doggie, on your wife or your brother or your father or your child, but the main thing is, after the hollering you dasn't leave the bad things hanging around—you've got to make nice. See? *Sweet* crazy.

* * *

If God gave my family plenty of trouble he gave them also the ability to laugh at it and to laugh at themselves.

Not long ago I was playing at the Palmer House in Chicago, and my Aunt Kate, my mother's sister, called up and said she wanted to come and see me. She had just been through a serious operation, and I told her I wouldn't allow her to come without her doctor's permission.

She got his permission, and as soon as she arrived at the Palmer House, she went right out on the dance floor and started doing her 1928 version of the Watusi with her husband, Dave, really shaking it up.

I got scared as hell. I walked out to Katie on the dance floor. "Katie," I said, "in your condition, you shouldn't dance fast like that."

"Allan," she said, "in my condition, I *have* to dance fast."

That's what I mean. God gave my family a gift of laughter.

Later that night Katie was remembering her school days at Tuley High School in Chicago. She said, "When I was in high school I had a very cute behind."

Her husband, Dave, said, "It's still cute. It's big, but it's cute."

"Shuddup," she said, "I'm talking to Allan. So I had this cute behind, and all the boys used to follow me home so they could watch my behind. There was this one boy, his name was Avrom Goldbogen, and he was really crazy about my behind. He always wanted to carry my books and take me for a chocolate phosphate, whatever, but I wouldn't give him a tumble. He was *fresh*—you know, a wise guy—"

Her son Kenneth interrupted, "So you know what happened? Forty years later there was an airplane crash and Michael Todd got killed. And they had the funeral in Chicago, and it turned out that Michael Todd's real name was Avrom Goldbogen."

Katie said, "See? If I had let him get near my behind, I could have married Michael Todd."

And Kenneth said, "How do you think *I* feel? I could have been Elizabeth Taylor's son!"

See? *Sweet* crazy.

I come from a typical Jewish background.

My father was a typical Jew. His name was Percy Copelon. He came from Birmingham, Alabama. He was a stock-car racer and an expert automobile mechanic. He had the Chicago agency for Auburn, Essex, Hudson, Nash and Cord. At one time he owned the largest garage in the Windy City. I remember him as a big fat man with a cigar in his mouth always. He had a rasping voice with a thick Southern accent. He was a generous man: I had a cellar full of toys when I was a kid. He was a reckless, free-spending, high-living, dangerous-living man. He flew airplanes at a time when only lion-hearted lunatics flew planes. He flew a pursuit plane in World War I. He loved machinery. He loved machinery that made you move fast. After the Armistice he flew in air circuses for a few years, doing Immelmann turns and flying upside down at carnivals and county fairs. Around 1922 he became a small-time Alabama bootlegger, and later he smuggled cargoes of booze into Illinois from Canada. But his real love was machines. He once invented a coal-mining machine that was widely used in southern Illinois and Kentucky. He adapted automobile gears to a machine that could chew into rock and bite out coal, saving labor.

My daddy had a brother-in-law, a dentist, who was a convert to nudism. He had a whole philosophy he had invented himself. It was about the benefits of eating uncooked vegetables and living on fruits and nuts, and what he called "naturism," which meant you had to go around naked all the time. His wife would answer the doorbell without a stitch of clothing on her. The doorbell was ringing at her house all day long.

My daddy had a most interesting family of eccentrics, but I do not know them as intimately as I know my mother's family, because when my father abandoned her he also abandoned me. When I became a celebrity, his family discovered me again.

My daddy did not like the garage business. He loved flying airplanes. And inventing. In 1928 he invented a new type of amphibian plane. He built it right in this immense garage he operated. It was so big, the plane, that when it was finished he couldn't remove it from the garage. He would have to wreck the garage if he wanted to get his plane out. He couldn't afford to build a new garage, so the plane remained there, unflown, until my father went busted. For all I know, it's still sitting there.

Daddy was a tough, hard-driving, hard-living, hard-drinking man. He drank bourbon whiskey by the glass like some Jews drink seltzer. Only he didn't drink seltzer. He was about as different from what we think of as a Jewish type as an American Jew could be back in 1924 when I was born on November 30th in the Lutheran Deaconess Hospital—and *there's* a typical Jewish hospital for you, huh?

Now my typical Jewish mother. Her maiden name was Rose Sherman. She was what they called a "flapper" and what we would now call a "swinger." She was a great Charleston dancer and she competed in Charleston dancing contests around Chicago, and she once won a loving cup at the Marbro Theatre on the West Side, and this loving cup was always displayed in a prominent place in our house. She was the first on her block to bob her hair. She wore short skirts. She began dating boys when she was twelve, and she was married at fifteen and divorced at sixteen, and then she married my father, and later she had two more husbands and I don't know how many boyfriends. There was always a man in her life. She loved music and dancing and singing and having a good time. She was a beautiful-looking little thing with brunette hair and mischief in the eyes, and she believed life to be a bowl of cherries. Neither of my parents spoke Yiddish around the house, and I doubt if my father knew ten words of it.

What is a Jew anyway?
I don't go to a synagogue. I don't wear a hat when I eat. I eat meat and drink milk at the same meal. I don't say prayers in the morning and evening. And yet, I am a Jew. I know I am a Jew. Everybody else knows I am a Jew. But why am I a Jew?

The first time I realized I was Jewish—the only incident of out-and-out anti-Semitism I have ever run into—happened one day when I was seven years old in Los Angeles. I was walking home from Cahuenga Grammar School. There was a Japanese gardener watering one of the lawns on my way home. In those days the Japanese in California were either gardeners or they worked in the open-air markets we now call supermarkets. As I walked past his lawn, this Japanese gardener turned the hose on me, full force, and no matter where I ran, he followed me, drenching my clothes, my books, my body, my face, and yelling insanely: "Joosh boy, go home! You bad, you Joosh! Go way, bad Joosh kid!"

I ran home and asked my mother was I really Jewish? And if so, what kind of an awful thing was this to be, that a perfect stranger should turn on me like that?

It turned out I *was* Jewish, and my mother couldn't explain why that should get people mad.

In 1964 I was playing the Cork Club in Houston, Texas. I was having a drink at the bar between shows when a tall, tough Texan came over and insisted on buying me a drink and then telling me about his success in the oil (he pronounced it "awl") business and how he had enjoyed my Jewish-type parodies of famous songs and the whole act. And then he said something that I believe he meant as a compliment, and that is how I accepted it.

"Mr. Sherman," he said, "I have been to Israel, I have seen *real* Jews, Mr. Sherman. I have seen Jews sweatin' and workin' and pumpin' awl out of the desert where you wouldn't think anybody could find awl, Mr. Sherman, let alone a bunch of Jews. But Ah saw those people with mah eyes, Mr. Sherman, and Ah want to tell you something: you ain't a pimple on a *real* Jew's ass!"

I seem to have my prejudices, too. I remember taking a plane from San Francisco to Chicago, and when I was deplaning I happened to walk by the pilot's cabin and I saw his name on the little plaque:

PILOT: CAPTAIN K. L. SHAPIRO

I felt terrible. If I had known my pilot was Captain Shapiro when I got aboard, I would have been worried all through the flight. I can't help it. I have this feeling that flying planes is not a job for a nice Jewish boy. I would have felt safer in the hands of a good white Anglo-Saxon, Protestant pilot—a John Wayne type, for instance. It's irrational, I admit, but I have this feeling.

My whole childhood is a blur. It was whirling from Chicago to Los Angeles, from Los Angeles to Miami, from Miami to New York, from New York back to Chicago.

Altogether, I attended twenty-one different grammar and high schools in New York, Illinois, California and Florida. Sometimes I was living with my mother and one of her husbands. When she was between husbands, she would park me with a relative or with her parents until she made a new connection. She was frequently between husbands. Somehow, though, I was always going back to Chicago. My grandmother and grandfather lived there, and when things got desperate for my mother, for one reason or another, I'd be shipped to my grandparents. They lived in an apartment on Kedzie Avenue across from Humboldt Park in northwest Chicago.

* * *

Grandma's name was Esther. Grandpa's was Leon. Grandma had two sisters, Annie and Fannie. Annie was married to Shaya. Shaya ran a hole-in-the-wall jewelry store on Division Street. Fannie was married many times, but she was unlucky in love.

Grandma had two brothers. One was named Leon, like Grandpa. Great-uncle Leon was a junkman. He drove a horse and wagon through the back alleys of Chicago, which was then a city of back alleys. Great-uncle Leon was the only member of the family who owned something. What he owned was the sway-back horse and the dilapidated wooden wagon in which he transported his junk. On special occasions, when I deserved a treat, Great-uncle Leon would take me riding with him through the alleys along his route. I loved it. I loved the other kids running along behind us, jealous of me because I was sitting on the wagon next to the junkman. I was fascinated by Great-uncle Leon's cry of *"Recksolayee! Recksolayee!"* Sometimes he let me yell it in my five-year-old voice—*"Recksolayee!"* It was almost something to sing; it was the traditional cry of the junkman, and it meant "Rags, old iron! Rags, old iron!" But somehow through the years the Jewish and Polish and Slovak junkmen in the alleys of American cities had turned it into "Recksolayee." Just a few months ago I heard Oscar Brown, Jr., the great Negro folk singer and songwriter; he sang a song about *his* uncle who was a junkman in Chicago. The title of the song was "Recksolayee."

Grandma used to take me on picnics to a place called the Milwaukee Woods, which she referred to as *Milvawkee-by-duh-Voodsuh*. She was crazy for Clark Gable. She called him "Clock." She'd look upward dreamily and murmur, "Oy, dot *Clock*. Oy, dot's a Clock!" She went three, four times a week to the big Balaban and Katz theatres downtown in the Loop—the State-Lake is one of them, or the Chicago, fancy theatres with vaudeville shows. Or she would go to the neighborhood movie houses; one was the Vision on Division Street. She usually went with her sister Fannie.

It was a principle of Grandma's life to avoid paying money to large corporations like streetcar companies, the telephone company, department stores, movie-theatre chains. Nine times out of ten she would not pay for the movies. She would make up some excuse, like her grandson was in the theatre and she had to go in and get him, or she had a message for a doctor who was in the theatre, or she had been inside an hour earlier and had gone out for an errand and lost her ticket stub. And Grandma looked so sweet and kindly—she had a face exactly like Albert Einstein's—that the ticket-takers always believed her. She had a heart full of love and kindness and humor—and a wide streak of petty larceny.

I loved her very much and I would have done anything for her.

I remember once she kept saying, "Oh, how I need it a *football*. If only I had a nice *football*." I had overheard her telling Mother she was having a big party for all the relatives that night, and she had to have this football for after supper. I was then about eight years old.

I don't know why it didn't strike me as peculiar that this little old silver-haired lady wanted a football. I loved Grandma. If Grandma wanted a football, I would get her a football. I counted up all my available cash, my nickels and pennies and one dime. It came to 73 cents. I asked about a football at the Army-Navy store. The cheapest was $2.98. On my block I knew of three footballs. First I went to Homer Dumbrowski's house. He wasn't home. Then I found Eddie Polonsky in the park playing touch football with his friends. I offered him 73 cents cash on the barrelhead for the ball. He laughed in my face. He said it was a $5 Spalding football and I should go to hell with my 73 cents together. Gudgie, my last Polack, gave me a punch in the nose when I offered to buy *his* football. Then he reconsidered and said he'd trade me his football for all the marbles I had plus an almost new Flexible Flyer sled which I had received for Chanukah last year. I made the deal.

I went to the gas station and filled the football up, nice and hard. Then I sneaked it into the house. I shined it up with brown shoe polish. Now it was a football worthy of Grandma's party. How proud my aunts and uncles would be when they saw it tonight! I put it on the dining-room table.

When Mother saw it, she hollered, "Allan, can't you put your things where they belong?"

I explained it was for Grandma—she'd said she needed a football for the party.

Mother burst into laughter. "A football for the party? Don't you understand Grandma's talking? Not *football*. She's trying to say *fruit bowl*. She needs a fruit bowl for the party."

So I went down in the basement feeling like an idiot, and I didn't want to come upstairs even when the relatives began arriving. I could hear the *clink-clink* of Grandma's best china and crystal, and every once in a while an explosion of laughter. I didn't even want to come up for supper, and nobody could drag me up. After supper Mother came down and said I should come upstairs and there'd be a surprise for me. So I followed her into the living room. Grandma was walking around like a queen, holding out to each of the aunts and uncles the biggest, the most magnificent cut-glass fruit bowl I had ever seen. It was filled with grapes, apples and oranges, and in the center of it was Gudgie's football.

"Esther," her brother Max complimented, "that's a beautiful football. Real cott-gless."

Grandma looked at Max the Genius haughtily. "Max, listen careful and you'll learn something. This cott-gless is called a *frutt boll,* not a *football.* The brown thing in the middle, *this* is a football."

"So tell me something—what for you got a football in your frutt boll?"

"Because today mine *Eln* [that's how she pronounced Allan] brought me a nice present, this football. It's beautiful, no?" Before Max could answer, she continued, "It's beautiful, *yes.* Because from a little child is beautiful *anything.*"

Grandpa was a quiet, melancholy drunk who did not speak much and did not eat much. He had been a presser "by ladies' coats." I don't mean a presser in a cleaning-and-pressing retail establishment; I mean a presser in a garment manufacturing shop—a "cloakmaker," he called it. Before they send out the finished garment, it has to be pressed, and it takes a special talent to do this, and Grandpa was a presser "by ladies' coats." He made a nice living for those times—$100 a week—but only during the *season.* There is a season when ladies' coats, wholesale ones, have to be pressed, and there is a season when they don't need you altogether. During the season Grandpa worked hard, overtime every night, twelve–fourteen hours a day—but he had only two three-month-long seasons, and the rest of the year he was out of work.

I guess my love for the Theatre comes from Grandpa, because during the nonworking season he used to take me to the Yiddish theatre, which is just like the American theatre, only more so; when they emote, they really emote. And the Yiddish theatre doesn't bother with subtleties or psychological nuances. It concerns itself with the big things of life: birth and death and marriage and incurable illness and infidelity and illegitimate babies. And the point is that every Yiddish play includes *all* of these things—otherwise the audience would walk out in the middle, because they didn't come there to see a lot of trivialities.

One of the most marvelous sights to behold in all the world is a death scene in the Yiddish theatre. There is Maurice Schwartz, or some other great Yiddish actor, and he has just discovered his wife in bed with another man, and he has a heart attack, and it is the end of him. But he doesn't die just like that. First he screams, "*I am having a heart attack! I am dying!*" Then he falls, and the fall itself takes a full minute onto the sofa, then he moans and groans; then he rises and stumbles across the room, knocking over furniture and all the while yelling, "*I am dying! I am dying! Oh, God, I am dying!*" Then he stumbles offstage, wailing and moaning; then he stumbles back on stage and clutches at the draperies and sinks to the floor. And by now the whole family is standing there watching all this, crying and shrieking, "*My God, he is dying!*" And when he finally lands on the floor, he writhes painfully and he makes a speech, gasping out each word. And this speech includes all of the philosophical Talmudic learnings of his life, and it is chock full of advice to his sons and farewells to his daughters and his wife, and this speech alone lasts six minutes. And then at long last he gives one great effort to stand up again, and he almost makes it, but just when you think he's going to be all right, he lets out this horrible, croaking groan and stumbles over the entire stage again, knocking over what's left of the furniture and the family, and finally he dies. This death scene always takes about fifteen minutes. If the play is a musical, it is exactly the same, except with singing and dancing and very melancholy music underscoring the whole thing. And the audience, which is composed of Jewish people who have troubles of their own, feel this man's great pain, and *they* moan and groan and weep, and when he is finally dead, they sigh with relief and they feel this wonderful sense of total satisfaction.

*   *   *

Grandpa also used to take me to the bathhouse on Division Street, where there was a steam room where I sat naked and listened to the wise words of the naked old scholars with their long beards and sideburns; and after sweating in the steam Grandpa would force me into the little eight-foot-square pool, which was filled, I think, with ice water. And we would lie on tables while the attendants bathed us with soapsuds and brushes that looked like feather dusters and were made of some exotic Turkish leaves.

Not long before he died I asked Grandpa if he had always been a coat presser, and he said no, when he first came to this country he had been a bricklayer, but in the old country, in Łódź-Gubernia, he had been what they called a *"grom."* A *grom* was a man who went around to weddings and parties and did *gromming.* What is *gromming?* you may well ask. I'll tell you. It's something like a minstrel.

My grandpa would go around to these weddings and parties and they would give him a list of the names of the guests, real names, and he would sing happy songs about these people, weaving the names into the songs and making up rhymes for the names and lines to fit the situation.

Honest to God: My Grandfather, the Folk Singer.

After the Great Depression, Grandpa became a heavy drinker —in fact, a drunk. He was *shikker* all the time. His eyes had a glaze on them of alcohol and tears, always. Grandpa didn't drink rye or bourbon or Scotch. Oh, no—he drank what he called "schnapps." Actually, it was some kind of cheap bootleg prohibition booze, but among Jews if you called it "schnapps" it was all right to drink it; but if you drank whiskey or gin, then you were a drunken bum. He spent his whole life drinking, and smoking Lucky Strikes in the green package.

Grandpa often warned me about the evils of alcohol. And My Grandma, the Poker Player—*she* warned me against gambling. Today I do both, though I'm not a compulsive gambler or drinker. *How is it possible to listen to people who do what they tell you not to do?* Besides, I didn't see that drinking hurt Grandpa very much.

His doctor once told him that if he didn't stop drinking immediately, he would die. And he did die—twenty-six years later he died, having outlived everybody who was sober, including his doctor.

Grandpa rarely ate anything. He just drank and smoked. He got all the nourishment he needed from alcohol, tars and nicotine—at least enough to live to be seventy-seven years old.

Grandpa's dislike for food made him unusual in our family. We were a fat, happy, laughing, high-cholesterol family. We ate with gusto. Especially Grandma—even when she got diabetes, she ate with gusto. They didn't use the word diabetes among the Jews. They called it "shugeh." They would say, "Esther has shugeh. *Tsk, tsk, tsk.*"

When insulin became popular, Grandma's doctor gave her a hypodermic needle, a syringe and the new drug, and told her to use them every day. He also gave her a strict diet. She didn't follow the diet and she seldom gave herself an insulin shot. The doctors told her with all her "shugeh" and how she's eating, she's going to be carried off in a wooden box any day. But she laughed in their faces and ate whatever she felt like eating, and the only time she'd take a shot of insulin was when she'd eaten a whole box of candy at one time. Grandma lived to be seventy-nine with her candy and her "shugeh."

My grandma's love for her family was expressed in the magnificent foods she cooked for us. When I was a boy, she cooked the most delicious food in the world. As I grew older, her cooking became less and less delicious. *Did my tastes change? Or did she lose her touch as the years passed? Or was Grandma's cooking lousy in the first place?*

I remember her standing in the kitchen with a big pot of soup steaming on the stove. I remember her standing there, tasting the soup from a long, wooden soup ladle, and then adding things and tasting again, and adding again and tasting again until it was exactly right.

Years later it made me think up a story. It was about this food chemist who works for a big food-manufacturing company, and one night he has dinner at the home of a Jewish grandmother like mine, and she serves a soup—the most delicious soup he has ever tasted—and he smacks his lips and it occurs to him that his company could make a fortune if they could put out this particular soup.

So he gets the old lady aside, and he tells her that if she'll give him the recipe, he'll give her a royalty and she'll be on Easy Street for life.

"Why not?" she says. And she takes him into the kitchen and starts to make the soup, and he takes out a notebook to write down the recipe.

"First," she says, "you put in pieces chicken."

"How much?" he asks.

"*Plenty*," she says. "If it's gung be chicken soup, let be *plenty* chicken, not stingy. Then soupengreens."

"What are soupengreens?" he asks.

"Soupengreens is soupengreens," she replies, and she mutters under her breath, "Some dummy."

"What next?"

"Onions."

"How many?"

"Not too much, but chopped, nice. And carrots."

"Not too many?"

"Just enough. And noodles. Plenty."

"Then what?"

"Then you'll boil. What else?"

"What temperature?"

"Not too hot. Too hot is no good. But hot enough—too cold is no good altogether."

By now the food chemist has given up taking notes. He asks: "How long do you cook it?"

And the old lady can contain herself no longer: "Dummy! *Till is findished!*"

Finally, the food chemist gives up. He gives up because he has never been able to discover what the missing ingredient is, what it was the old lady was putting in the soup that all the food chemists in the world can't put into a can of soup.

If they had asked me, I could have told them what it was. It was the same ingredient my grandma put into *her* soup—love.

She would stand there in the kitchen and taste the soup with her wooden spoon, and then she would look out at all of us sitting in the front room, and the love in her heart would say to her, They will want more salt. And she would put in more salt, and taste it again and look at us again until the soup was just exactly perfect, just exactly the way we would want it. Nice.

At Grandma's big Friday-night family dinners she would prepare a roast duck or a roast chicken, and there was chopped liver and soup with *kasha* or *kreplach,* and vegetables and honey cake and tea. It's unbelievable how my family could eat. Right up to dinnertime, we'd be in the parlor, hollering and arguing and insulting each other, my mother, her sister Kate, her brother Maury, various aunts and uncles and great-aunts and great-uncles; but as soon as Grandma said, "Come, eat!" the arguments ceased. Everybody gathered worshipfully around the long table with the lace tablecloth and the silver, the heavy silver. Everybody picked up his knife and fork so when the food was actually placed on the table he or she could be the first to get the most. And we leaped upon the food with a zest and an enlightened self-interest that can hardly be described. You had to be there.

I saw nothing comparable to it until recently when I appeared at the Diplomat Hotel in Miami Beach.

At the cocktail hour in Miami Beach, all the hotels bring out a beautiful spread of food, absolutely free, a magnificent buffet with designs of culinary architecture: an Empire State Building made of chopped liver, heaps of pastrami sculptured in the shape of the Matterhorn, an American flag made out of alternating stripes of lox and cream cheese with radishes for stars, and there's turkey and sturgeon and corned beef shaped like the Mount Rushmore faces, and schmaltz herring and pickles and scallions and rye bread and all kinds of crackers. And the waiters wheel all this onto the terrace on rolling tables, but before the waiters can reach their destination the hordes come out from every room in the hotel and attack. It's unbelievable. You've got to see it. From the twelve floors of the hotel, out of every room, they come; and from strange hotels, even from nearby cities. Like Pavlov's dogs. No whistle blows. Yet somehow, instinctively, everybody knows it's five o'clock and there's free food.

In a matter of minutes the Empire State Building is reduced to rubble, and there's no more Mount Rushmore, and of Old Glory nothing is left but a lonesome, half-eaten radish.

This was how my family would eat, and everybody in the family was short and fat and jolly—everybody, that is, except my Great-uncle Max (Grandma's brother), who was the Genius of the family. He was skinny; he had always been skinny— no matter how much he ate. He was a fiddler, a violin player, and he *looked* like a violin player.

There are certain people who look like what they are in life —and there are others who don't. Max looked like a violinist. He looked more like a violinist than anybody else in the world. Jascha Heifetz—you pass him in the street, you could mistake him for a certified public accountant or the vice-president of Hart, Schaffner & Marx. But the first time you see my Uncle Max you think, *There goes a violinist.*

He isn't very tall—but he looks tall, if you know what I mean, and in his face are many deep lines, wrinkles that show he's a man who worries about Life, like a real violinist. He has high cheekbones, like an Indian's—two little hills standing out on each side of his big, sad eyes—and long black hair and long black sideburns and heavy eyebrows, always wrinkled, like he's in Deep Thought. And his head is tilted over to the left side, as a violinist's head should be. The rest of the family, Grandma and the other sisters and brothers—five of them—were short and round and jolly, but from the time he was four years old Max was given a violin to study and he was the Genius and Hope of the family. The others were told to go out and play and get fat and jolly, but all the hope and attention went to the little Genius.

In those days it was the dream of every Russian-Jewish family to have a son a violinist, another Elman, another Kreisler. At age nine my Uncle Max played fiddle for the Czarina, and she gave him a little gold medal, and this medal my great-grandfather, the bass-player, wore every day as long as he lived. At sixteen my Uncle Max was Assistant Concertmaster of the Imperial Russian Symphony. At twenty my uncle, by then married to a plump, jolly lady named Dora, came to America where the streets were Paved with Gold.

Here he didn't make out so good. He ran around Chicago, playing a *bar mitzvah* here, a wedding there, getting a week's work in a moving-picture theatre playing music for the silent movies so they wouldn't be so silent. But he didn't work steady. Grandpa worked more steadily than Max and made "union wages," as he put it. There was a mixture of admiration and jealousy on my grandpa's part toward his brother-in-law, and you can't blame him, because my grandma's family all worshiped the Genius. They worshiped him, but Grandpa was *supporting* him.

One Friday night, when I was five years old, Grandpa handed me a long package. I untied the strings and unwrapped it. It was a violin, a real one, but child's size. I held it in my left hand, trying to imitate my uncle. Then Grandpa turned to Max and spoke a command.

"Well, Max—make from Eln a genius, too."

Was he being sarcastic? Who knows?

But I wasn't a violinist, even though my uncle did his best. I could make my fiddle scratch and squeak and sound like an alley cat in heat, but I couldn't produce music. Uncle Max would sit there during my lessons, looking wise beyond all wisdom, and smiling—serene in the knowledge that there was still only one Genius in the family.

Nobody in my family ever had any stocks or bonds or securities or anything like that. Still, when the market crash came, they all managed to get wiped out. How, I don't know. Maybe there's some law of economics involved. All I know is, something happened on Wall Street on Black Thursday which ruined the coat-pressing business on the West Side of Chicago, and from Friday on, for the rest of his life, my grandfather was on relief.

I guess the only business that withstood the crash was the Genius business. Uncle Max came through it beautifully; in 1930, when everybody else was looking really silly, Uncle Max looked even wiser, even deeper than before.

My grandmother kept having the Friday dinners, only they weren't as fancy as before the crash. Uncle Max and Aunt Dora showed up every Friday night. Sometimes they brought a pot of soup or a sponge cake and a bottle of wine. My grandmother would apologize for the *nebbish* dinner, and for the fact that her husband was out of a job. She blamed the 1929 market crash on my grandfather, personally. At first he argued the point, but after a while he got used to it and admitted it was his fault.

My grandpa became a bitter man. One Friday night, at the dinner table, he took out his leather change purse—the one he used to keep rolled-up dollar bills in. Instead of dollar bills, he was saving clippings from the *Jewish Daily Forward*—which he called the *"Forvitz"*—which he read aloud at the table so my grandmother and Uncle Max could hear. One was an interview with Fritz Kreisler that told how well he was doing. Another was a rave review of Mischa Elman. Another told of a boy genius, Yehudi Menuhin. After Grandpa read the clippings, he passed them to Uncle Max to examine, and sat back in triumph.

But it was a good year for Uncle Max. He held the clippings up high so everyone could look at them. "You see?" he said. "By music is no crashes. Music is always the same. Music is music." And, having said something really deep, he returned to his noodle soup.

But Grandpa had waited ten years to say something, and tonight he was going to say it. He took off his gold-rimmed glasses and wiped them with the tip of his necktie. Then, with a bravado we never knew he had, he shouted:

"You listen to me, Max. I'm gung tell *you* something!"

He looked around the table to make sure all of us were paying attention. We were. And the next few words he delivered magnificently—like Clarence Darrow, setting up Uncle Max for the kill:

"Maybe you right, Max. Maybe music *is* music. But one thing you forgot in ten years, Max. Just one thing!"

He stood up and leaned across the table toward Uncle Max. Then he said it. *His* philosophy:

"Ladies' coats is also ladies' coats!"

This struck me funny, I don't know why, and I giggled out loud.

All my life I will be sorry I giggled then, because my grandpa looked at me as though I had cut him with a knife. It was the only time I ever saw bitterness on his lovely face.

34

After that night I never heard him shout again. And after that night was when he started *really* drinking.

What kept him alive, I think, was the same thing that kept him drinking. His dream of vengeance, sweet revenge on his brother-in-law, on the Genius of the Violin, on my Uncle Max.

My grandfather lived only because he had to prove somehow that music *isn't* music.

And I'm happy to say he *did* prove it.

Just after The Night of The Argument, Uncle Max and Aunt Dora stopped coming to the Friday-night dinners. Not because they were insulted—we don't get insulted in our family. We holler and we fight, but if someone's serving dinner, we show up. *Eat first, later we'll talk*—that's our family motto.

Uncle Max and Aunt Dora stopped coming to the Friday-night dinners because they moved to Hollywood, California.

The whole world was in the middle of the terrible Depression except my Uncle Max. All of a sudden Uncle Max was rich. He had a Willys-Knight touring car, and a Spanish hacienda with genuine stucco walls, and a palm tree. I wouldn't have believed it, but I saw the snapshots myself. My grandma carried them around in her pocketbook and showed them to people. Mostly to my grandpa.

Another mystery of economics: from nowhere, in the mid-Depression, silent pictures became talking pictures. And for the talkies they needed musicians, quick, and they were paying plenty.

For the talkies they needed a very special kind of musician who not only played but *looked* like a musician. They needed saxophone players who *looked* like saxophone players, and drummers who *looked* like drummers. These were very hard to find.

But when they needed a violinist who *looked* like a violinist —that's when Uncle Max got rich.

Warner Brothers was the company that originally brought Uncle Max out to Hollywood, but they goofed. They forgot to sign him to a long-term contract. After a few pictures at Warners, MGM grabbed him for *The Great Waltz* and they gave him a close-up. After the close-up there was no stopping him.

You've seen my Uncle Max a thousand times. Sometimes he's in a symphony orchestra, and while the music soars, the camera gets beautiful high-angle shots of Uncle Max fingering and bowing like mad. Or sometimes he's a Gypsy. It's very effective; Uncle Max looks more like a Gypsy than any other violinist in the world. Sometimes you see him in a big-name band. He had three close-ups in *The Glenn Miller Story*. Uncle Max is everywhere—and the older he gets, the more like a violinist he looks.

So my Uncle Max, the Genius, got rich, and the rest of the family stayed poor.

About two years ago, just before my grandfather died, Uncle Max and Aunt Dora flew to Chicago to see him in the hospital.

Grandpa was resting. There was a television set in the hospital room, and the whole family was sitting around, watching an old Fred Astaire movie.

And there it was—a great big full-screen close-up of Uncle Max playing away dreamily. *No kidding—they took the camera off Fred Astaire to show Uncle Max.*

My grandfather stirred. "Max," he said, "I got to tell you something."

Uncle Max said, "Yes, Leon?"

My grandfather said, "You was smart, Max. I got to give you credit."

"What do you mean?" Uncle Max asked.

"What I mean?" My grandfather pointed to the television set. "I mean, listen, how beautiful. You was right, Max. Music is music."

Just then the TV music swooped up in a beautiful crescendo, and there was a poignant melody for the strings, and there was a handsome close-up of Uncle Max, the camera looking across his profile at his long, sensitive fingers on the bow.

Uncle Max walked over to the bed and took my grandfather's hand. "Leon," he said, with his eyes closed. "Listen to me, Leon. I'm gung tell *you* something."

"Okay," my grandfather said. "Tell."

"Leon, this—what I'm gung tell you—I never told nobody. Just you. But you I got to tell, because *you* was right and I was wrong."

"Max, I'm a sick man," my grandfather said. "Don't make me crazy."

Uncle Max continued: "Leon, you was right. Music isn't music. Since I was a baby I studied. All my life I practiced. And now—my music isn't music."

"What are you talking?" asked Grandpa. "Listen to the television. Look. On the picture is you. See? You playing beautiful! Nice."

Uncle Max continued: "Leon—I'm ashamed. Terrible. On the picture is me, yes. But the music—no. The music is playing somebody else. I don't even know who."

Grandpa said, "Max—you crazy, something? Can't you see who's playing? *You!*"

"No, Leon! Not me!"

"*Not you?*"

"I'm moving the hands, and I'm shlepping the bow, but I'm not playing. No."

My grandfather thought for a moment. Then he asked, "So who's playing?"

"A *record*," said Uncle Max. "A record, from a Victrola. Not me. This they call pre-recording. It's not me."

"In all those pictures you didn't play?" asked my grandfather.

"No."

"Max—twenty-three years you're in Hollywood, *you didn't play yet?*"

"Not even one peep."

My grandfather sighed. "How you like that?" he said to God. *"Music is not music."*

Uncle Max said, "No. Absolutely not."

My grandfather felt no sense of victory. Instead, he felt sorry for Uncle Max.

"What's the matter with them?" Grandpa said. "Don't they know you a Genius?"

"They like better how I *look*," said Uncle Max.

"All right." My grandfather had decided. "Enough is enough. You'll sell the house, and you'll move back to Chicago, and you'll play. At least you'll *play*."

"No, Leon."

"Why not?"

"Leon, listen to me. Twenty-three years, every day working, getting up six o'clock in the morning, make-up, costume, lights, camera, action, retakes . . ."

"So?"

"So. Every night busy, cocktail parties, gin rummy, night clubs, running around, keeping up."

"So?"

"So. Twenty-three years, Leon, no time for practicing. Not a minute."

"*Tsk, tsk, tsk, tsk,*" said my grandfather, and he shook his head slowly from side to side. "*Tsk, tsk, tsk,*" he kept saying, as Uncle Max said:

"Leon—I forgot how to play the violin."

Because of Uncle Max's success in Hollywood, my father and mother decided to try their luck in California in 1930. Daddy's business had been wiped out by the crash, so we all piled into the car with suitcases and possessions tied on the roof and onto the trunk in the back, and we took Highway 66 to Los Angeles.

I remember it wasn't all paved yet and there were times after

*a rain when it was so muddy the car got stuck and wouldn't
move and Daddy had to go find the nearest farmer and they'd
bring a team of mules and pull the car out of the mud.*

When we got to Los Angeles, Daddy had to start all over from
the beginning. He went into the only business he knew—the
automobile business. He opened a small gas-and-service station
in downtown Los Angeles. We moved into a miserable two-
room flat in the El Capitan Bungalow Court, a cracked stucco
monstrosity. It was next door to the Los Angeles Coliseum,
which was then being built. It was a gigantic stadium to hold
100,000 persons when it was finished in time for the 1932 Olym-
pics. In later years I vended hot dogs and Coca-Colas at USC
football games in the Coliseum.

Daddy's business was bad. What money he had he blew on
booze. Mother and he were arguing, hollering all the time.
Then she would slam the door and run out to the poker palaces
and the beach amusement piers near Santa Monica, and he'd
sit down at the kitchen table with a bottle and drink himself
into a snoring stupor. I was six years old.

*We were about to sit down to dinner one evening—I remem-
ber it clearly. There was the smell of lamb chops broiling in the
oven. The table was set in the kitchen. I was playing outside in
the courtyard. Mother called me to come in. I was very hungry.
I always had this big appetite. But instead of serving dinner, she
asked me to come into the living room. My father was sitting in
the kitchen, at the table, with a bottle of whiskey and a shot-
glass. He didn't say anything. My mother closed the door so we
were alone. She was crying. I can't stand it when women cry. To
this day, I fall apart when a woman cries.*

She put her arm around my shoulder. She said, "Your father
and I are going to separate."

My eyes filled up with tears. I didn't know what to say. I
could smell the lamb chops burning. I could see she didn't care
if the whole house burned down.

"Allan," she said, "you have to choose. Which one of us do you want to live with?"

I think all the indecision and disorganization in my character since then comes from having been asked to make such a decision so early in life. It's absurd, it's damaging to a child's soul to be asked to choose between his mother and his father at the age of six. Well, I chose my mother, because she was in the room with me and I didn't dare reject her to her face. If my father had asked me the same question, I would probably have chosen him. Since that day, I can't say no to anyone; I can't reject another human being.

When I had made my choice, my father moved out of the house. I did not see him again until I was eighteen years old.

When the 1932 Olympic Games took place in Los Angeles at the Coliseum, my mother opened a little stand where she rented binoculars, and I worked with her after school and on weekends. One of our customers was a soft-spoken, kindly man, a German refugee named Dave. He became Mother's boyfriend, and they were married as soon as she got her divorce. He was kind to me. A year later he got diabetes and went blind and died.

So my mother moved in with my Uncle the Violin Genius, but there wasn't room for me, too, so I got shipped to another aunt and uncle. My mother's life was miserable. My life was miserable. If I wanted an extra piece of bread, they resented it.

Finally my mother shipped me to Grandma's, back to Chicago.

I was appointed Captain of the Toilets at James Russell Lowell Grammar School, near Humboldt Park. In the last few years I have had many honors; I have met two Presidents, but never have I been prouder than I was when they made me Captain of the Toilets. This is no mere honorary job; it is a high-level executive position with great responsibility.

All the teachers were ladies, so they couldn't go in the little boys' room. And little boys in grammar school, when they go to the toilet, they don't know exactly what to do, or how to button up their pants (this was before zippers), and, secondly, a lot of them go into the toilets and are never heard from again. They never come out, because they hate school, and besides they are busy writing on the walls. And so the teachers have to appoint a Toilet Captain to make sure every boy who goes in comes out, and every boy who comes out does so with his pants buttoned.

Although my grandma loved me and I loved her, it wasn't in her nature to be motherly. She was a swinger, like my mother. She was, in her day, a hot number. I remember her son, my Uncle Maury, describing his memories of how peddlers or door-to-door salesmen would come knocking at the door, selling one thing or another, and wind up necking with Grandma. Of course, it's hard to think of your grandparents in terms of lust and passion, and when I knew her she looked like a sweet, wholesome, silver-haired Jewish grandmother. But she wasn't. Every afternoon she went to horseparlors and bet on the races. In the evening she played poker. And Grandma cheated whenever she could. She cheated because it was a much more scientific and surer way of winning than trusting to luck.

Once she was playing poker with a group of old ladies and they needed another hand, so she got my Uncle Maury into the game. The first hand he picked up, he saw she had dealt him four kings. She was a very slick second-dealer—what they call a "mechanic" in Las Vegas—and Maury knew his mother had slipped him the four kings, and he was embarrassed, so he went out of the pot. Next time it was her deal, she dealt him four kings again. He went out again. She kept on dealing him the same four kings, hoping to make him win, and he kept going out. Finally she went into the kitchen for a glass of water, and he followed her and said, "Listen, Ma, please stop dealing me four kings. *Please.* I don't want to win like that with four kings."

So the next hand she dealt him *three* kings.

In those days the phone company put nickel pay phones in private dwellings. Grandma had a pay phone in her flat. She figured out many ingenious ways to crook the phone company. Like she'd put in a nickel, make a call, and then get the operator and scream, "Operator, you cott me opp!" She meant the operator had cut her off, and so she got her nickel back. Every month a man came to open the coin box and collect the nickels. Grandma played Casino (she called it "Kereseno") with him for the nickels, and won them all back, every month.

Once I was sent to New York to live with my Uncle Maury and Aunt Edith, who were then newlyweds. Grandpa came to visit, and Edith, who was new to the family and did not know what a crazy set of relatives she had acquired, wanted to make an impression on her new father-in-law.

Edith decided that Grandpa would be very impressed if he saw that she could cook a real Jewish meal, featuring a roast chicken. She wanted him to be completely satisfied, so the first thing she did was take Grandpa to a kosher butcher shop so he could be there in person and make sure the bird was killed in the proper ritual manner by a legitimate *shochet*. (A *shochet* is a man who kills poultry for Jewish people in the kosher manner; as I understand it, that means so swiftly that there is, at least in theory, no pain.)

There were hundreds of chickens in the store, and Grandpa made a great ceremony of feeling all of them, arguing with the butcher about which was the plumpest and the tenderest, and after much Talmudic philosophy had been exchanged, Grandpa chose a bird, and it was *flicked* (the feathers were removed), and Grandpa and Edith took the chicken home.

Then Edith asked Grandpa did he think roasting was nice.

And he answered, "Why not?" And so she began to roast the chicken.

Grandpa supervised Edith's every move, the salting and the seasoning and the basting. For two hours he stood over her shoulder in the kitchen, making sure everything she did was perfect.

When the chicken was finished to Grandpa's satisfaction, Edith took it from the stove and put it on a platter and brought it to the table.

Then Maury took the carving knife, and Grandpa supervised the carving. He studied and deliberated over each slice like a consulting surgeon. When the carving was finally done, Edith took Grandpa's plate and turned to him and asked, "Papa, darling, which part do you like the most?"

Grandpa looked at Edith as though she were the village idiot. Astonished that she could be so stupid, Grandpa said:

"Who eats chicken?"

My Uncle Maury, who died too young, was a sweet soul with a delightful pixie sense of humor. He was the first and only person in our family ever to have a steady job, and he didn't have it long. When he graduated from Northwestern University, he went to work for the International Paper Company as a salesman in the Seminole Toilet Paper Division. The slogan of Seminole Toilet Paper was "One thousand sheets—not the usual 650." Uncle Maury used to say, "Who counts?"

Uncle Maury had a beautiful comic spirit. Even when he was out of a job, even when the illness that was going to waste him to death was already growing inside him, he could laugh at himself and at the whole human predicament.

Once Aunt Edith gave him a sandwich for lunch.

He looked at the sandwich and said, "Edith . . ."

"What, Maury?"

"There's a piece of cellophane in this sandwich."

"So?"

"So I asked for tuna fish, not cellophane."

"So take out the cellophane and eat just the tuna fish."

"But why did you give me cellophane? I didn't ask for cellophane."

"Please, Maury, take it out already."

"If I wanted cellophane, I'd have asked for cellophane."

"You think I put in cellophane on purpose?"

"How do I know? Maybe you thought I wanted a tuna-fish-and-cellophane sandwich."

"Shuddup and eat, you're making me cràzy."

"It isn't that I don't *like* cellophane."

"I'm glad you like it. Now leave me alone."

"If you really want to know, I *love* cellophane. If I knew you had cellophane, I wouldn't have asked for tuna fish."

This was an actual dialogue between Uncle Maury and Aunt Edith, word for word as I heard it.

I didn't stay with Uncle Maury and Aunt Edith as long as I would have liked, because my mother married again, Husband Number Four and, for me, Father Number Three. My new stepfather—I'll call him Dave Number Two—was a bad person. He was a promoter, a con man and a grifter who operated between pure larceny and shady business. He had connections with gangsters and mobsters in Miami, Chicago and New York.

Once, when I was about twelve, my mother was pregnant with my half-brother, and Dave Number Two started beating her up. I went into the kitchen and took the carving knife and held it out toward him and screamed that if he didn't take his hands off her I would kill him. This is the closest I have ever come to committing an act of violence. I'm glad I did it, because he stopped hitting her.

Dave Number Two shot and killed himself two years ago in a San Fernando Valley motel.

* * *

I had to get out of the house. I started going to thc movies.
They only cost a dime then for kids under twelve, and I'd say
I was under twelve, and I'd go in and sit there all day long seeing
the same pictures over and over. I was crazy about the Marx
Brothers pictures, and I loved the musicals. I saw them all. The
Fred Astaire and Ginger Rogers ones ("Isn't It a Lovely Day to
Be Caught in the Rain?"), the Dick Powell and Ruby Keeler ones
("Oh, Baby, What I Couldn't Do with Plenty of Money and
You"), the ones with the big, crazy Busby Berkeley dancing-girl
routines. I fell in love with popular music, with songs and with
show business, sitting there all day watching those musicals. I
memorized all the songs. I can sing them for you today, word for
word. I think I know as many songs from the movies, the Broadway theatre and Tin Pan Alley as anybody in the world.

To get the dimes to go to the movies, I got a job. There was
this man who came around the neighborhood recruiting kids to
sell magazines. It was 1936, I remember. The man gave you a
canvas sack that you hung over your shoulder, and every week
he gave you twenty magazines to sell, and for each magazine you
sold, you kept three cents for yourself. The name of the magazine I chose was *The Literary Digest.* More important than the
three-cents-a-magazine commission was the fact that you could
gct real good things if you sold a lot of them. For every twenty
magazines you sold, you got a brown coupon, known as a
Brownie. Twenty-five Brownies got you a Greenie. One hundred
Greenies got you a Goldie. And for seventy-five Goldies they
gave you a genuine Ranger bicycle with balloon tires, headlight,
speedometer, chromium chain guard, Troxel saddle and New
Departure coaster brakes. That bike was what I had my eye on.
    Unfortunately, I wasn't too good a magazine salesman. The
biggest week I had, I sold four. I made my mother buy the rest
so I could get a Brownie. This went on for weeks. Not only was I

a lousy salesman, but *The Literary Digest* was not the most popular magazine in America, either. It spent that entire year of 1936 predicting that Alf Landon would beat Roosevelt by a landslide. That was the result of its Official Guaranteed Accurate Poll, but there must have been some slip-up, because Roosevelt sneaked through and won that year, taking every state except Maine and Vermont, and the next thing I knew, *The Literary Digest* was out of business and I was left holding my canvas bag.

By now I had two Greenies and eleven Brownies. *I still have them, and if* The Literary Digest *ever goes back into business, I am going to be out there with my bag selling, because, Goddammit, I never did get a bicycle.*

We always had music in our home. There was always a piano, but I never stayed put in one place long enough to learn how to play the piano. *I never learned the technique of anything. I can't do anything.*

My mother could play only one selection on the piano: "Some of These Days." She played it and sang it, and what she played and sang was Sophie Tucker's arrangement, with all the riffs and breaks of Sophie Tucker's rendition. No matter where we were and no matter how poor, my mother always managed to buy or rent a piano and she'd do her impersonation of Sophie Tucker singing "Some of These Days."

We always had books in the house, too—all kinds of wonderful books, the classics, modern books, novels, essays, biographies, the whole literary spectrum. Not because my mother was a big reader. She wasn't.

Mother bought books according to how well the color of the jackets went with the interior decorating. I remember we had *The Meditations of Marcus Aurelius*, which I thought was high-class reading, and I admired my mother for her literary taste, but it turned out Aurelius matched the drapes. So my introduction to literature was the result of how well the books went with the drapes, which is probably as good a way as any.

My favorite author during childhood was Horatio Alger. I loved his stories. I devoured them. I will always be grateful to my mother for buying me a complete set, used, of Horatio Alger—even though he didn't go with the slipcovers. I read his books and reread them and identified with all his heroes.

Horatio Alger kept saying that if you were a nice person and worked hard, something wonderful would happen.

His stories were all the same. There's this shoeshine boy who is working hard shining a rich man's shoes, and then he saves the rich man's daughter from a runaway horse, and the rich man gives him the daughter and the chemical factory. Alger overlooked the fact that the poor but deserving lad might not know a Goddam thing about chemicals, and maybe he hates chemicals, and he hasn't got the least idea how to run a chemical factory, and he accidentally blows up the Goddam chemical factory and the whole typical American town it's in.

I don't care. I loved those books. And I still do. Right now, today, if I could find a book of Alger's that I hadn't read before, I would pick it up and read it right away. Those Alger books had a strong influence on my way of thinking, my way of living, my increasing withdrawal from reality.

Horatio Alger taught me that nothing is impossible and that what is an illusion in my mind today may be a reality tomorrow if enough people accept it.

The difference between reality and unreality is that reality has so little to recommend it. Unreality is so delightful; it is Disneyland and the World's Fair and the movies and the songs we sing and the paintings we see and all the springs of the imagination that pour pleasure into us. Unreality is the vast source from which all creative things come; it is the wonderful infinite world of the imagination; it is literally fantastic. Somewhere in Robert Fulton's imagination one day there popped up a picture of

47

a totally unreal thing that seemed to him, and to him only, to be a steamboat, and it was unreal and without substance. But because Mr. Fulton saw that unreal thing, because he never stopped seeing it, it came to pass in good time that there were *real* things called steamboats substantial enough to carry real people up and down real rivers.

All my life I have refused to face reality. I have lived in a Walter Mitty world of great expectations and daydreams where I could be Cary Grant or Fred Astaire for a few minutes if I wanted to, and it doesn't really hurt anybody, does it? That's why I was so drawn to the Horatio Alger books, and now look what's happened to me. Whammo, like the man said, I'm a genuine living Horatio Alger story myself. All of a sudden, it happened—a rich man came along and said, "Allan Sherman, you've been a good boy. Here's the key to my factory, here's my daughter's hand in marriage, it's all yours."

The idea of becoming a writer came to me very early in life—sometime when I was in grammar school and was maybe twelve, thirteen years old. There was a woman, Elsie Robinson, and she wrote a syndicated column which appeared in the Los Angeles *Herald-Examiner*; she published poems and little stories and humorous sayings sent in by contributors. My first appearance in print was with a humorous four-line poem which I sent to Elsie Robinson. She published it word for word, like I sent it in, and I was very happy and proud to see my name in print for the first time. The poem was:

TREES
by Allan Sherman

I think that I shall never see
A billboard lovely as a tree.
In fact unless the billboards fall—
I'll never see a tree at all.

Unfortunately, I had stolen it, word for word, from Ogden Nash. I saw Mr. Nash's satiric quatrain somewhere, and I thought it was good, and thus I began my literary career, albeit as a plagiarist. I didn't realize there was anything wrong with this. I had the idea everybody who sent in a contribution to Elsie Robinson had read it some place else and she gave the credit to the person smart enough to send it in, or to the one with the earliest postmark, or something.

At John Burroughs Junior High School, in Los Angeles, I began writing original squibs for the paper, *The Far and Near*. I also went to high schools in New York, Chicago, Miami and Los Angeles. At the Fairfax High School in Los Angeles, I became editor of the school paper, *The Colonial Gazette*. I was also beginning to write song lyrics and librettos, and finally I wrote the senior class musical show, *Yankee Doodle Presents*, the star of which was a classmate, Ricardo Montalban.

I was also an outstanding member of the debating team. I invented the Sherman System of Rebuttal, which was based on the Sliding Defense. You use the Sliding Defense when you're in trouble and you have to slide from what you just said to the exact opposite, without letting anyone realize it. I had already discovered that people are impressed by statistics and by quotations from Learned Authorities. Well, in a school debate you have little three-by-five cards with things written on them, and you may quote from whichever authorities you wish. I didn't want to waste a lot of my valuable time going to the library and doing research for quotations to quote.

I remember one debate where the topic was "*Resolved:* that Installment Buying is Beneficial to the American Economy." My team had to take the negative. Well, I was born with a gift for parody and an ability to invent titles of books and names of authorities, and so when I had to stand up in rebuttal to the opposition, I read from a blank three-by-five card (making it up as I went along), "I would now like to quote from *Problems of*

Consumer Debt by Carruthers and Kiekhofer—that is, Smedley W. Carruthers of Yale University and Alvin E. Kiekhofer, also from Yale—in which they state on page 149, quote, 'The rising curve of fiscal delinquency and repossessions of consumer products poses a threat to the inventory system of this nation,' end quote. Need I say more, ladies and gentlemen?" *It never failed. I always demolished the opposition.*

Somewhere between movies like *Mr. Smith Goes to Washington,* and my Civics class in high school, and my first excursions into the writings of Thomas Wolfe, I fell in love with the United States of America.

When I discovered the *Federalist* papers, I read them over and over and over, and I memorized the Bill of Rights, and the whole splendid idea of this country burst upon me. This small group of men, so poor in material things, and so rich in sensitivity and intelligence and foresight that they could create together the fairest, most just, most democratic nation since the world began. To live in a country, even in a *world,* where Abraham Lincoln had lived! To know that as long as I lived Thomas Paine would watch out for my rights, and if anybody threatened them, he would cry out and kick and fuss to preserve them for me. To grow up in the living presence of Franklin D. Roosevelt. That was *something.*

I entered the American Legion public-speaking contest. The subject that year was the Constitution of the United States. I was one of the winners in Los Angeles, but I was eliminated in the state-wide finals, and I didn't get to go to Washington to compete in the nationals.

Maybe it was just as well I didn't win.

As I grew older I found I cared less and less about the problems of Installment Buying, and when spring came and the girls began to show up at school in their summer dresses, it dimmed my enthusiasm for our great Constitution and the men who had framed it. By the time it was summer vacation and the dresses were even thinner and I could go to the public swimming pools and see sixty to seventy percent of a whole girl—by the time *that* happened, I couldn't have cared less about Thomas Jefferson and the Supreme Court, and I lost any ambition I might ever have had of becoming our first Jewish President.

I was ashamed. My mind was becoming obsessed with girls, sex and depravity. I couldn't understand it, because all the heroes of the Horatio Alger books, all those newspaper boys and shoeshine boys I had always admired and emulated—they never had any sexual desires at all. They must have been fags or eunuchs or something. Whatever they were, they were not interested in sex, and this is where Horatio and I parted company, because by this time there was damn near nothing else on my mind but sex, sex, sex.

Warning: The next chapter is pretty sexy. It's all about puberty and adolescence and girls and nakedness, and a lot of people said I shouldn't put it in this book because it would spoil my image. So if you like my image better than you like me, please skip the next chapter. For good or bad, though, it's true; it's an honest chronicle of my own years of discovery of sex, and that's why I put it in. For that matter, those who are expecting something like The Carpetbaggers *might as well skip the next chapter, too.*

I'm sexy, all right, but not that *sexy.*

CHAPTER 3

Puberty Revisited,

OR Sex and the Single Me

WHEN I WAS A LITTLE BOY and we lived in Chicago, I had a whole basement full of toys, and the one I remember best was a set of electric trains—passenger trains, each car more than a foot long, with all the accessories, signals going up and down, stations, blinking lights, water towers and coal chutes—the works. Then the Depression came, and my father lost his business, and we had to move to California.

I remember one day going down to the basement to play with my trains, and *there were no trains.*

No tracks, no blinking lights, no stations, no water towers. My trains were gone. So were all my other toys.

Sometimes when I am in New York, even now, I go up to the second floor of the F. A. O. Schwarz toy store and wander around for two or three hours; meanwhile people are trying to get me on the phone, and nobody knows where I am, and I'm lost as far as the world is concerned, but I'm up there on the second floor of F. A. O. Schwarz having a ball playing with the toys. I'm working the electric trains and playing all the new games and fitting the plastic pieces of model kits together, and I guess what I am really doing is trying to make something in my life continuous, because from that day when the trains were suddenly gone—those large, solid trains with lighted cars and the passengers' silhouettes painted inside the windows—from the day they disappeared, something else disappeared with them: my ability, or at least my desire, to distinguish between what is reality and what is fantasy.

I wonder why, when I started to write a chapter about sex, I began with the missing trains.

I guess it was because I wanted you to understand, and I wanted myself to understand, that since the morning those trains disappeared in Chicago, since the night my family fell apart in Los Angeles, since the first time I was sent away to live with distant relatives, I have lived with the terror that there is nothing tangible, that there is no one who really wants me, and that anything that is any fun—anything in the world that is any fun—is not going to last. One morning I'll look for it, and it just won't be there any more.

Nobody ever told me anything about sex. I mean, by the time I was ready for a heart-to-heart, father-son talk, I no longer had a father. My mother was embarrassed to discuss it, and was also, I now realize, involved in her own sex problems. The only preparation I had, I got by osmosis. I was a nice Jewish boy, so I knew you shouldn't *do it*, whatever *it* was, to nice girls. And all my life I have been attracted to nice girls—the kind you aren't supposed to *do it* to—and they, too, have been brought up, at least in my generation, that they shouldn't *do it* either. How *it*

ever gets done between nice people is a mystery to me. What I
think happens is, nice people do it, but their hearts aren't in it.

The first girl I remember was Natalie.

I was living with a distant aunt and uncle in New York, in an
apartment house on Audubon Avenue on the upper West Side.
I was about ten years old, and so was Natalie, and she lived on
the same floor, and we played an interesting game. I imagine we
had to invent this game to rationalize our sexual explorations of
each other, because without the game it would have been a
blunt admission that we were curious about each other's sex organs, and this of course was a nasty and dirty thing.

We played the game in the hallway. The idea was, we would
run across the hall, and the first one to touch a certain doorknob at the other end of the hall was allowed to see and touch
the other's privates, and this was a real good game. *Oh, boy!* I
tell you, I couldn't wait to get home from school and get the
game started. And the more we played this game, the more it
was a good game. It sure beat football and stickball and Monop-
oly, which was also popular at the time, and Ring-a-Levio and
Kick-the-Can, and even if Scrabble had been invented then, I
wouldn't have wanted to play Scrabble, because the highest
triple word score in the world would not have expressed how
much I liked the game Natalie and I played every afternoon.

We had no name for our game. The rules came natural to
both of us, and the rules got more relaxed as the game continued. We never argued about who won, because losing was just
as much fun as winning. I knew I had a good thing going,
and I didn't tell any of the other little boys about my secret
game. At the time, I thought Natalie was the only girl in the
world who would play such a game, but now I realize that I
might have made a fortune with Parker Brothers or Milton
Bradley if they could have seen their way clear to put out something called *The Natalie-and-Allan Doorknob Game.* It would

have been a big seller, with very simple instructions and no plastic pieces to get lost.

It was terrible when I had to leave New York and go back to Los Angeles because my mother had a boyfriend there. My heart was broken. I guess in a way—in a ten-year-old's way—I had fallen in love with Natalie.

Back in Los Angeles, there was a girl in junior high school—Geraldine.

I thought she was beautiful, and I was in love with her. I followed her from a distance. I thought about her all day and I dreamed about her at night. Finally I got up enough nerve to ask her to go to a school dance with me. She laughed in my face and said I didn't appeal to her because I had a hooked nose.

I looked in the mirror. I knew I wasn't a handsome devil. I knew I had a tendency to plumpness. A Clock Gable I knew I wasn't, but now what I saw in the mirror was a fat, ugly gargoyle with a hooked nose like the beak of a vulture. Well, from that day until June 6, 1944—for ten years—I felt such a shame about my ugly nose that I would not sit in profile to anybody. If I was with a person, I always sat directly in front of that person. If I was traveling in a bus or streetcar full of strangers, I would sit with my hand over my nose and pretend to be rubbing it thoughtfully. I had this sense of shame that I had something awful on me—something I couldn't cover up, and people could see it wherever I went.

When I got out of the Army, I took my $200 mustering-out pay and I went to a certain Dr. Oscar Becker in Chicago. On June 6, 1944 (it was D-Day), at the Michael Reese hospital, he performed a submucous resection on my nose—what they call a plastic job. He supposedly gave me a beautiful Greek nose. Also I am supposed to breathe better, although this hasn't happened yet and my new nose was twenty-one years old in June.

In those days Dr. Becker was a famous man among self-conscious Jewish girls and boys. His fee was $200, and it included hospital, surgery and pre- and post-operative treatment. I suppose now it is probably around $2,000.

I was terrified of the operation. Dr. Becker gave me a local anesthetic, so I was conscious while he was chipping away with a little mallet and chisel on my formerly ugly nose. To forget my fears during the operation, I started singing a current song hit, and Dr. Becker sang the alternate lines.

I sang: "Won't you tell me when . . ."

Dr. Becker: "We will meet again?"

Together: "Sunday, Monday or always?"

After I came out with my new nose, nobody noticed that I looked any different. But *I* felt better, and this shame about my nose went away. It was soon replaced by different shames, of course.

Among my counterparts at the University of Illinois, Northwestern University and the University of Chicago, Dr. Becker's noses blossomed everywhere. You could recognize a Becker nose. It had a special and distinct design, like the postwar Buicks with the three holes. I hasten to add that Dr. Becker's noses have only the standard two holes.

Between Geraldine's disparaging remark and the Dr. Becker nose, ten years elapsed. Ten years in which I was unable to make overtures—let alone first acts—to lovely, nice girls for whom I yearned. But I did not starve for feminine companionship, thank God.

There was Shmoozie.

It was during one of my periodical migrations to Chicago. I was attending Tuley High School and living with Grandma and Grandpa across the street from Humboldt Park. Shmoozie was a girl on the block.

I believe that on every block in America there exists a Shmoozie. Of course, neighborhoods don't have blocks today. Blocks aren't what they used to be, because now they have those garden housing developments with subdivisions and play areas, and the streets are curved and don't begin and end the way a real street should, and people don't live on square blocks any more. And nowadays they wouldn't write a song like "Love Is Just Around the Corner," because there is no corner.

But in those days there was a corner on every block, and there was at least one Shmoozie on every block. She was a girl who was anybody's girl. Shmoozie was all we ever called her, and nobody ever knew her by any other name, first or last. Shmoozie was a girl that, when it came time for sex education, you went to Shmoozie. Usually another boy fixed you up with Shmoozie, and you went to Humboldt Park after twilight in the summer evenings, toward ten o'clock, and you crept into the bushes there, and Shmoozie let you fool with her privates—or, in her case, her publics.

There was a whole summer in Chicago when I was hiding in the bushes with her every night, practically, and it got me real hot and crazy.

Shmoozie, wherever you are today, and whatever high position you may hold in the councils of American womanhood, I shall be forever grateful to you.

I do not know what has become of the Shmoozies of America, but from what I hear, I think what has happened is that *every* girl has opened up a little Shmoozie department of her own. But in the days of my youth, before World War II, there was still a difference between the so-called respectable girls and the Shmoozies; the former wouldn't, and the latter would. Maybe the Shmoozies had neurotic problems that made them shmooze quickly; I don't know. Because when any guy on the block had a date with Shmoozie, it was with the express purpose of going behind a bush in Humboldt Park and petting her. You didn't have to take her to the movies. You didn't have to buy her a soda. You didn't have to give her a buildup or use a line or per-

petrate a snow job. She just put out. It was her way of making
friends—and of me she made a lifelong friend.

*Sad to say, I can't for the life of me recall what she looked like
or the color of her hair or her eyes, because I never saw her except in the dark.*

But I must tell you that even after that long, hot, crazy summer with Shmoozie, when I left Chicago to go back to Los Angeles I was still a virgin.

When next we find me, yo-yo that I am, I was bouncing in
Los Angeles again. This was during my all-day movie period. I
was about fourteen or fifteen, and my sex life consisted of wild,
passionate dreams which co-starred Alice Faye and/or Betty
Grable and/or Ginger Rogers. (Much as I loved the Marx
Brothers pictures, I was never able to get up any sex fantasies
featuring Margaret Dumont.) But now, looking back on these
torrid dreams—now when I see Miss Faye or Miss Grable or Miss
Rogers on the *Late Late Show*—they seem as virginal and innocent as I was then. Compared to Romy Schneider and Marilyn
Monroe and Elizabeth Taylor, the sexpots of my puberty could
have banded together and opened a nunnery.

Next came Conchita.

My stepfather, Dave Number Two, had begun wheeling and
dealing, and for a while there he was in the chips, and my parents had a sleep-in maid. This luscious Mexican creature, Conchita, got my libido all fired up, and she knew it. She was
about seventeen years old, and unreasonably well developed,
with long black hair, and hips that operated on a 24-jewel movement as she slithered around the house. Conchita could single-
breastedly have laid waste the entire Boy Scout movement.

I followed her around like a hypnotized bird following a
snake. I had the constant hots.

After a few weeks Conchita had *me* doing the housework,

pushing the carpet sweeper or washing the dishes while she stood in the corner with her motor running, eating my mother's candy and singing "Perfidia" or "La Cucaracha" in Spanish.

That was when I got the mumps, and the doctor came to the house and warned me not to get out of bed until I was cured, because the mumps can be very serious to a young boy (one's testicles can atrophy). But how could I stay in bed when all through the day I could hear the suggestive rustlings of Conchita's dress and the sensuous strains of her off-key "Perfidia," and every few minutes she would insinuate her bosom into my room to see if I was all right? I crawled out of bed. Just to see her smile. Just to be in the same room with her. I followed her around the house, oblivious to the pain in my groin, thinking it was passion when actually it was the swan song of one of my testicles.

I am pointing this out, not for sensationalism but because I am trying to give this chapter all of the suspense and cliff-hanger aspects that it had in real life. I only want you to know that when Conchita ran away to get married a month later, there I was, a mere youth of fifteen, with only one ball left, and *still* a virgin.

Now we come to Miss Giggle.

I guess it was my junior year in high school when a bunch of my friends decided that I had been a virgin long enough, and they took me to San Berdoo.

San Berdoo is the nickname of a town called San Bernardino, fifty-five miles from Los Angeles. If you are old enough to have listened to the old Bob Hope radio show, you will remember that he used to make a lot of jokes about San Berdoo, and you probably didn't understand why the studio audience laughed their heads off. It was a Southern California inside joke. Everybody in Los Angeles knew that San Berdoo had a street, D Street, on which every house was a whorehouse, ranging from what they called the bull pen, where you walked into a little courtyard and all around you in tiny stucco houses there were girls hanging out of windows, asking if you wanted to "have a little party," where the price was one dollar, on up to the first-class houses where the price was *two* dollars.

The whole idea sounded very racy to me. A horny group of five of us was organized by my friend Morton, and one Friday night we drove out to San Berdoo. I was pretty nervous and shaky, but Morton was a model of self-confidence. He parked the car, and we trooped up the stairs of a large frame house, and Morton rang the bell. A middle-aged, white-haired woman opened the door.

"*Why, good evening, Morton,*" she said, "*and how are you?*"

I don't think I will ever be quite as impressed again as I was at that moment when the Madam called Morton by his first name. And this was one of the fancy two-dollar places.

We went into the house, and there was a parlor, and five girls came out, one for each of us, and we all had the hots in two seconds. The one with me was not the one I really wanted. She was a plump bleached blonde with a weird giggle. The one I liked was fooling with one of my friends. She looked a little like Conchita, but I didn't have the heart to reject the prostitute sitting on my lap.

I have never been able to say to any other human being, man, woman, child, prostitute or President, "I don't want you. I want the one over there."

So I went upstairs with Miss Giggle, into a little bedroom which was her working quarters.

"Take off your clothes," she said.

"What for?" I asked.

"*What for?* What do you mean, what for?"

I had never been naked in front of any female except my mother in my life.

"Just a minute, here!" I said.

Miss Giggle unbuttoned or unsnapped something in back of her, and all of a sudden she was naked. She was the first all-naked girl I had ever seen.

"See," she said, "*easy*. Now I'll help you."

She did, and she was very efficient.

Then she went and got a pan and filled it with warm water and soap.

"What are you doing?" I asked, standing there naked, trying to cover myself with my hands, like September Morn.

"First I wash you," she said.

Cleanliness, I thought, *is next to Godliness*.

I should have said, "Oh, no, you don't."

Because it had nothing to do with cleanliness. The fact is that Miss Giggle and her associates had a lot of clientele like me, fifteen or sixteen years old. You were very horny and standing there naked with a naked lady for the first time in your life, and by the time your hostess had finished soaping you—forget it, Charlie, *it was all over*.

When I went down the stairs, I gave the other guys the signal, as if to say it had been real great. Because, Goddammit, I was not going to admit that I had now been to a whorehouse and *still* hadn't gotten laid.

I was finally deflowered by a girl for whom—to this day—I have mixed emotions which run from gratitude to rage, and back.

Her name was Eleanor.

I had a reputation, even in high school, for being funny, and Eleanor kind of liked me, and a bunch of us went to Santa Monica on a weenie bake. It was night, and we roasted hot dogs and toasted marshmallows and drank Cokes, and later when the fire became glowing embers we went in swimming, and afterward we huddled together on the sand in the blankets we had brought to keep warm. Not only did one thing lead to another, but I made every effort to speed up the whole process, and Eleanor made very little effort to slow it down, and the next thing I knew we were *doing it.* We were doing it pretty good, as far as I was concerned, and I remember thinking, *This is even better than it's cracked up to be,* and then I remember losing track of what I was thinking, and then, just at the very moment when she should have said almost anything else, Eleanor whispered the most crushing words I had ever heard:

"Say something funny," Eleanor said.

Well, there you have it. There you have my six years of puberty, and as I look back over them and realize that I have two children, both going through these awful years, I wonder—oh, God, I wonder—why it has to be like that. Why does it have to be that every human being I've ever met is hung up and mixed up and tortured all his life by the mistakes and fumblings and shames and guilts of those years? Why can't there be a simple way, a beautiful way, for a child to encounter this loveliest experience on earth for the first time?

CHAPTER 4

Chug-a-Lugging,
AND Other Things I Learned in College

I WAS SITTING in this class in Public Speaking and looking outside at the brown-and-gold leaves of October in the year of 1941 on the campus of the University of Illinois—a nice college located either in Champaign, Illinois, or Urbana, Illinois, depending upon what classroom you are in, because the campus straddles both towns.

My time was running out. The other students got up and delivered their five-minutes speeches with clarity, firmness and conviction. Finally it was my turn, and I still hadn't thought of anything to say. I walked to the lectern. I hemmed. Then I hawed. I cleared my throat. Then I said:

"I shall give an illustrated lecture on the interior of the human mouth—the teeth, the tongue, the upper palate, the lower palate and other points of interest."

Then, to illustrate my lecture, I stuck my finger in my mouth, as if to point out the various things I was talking about, and for five solid minutes I spoke totally unintelligible gibberish, never removing the finger from my mouth, and sometimes inserting my entire fist.

At the end of five minutes I removed my hand and said, "I hope this has given you a new understanding of the human oral apparatus. Thank you."

The next assignment was a practical how-to-do-it lecture. The other students demonstrated things like How the Internal-Combustion Engine Works, How to Ski, and How to Make Your Own Short-Wave Radio. I gave my demonstration speech on the Art of Doughnut Dunking. I brought to the lectern with me a bag of doughnuts and a cup of hot coffee. I gave the entire speech with a mouthful of dunked doughnut, and it was impossible to make out what I was saying.

Another student in the class was Sheldon Keller, a very funny fellow (recently the head writer of Danny Kaye's television show), and he was the first to catch on to my Great Master Plan. Sheldon began to laugh hysterically during my doughnut speech, because he realized that it was my intention to go through the entire semester of Public Speaking without ever uttering one single intelligible word.

I damn near made it, too. But about two thirds of the way through the year the professor caught on.

After the doughnut speech Sheldon came over and said he thought I was a very funny person, and if I wasn't doing anything after class we should go over to Bidwell's and have a beer. So I cut my three-o'clock class in Modern European History, and we went over to Bidwell's and we had a beer. There was a front room and a back room at Bidwell's. The back room was where you went when you had a date. The lights were low, and there were intimate booths, and you carved your initials and your date's initials into the tables or the paneled walls. Keller and I went into the front room. They served only beer at Bidwell's —Schlitz, Foxhead 400, Pabst and a beer from St. Louis which was very popular with the evil-minded Illinois undergraduates. It was called Griesedick Brothers' Beer, and we would ask for it by shouting, "Gimme a Greasy Dick!"

The first song parody I ever invented was in 1942, to the tune of "Won't You Come Home, Bill Bailey?" Here it is:

> *Burn down that Union Building,*
> *Burn Lincoln Hall,*
> *But, please, boys, don't burn down Bidwell's!*
> *Burn down the football stadium,*
> *Huff Gym as well,*
> *But, please, boys, don't burn down Bidwell's!*
> *We know you love this campus, we think it's swell,*
> *You can burn it till it flames like hell!*
> *But if that backroom's found in flames,*
> *We're gonna call you dirty names,*
> *So don't burn Bidwell's down!*

It swept the campus like wildfire. Within twenty-four hours the whole student body was singing it. And they never forgot it. Twenty years later I still have total strangers come up to me and sing, "Please, Boys, Don't Burn Down Bidwell's."

So Shelly and I had a few Greasy Dicks there in Bidwell's, and we told some stories and made some jokes and decided we liked one another. He asked me if I had pledged any fraternity, and he identified himself as a member of Sigma Alpha Mu. They were called "Sammies," and in those years only Jews could join. *Last year, in San Francisco, a Japanese boy gave me the secret handshake.*

I said I was afraid I was doomed to be an independent because my family didn't have the money to support me in a fraternity. He said I shouldn't worry about money, and he invited me to the SAM house for dinner, and I was introduced to the other SAM members—about forty-five or fifty of them—and they seemed like a cheerful crowd.

Like a typical Jewish boy, I had been living in the Catholic dormitory, Newman Hall.

I was not happy in Newman Hall. It was like being with strangers in a big hotel. On the other hand, I felt very much at home in the SAM house. And the brothers looked me over, and Shelly made a big pitch for me, telling them I had a great sense of humor and, even though I was kind of a slob, I was active in outside activities and was going to be a Big Man On Campus.

I had joined the staff of the paper, the *Daily Illini*, and the Debating Society, the Drama Club and the Illini Union, which put on musical shows. I was to write three musical shows before I finished college—or, rather, before college finished me. I was one of the thirty-two freshmen pledged to Tomahawk, the sophomore honorary activity organization. It was considered a big honor, and they had a traditional ceremony, initiating us by the Tomahawk Tree, south of the Illini Union Building.

So Shelly told me the SAM's liked me, and I said I liked them, too, but I couldn't afford the $55 a month for room and board. He said they would arrange for me to wash dishes and help in the kitchen, and this would pay for the food and then the rent would equal what I was paying for room and board at Newman Hall. So I pledged SAM.

I was terribly ignorant of the amenities of life, like how to make girls and how to dress properly and carry on social conversations. I didn't have much of a wardrobe. My basic outfit was a pair of brown corduroy pants, a dark green sports coat two sizes too big, and a striped green shirt.

The first thing SAM did for me, a Haberdashery Committee was appointed to guide me, and they took me to Lou Overgard's, a shop that sold college-type clothes. And the Committee explained to me that you don't wear a purple tie with a green-striped shirt. They introduced me to color harmonies. They advanced me the money to buy a natural-beige cashmere sweater, a Shetland sport coat, some white button-down Oxford-cloth shirts and brown-and-white saddle shoes. I had to rub dirt into them because you weren't properly dressed unless you were wearing dirty saddle shoes.

At first I felt conspicuous in my cashmere sweater and dirty saddle shoes. I felt like Robert Benchley, who once wrote a beautiful piece about his first white Palm Beach suit and how he felt ridiculous walking down the street in it, like everybody was looking at him and snickering, and finally he was sorry he bought the suit. *I was reading a lot of Benchley and Mark Twain and Dorothy Parker and Thurber and Perelman and Stephen Leacock and all the humorists available.*

In 1942 it was more important to chug-a-lug a stein of beer than to prepare oneself for a career in comedy. One's ability to absorb beer was a status symbol then.

A Beer-drinking Committee was appointed to teach me chug-a-lugging. To chug-a-lug means to drink a whole stein of beer in one long swallow without lowering the stein or taking a breath. You tip the stein to your lips and start gulping, and your friends keep yelling, "Chug-a-lug, chug-a-lug, chug-a-lug!"

The Jewish Greek-letter societies exchanged lunches and dinners, and if you didn't have a date, they arranged a date for you from one of the three Jewish sororities. A Dancing Committee was appointed, and my SAM brothers showed me how to do the Lindy and the Suzy Q. A briefing meeting was held, at which all known information was exchanged about how readily various girls would kiss and neck and pet.

Such sex as was accomplished in the University of Illinois in the early 1940's was accomplished either in the back room of Bidwell's (students were not allowed to have cars) or in a part of the college known as "South Campus." If you were caught having a rendezvous in this secluded garden of love, you were liable to be summarily expelled from school. I would usually have to take my dates either to the back room of Bidwell's or into the fraternity-house chapter room. The chapter room of the SAM house was scientifically designed to ensure the greatest possible facility in necking. Yes, *necking*. In those days, even if you were in love, it was the exceptional girl who went all the way.

There was very little actual cohabitation going on. A Cohabitation Committee was appointed, but it didn't help. Well, the SAM parlor's lights were the lowest possible, and there were deep leather couches into which you and your girl could sink, and there were romantic records of Harry James ("Instead of making conversation, Make Love to Me") and Glenn Miller ("Mister Whatchacallum, whatcha doin' tonight? Hope you're in the mood because I'm feelin' just right").

The only things that interfered with my sex life were my studies, which I put aside, and washing dishes to pay for my meals, which I could not put aside.

One day my mother wrote and suggested that I ask my father to send me some money. He had never given a cent toward my upbringing or education. He had remarried and was living in Birmingham, Alabama. I had not seen or heard from him for twelve years.

I took a bus down to Birmingham. I went to his place of business. He had a small factory which wound armatures for generators. I had not written him that I was coming. I stood outside his factory for an hour, getting up my courage. And then I walked in, and there was this great big fat man sitting in his office— Percy Copelon. He looked up at me.

"I'm Allan," I said, "your son."

His eyes filled with tears. He got up from the desk and put his arms around me. He hugged me. We talked all afternoon and then we had dinner, and he began pouring out all the bad things he could think of about my mother. I changed the subject to my college education and my future, and I asked for his help. He agreed to help me. The price he exacted for his help was that I change my name back to my legal name, his name—Allan Copelon. I agreed.

As soon as I returned to school, I told everybody my name was now Allan Copelon. I was writing "The Campus Scout," a daily column of gossip, humor and crazy poems for the *Daily Illini*. I had to give *some* explanation of why a Sherman overnight becomes a Copelon. So I wrote this column:

THE CAMPUS SCOUT
by Allan Copelon
(Formerly Allan Sherman)

On a recent trip to Birmingham, Alabama, I was standing on a corner when a strange man came up to me and said:

"I am Brown from the Birmingham *Sun.*"

Retorted I: "I don't care if you're black and blue from the Birmingham *Post.*"

It turned out he was a reporter, and he asked me many questions. When he was finished, he said, "May I use your name?"

I replied that he could not only *use* my name, he could have it for keeps.

And that, Dear Readers, is why you are reading another name at the top of this column. To be exact, Allan Sherman is now Allan Copelon.

I sent the column to my father, to prove to him that I had kept my promise.

I did not get any money. Not a nickel. I did not even receive a letter. I couldn't understand it. I wrote him a few letters. He didn't answer me. I was furious and I was miserable. I changed my name back to Sherman. Now I had to write another column to explain why I was Sherman again. It was in dialogue:

THE CAMPUS SCOUT
by Allan Sherman

Who?
Allan Sherman.
Are you sure?
Sure I'm sure.
But didn't he change his name some time ago?
Yes, but he was just going through a phase.
But why did he change it back again?
Well, he was standing on a corner and a reporter came up and said, "I'm Warren Brown from the Chicago *Sun*."
So he answered, "I don't care if you're Warren Peace from the book of the same name."

Say something funny say something funny say something funny . . . to cover up this terrible experience, from your friends, from the whole world, most of all from yourself, because how can you look reality in the face and think, My God, my own father doesn't care whether I live or I die?

Six years later I was writing jokes for television comedians with Louis Quinn, who was then a writer. We were working in his place at the Beaux Arts Apartments. I was sitting at the typewriter, and during a lull in our work Louie picked up a copy of the New York *Journal-American*.

"Hey, kid," Louie said, "you want to see a funny picture?"
"Come on, Louie," I said, "let's stop futzing around and

write the jokes."

"No kidding," he said, "this is really weird. Listen: *'Perched atop a flagpole until he starves away half his 350 pounds is Tarrant City, Alabama, fat-man Percy Copelon, who . . .'*"

I grabbed the paper out of Louie's hands. I couldn't believe it. I called my mother in Chicago and she said she had already seen it in the newsreel. She was crying. She said she had hoped I wouldn't see it in the newsreel or the papers. She was afraid I would think my father was insane.

A few weeks later I was over at Louie's place again and he said, "Too bad about your Daddy."

"What?"

He showed me the headline:

DOWN FROM FLAGPOLE,

KILLED IN BATHTUB FALL

I don't understand. *I don't understand the way my father lived or the way he died.*

In December 1942, I enlisted in the United States Army.

My Army career was short and stupid. I was sent to Camp Grant, Illinois, and they gave me all kinds of classification tests and determined my wide range of qualifications and skills, and because they appreciated the fact that I was a college man, they put me in the Infantry. My dog-tag number was 16121278.

They gave me a uniform, too long, and a haircut, too short. Then a bunch of us were shipped out on a Pullman train—of course, since there was a war going on, everything was kept very secret, and we weren't told where we were going.

When the train stopped, it was at Camp Wolters, Texas, a non-oasis in the desert, fifty miles west of Fort Worth and five miles from Mineral Wells, Texas, where they make Crazy Water Crystals. I understand this is a laxative, and it's a good thing they had it there in Mineral Wells, because it gave you something to do if you got a pass and were able to get into town for a few hours.

I hated the Army. It was too damned organized. When I went in, I was very patriotic, but that was before I knew that they would insist that I wake up so early in the morning, and do what everybody else did, and take orders all day long.

I got a terrible attack of asthma. I could breathe in, but not out. *After you've breathed in several times in succession without breathing out, it not only gets boring but it is dreadfully painful.* I went on sick call and they put me in the camp hospital. My treatment was administered by a nurse. She'd bring me a glass of water and a glass full of aspirins and say, "Take as many as you want."

Nice ladies from Fort Worth came to visit us in the hospital, and they brought us jigsaw puzzles, to while away the time. We were delighted to get those jigsaw puzzles because after the nurse went to bed, we opened them all up, mixed them together on a table top, distributed them, and used them for poker chips in an all-night poker game that we had going secretly. The chips represented real money, and I lost more than $100 to a young soldier just out of Harvard. He came from New York and his name was Jerry Weinstein. I never paid him, and, as you will see later, I owe him much more than that hundred dollars.

Then they gave me allergy tests.

I was allergic to thirty-one different things: sheep dander, horse dander, palm fronds, corned beef and Brazil nuts.

My Uncle Maury wrote me, "Is there no way we can win the war without your having to eat Brazil nuts?"

I guess there wasn't.

I was medically discharged in May, 1943, and back I went to the fraternity house on the Illini campus, and there I took up with a vivacious, dark-haired, dark-eyed girl from Missouri—Dee

Chackes. She was beautiful and slim and intelligent, and she had a great sense of humor. I knew this because she laughed longer and harder at my jokes than any other girl I had ever met.

Dee was like a girl from a poem.

There was and is a rare, unusual beauty about Dee—a beauty in the slenderness of her figure, the charm of her face, the wistfulness of her smile, the humor lighting up her dark eyes. And there is a beauty in her soul. A sweetness. My grandmother called her a *"zisseh neshumah"*—a sweet soul. And she was sweet from the inside out. She was someone completely unusual. I wrote a serious love song recently that says some of what I feel:

> *Oddball—*
> *You're something else, that's the rumor,*
> *What an oddball—*
> *With that wild sense of humor . . .*
> *Why do you do those strange and peculiar*
> *   things you do?*
> *Everyone else in the world is in step,*
> *   but no, not you.*
>
> *You're just an oddball*
> *All the time nonconforming.*
> *Tell me oddball—*
> *What makes you so heart-warming?*
> *You're not too good-looking;*
> *You're way out of style—*
> *And even when you make a serious face,*
> *I've still got to smile.*
>
> *'Cause you're an oddball*
> *Is there no one to love you?*
> *Little Oddball,*
> *Do they all make fun of you?*

Well, you're one of a kind,
And that's what I find refreshing and new—
And I guess I'm an oddball, too—
'Cause, Little Oddball, I love you.

Once I was out of work and we were broke and it was Christmas and she went to work at a Doubleday bookstore. I sat home all day, waiting for the phone to ring. Dee was out selling books, standing on her feet all day. And still, when she walked in the front door, she lit up the whole one-room apartment with her smile. And she didn't complain. And she prepared dinner. And she laughed at trouble. And she always had faith in me, no matter how badly things were going. And she never wanted anything for herself. Just to give, always to be giving.

She's one of a kind.

I gave her my fraternity pin. Why she took it, why she chose me, I still don't understand. All kinds of good-looking fellows, and wealthy ones, were after her.

But Dee took my fraternity pin, and that night the whole fraternity, all the brothers, gathered on the lawn in front of Dee's sorority house, and we serenaded her, and I had tears in my eyes because I knew our love would last forever.

A week later she returned my pin.

I asked her, "Why?"

"Because I'm not in love with you," she said. "I love you, but I'm not *in love* with you. I could not be serious about you in the future."

"How can you say such a terrible thing?"

"Because I can't picture us being married."

"So don't picture it," I said, all choked up. "Why should you have to picture anything like that?"

"I'm the type of person who pictures," she said coldly. "You see, that's another difference between us. You don't picture. We live in two different worlds. One with pictures, one without."

"All right, all right," I said. "Picture anything you like. Picture to your heart's content."

"Very well," she said, "so I can't picture us being married. Here's your pin. But I'm not going to leave you in the lurch. I have a nice girl picked out for you. This girl is good-looking and she is more the intellectual type than I am. She's your kind of a girl, Allan, much more your type of girl than me. I can *picture* you with her."

"Who? I ask you, who?"

"I was thinking of Stella Kane. She's an A.E.Phi. She's got eyes for you."

"I can't picture Stella Kane and me being married," I said.

But, on the rebound, I went around with Stella Kane. She wrote poetry. She introduced me to Wordsworth and Shelley and Swinburne. Stella and I went steady for a few weeks, but my heart was longing for Dee, and her heart was longing for me, and we got together again. Inevitable. Kismet.

This time I gave her the pin quietly, in the back room of Bidwell's.

I wrote the libretto for *Nothing Ventured,* the varsity musical show of 1943, and the lyrics to Bill Pilkenton's music, and I played the part of Adolf Hitler. We played to capacity audiences four evenings. The drama critic of the *Daily Illini*, Nick Shuman, wrote: "Any deficiencies in the singing voice of Sherman Shickelgruber were dissolved by the sophomore's quaint expression, carried over from everyday living, and his general stage charm which couldn't help but win the audience for him. . . . The need for more rehearsing was displayed frequently by the cast, which missed cues and fumbled lines more than once."

Another show I wrote, also with a patriotic theme, was a parody of the entire show *Oklahoma!* In my version the title song became "Yoooooookohama, where the planes come sweep-

ing through the wind!" And another one became "Everything's
Up to Date in Berchtesgaden."

By this time I was obsessed with the idea of show business. I
was writing songs and parodies and sketches for the "stunt shows"
which our fraternity put on every semester, and I helped out
with the material for Sigma Delta Tau, which was Dee's sorority.
Dee and I even worked up a little act with songs and hoofing
and snapper patter.

The college had encouraged the students to open a nonalco-
holic night club in the Union Building to keep us out of trou-
ble in Bidwell's and even more depraved places. It was called
Club Commons and its manager was my SAM brother Marshall
Migatz. The act of Sherman and Chackes played Club Com-
mons many times. But Dee did not picture herself as an actress.
So I put together an act with my old buddy Shelly Keller, my
Public Speaking classmate and SAM frater. We were a big hit at
Club Commons.

Keller & Sherman were a hotter act than Sherman & Chackes.
Our act started at the bottom and went downhill. Here's an example:

KELLER: I'm homesick!

SHERMAN: But you *are* home.

KELLER: I know, but I'm sick of it!

We even opened up some unexplored areas of questionable
taste:

SHERMAN: Boy, am I happy! Boy, am I happy!

KELLER: Why are you so happy?

SHERMAN: Because my girlfriend has syphilis.

KELLER: What's so good about syphilis?

SHERMAN: *It* must *be good. The Chicago* Tribune's *against it!*

There was a fellow in the fraternity whose father was Danny
Thomas' dentist, and he was overcome by what he thought were
the great talents of Brother Keller and Brother Sherman. He

said we had to have a wider exposure than Club Commons. So he spoke to his father the dentist, who spoke to Danny Thomas, and I went to Chicago and was introduced to Thomas, and he was friendly even when I told him we were doing his "no-jack" routine in our act.

He said, "I'll tell you what, kid, the next chance you get, come over to the 5100 Club with your partner and I'll put you both on and we'll see how the act goes in front of a real audience."

"How about the day after tomorrow?" I said.

"Sure," Thomas said.

I telephoned my mother and told her the good news that I was breaking into show business, real authentic show business. She said she was proud of me and she would reserve a ringside table.

"Please, Ma," I begged her, "*please* don't come. It's our opening night. I'm gonna be very nervous. Don't come."

I never could be funny in front of my mother.

So she promised she wouldn't come.

I was getting more and more frightened, and by the time Shelly and I got to the 5100 Club I was in a panic. They were full to capacity that night—everybody was drunk and laughing and having a good time. On every table were big knockers, made of wood, so people could knock on their tables instead of applauding.

Danny Thomas gave us a beautiful introduction:

"And now, ladies and gentlemen, I take great pleasure in presenting to you, from the University of Illinois, two of the freshest, brightest young comedians you've ever seen in your life. And now for the first time they are appearing on the professional stage, and I venture to predict, ladies and gentlemen, that this will be a historic night which none of you will ever forget in the annals of show business."

Mind you, he had never seen our act—and he said all those

wonderful things.

If he had seen our act, he would never have said those wonderful things.

We walked on and the spotlight hit us and the audience gave us a big round of applause and there was drunken cheering and suddenly I lost my nerve completely. My mouth was dry. I could barely get out the words, "Boy—am I happy!"

Nobody could hear me. Some of the customers were yelling, "Louder! Louder!"

Shelly said, "Why are you so happy?"

I couldn't remember the joke. I could only say, "Yeah, yeah." I kept muttering "Yeah, yeah," whenever it came to a punchline.

Now the customers started hollering, "Louder and funnier!"

And "Go back to college, you bums!"

And "Drop dead!"

Then they began throwing their knockers at us.

From all sides of the room we were being pelted by knockers and noisemakers. I was trying to duck them. I no longer cared about the act, the jokes, the routines, the comedy songs and parodies. It was *survival*. I only wanted to get out of there with a whole skin. I thought they were going to kill me.

Shelly bravely went on doing the act, with me muttering, "Yeah, yeah, yeah." And finally I just walked off the stage, leaving him there by himself, and I walked out—not through the stage door, but right down the floor, passing through the tables, my hands over my face to protect myself from the flying knockers, and through the cocktail lounge in front.

My mother was sitting at the bar, and she was crying, and when I started to talk to her I realized that she was plastered. For the first and only time of her life she had gotten stoned. She had witnessed my humiliation from start to finish.

Last year I met Danny Thomas at a party, and we had a drink and I reminded him of this whole story. But he didn't remember it at all. He had successfully blocked it out of his mind.

After my fiasco at the 5100 Club I gave up all hope of ever becoming a performer and decided to become a playwright. In my senior year I stopped attending classes and I sold all my textbooks and I took my weekly allowance and Dee's weekly allowance and I bought every book of plays and every book on how to write plays that I could find. I holed up in the fraternity house like a hermit, and I read George Jean Nathan and George Pierce Baker and studied every play from Aristophanes to Kaufman and Hart. I wrote hundreds of pages of dramatic scenes and began to get the reputation around the fraternity house of being some kind of a nut.

Nobody believed in me except Dee, and Dee has never stopped.

Dee and I didn't want to be apart all summer, so we decided to go to the summer session at Illinois so we could be together.

One afternoon we went into the Taylor-Fisher Music Shop to buy an album. It was understood between us that we were going to get married, and we had already started to build a record collection together. We picked out Liszt's Piano Concerto No. 1.

That night we had a double date with my fraternity brother Steve, now a prominent Chicago attorney, and his date, Laura. First we had dinner and then many beers at Bidwell's, and then Dee and I told Steve and his date about our new record album, and we decided we would go listen to it and neck. The only decent phonograph we knew of was in Dee's sorority house, which was closed for the summer. I said that was no problem, and we walked over to the SDT House. It was about ten o'clock, and, emboldened by all that beer, I broke a window of the SDT House and I climbed in and opened the front door, and then we all went into the parlor and put the Liszt Piano Concerto on the phonograph and it sounded real nice—very good necking music.

All of a sudden we heard a thumping and clumping.

The next thing we knew, two policemen came into the room, shouting, *"Don't nobody move!"* They had their revolvers out. We put up our hands. We were frisked and then taken to the Urbana police station and questioned for hours, like hardened criminals. We were charged with breaking and entering, listening to Liszt's Piano Concerto No. 1, and necking with someone of the opposite sex.

They finally released us, but the University's Dean of Men and Dean of Women brought us up on charges. We were given a hearing. My mother came before the Disciplinary Board and kept saying, "Don't expel my son. Let the punishment fit the crime. *Let the punishment fit the crime.*"

But Dean Turner, then Dean of Men and now Dean of all students, took a strong stand, and on July 20, 1944, I was expelled and Dee was suspended.

Dean Turner, if you are reading this book, I wish to assure you once again that all we wanted to do was hear Liszt's Piano Concerto on a good phonograph and neck. But we were arrested early in the second movement, and I never did find out how it comes out. Maybe you should have followed my mother's and Gilbert and Sullivan's advice and let the punishment fit the crime. All I know is, Dee and I have been married twenty years now, and we still don't talk about the incident because it still makes us feel ashamed and guilty.

CHAPTER 5

In Which I Go to New York
to Seek Fame and Fortune
and I Marry the Girl I Love
and I Declare War on the Lincoln Hotel
and If I Tell You Any More You Won't
Need to Read This Chapter Altogether

I WALKED OUT into New York City from Grand Central Station at eleven o'clock on the sunny morning of May 7, 1945, carrying in my left hand a suitcase containing what clothes I owned, and in my right hand a cardboard box filled with roughly seventy-five songs which I had composed, including love songs, torch songs, novelty songs and comedy songs.

I got into a taxi and told the driver to take me to the Edison Hotel, and he had me pegged for a rube, because he took me there by way of the Bronx and Staten Island, and it took an hour to get to the Edison, which is six blocks from Grand Central, just off Times Square.

I have never in my life seen such an excitement as there was in Times Square that day. There were easily 500,000 people milling around, kissing each other, yelling and screaming, singing and shouting, and on top of a lamppost I saw an English sailor, completely nude except for his sailor's hat. He had shinnied up the lamppost and he was singing an English song, "Roll Me Over, Lay Me Down and Do It Again." I passed by the Brill Building and I looked up. From every window, people were looking out and waving and throwing down torn-up sheet music.

New York, New York, a helluva town, I thought.

New York, I'll lick you yet, I thought.

And if this is how it's going to be, half a million people jumping around, and all this miscellaneous kissing, I decided I'd better get right in there where the action was, real fast.

So as soon as I was all checked into the Edison, I went right back out into Times Square and I did a little kissing myself. None of the women I kissed seemed to mind. They were kissing anybody, *anybody.*

I was crushed when I found out this was not a typical day on Broadway.

No sirree, it wasn't typical at all. It was V-E Day, and all the kissing was to celebrate our Victory in Europe.

I had been on the train for the last twenty hours and hadn't heard a radio or seen a newspaper, so I didn't realize that the Nazis had surrendered.

May 7, 1945. I had $150 in my pocket, and I figured this ought to be enough to last me three or four weeks, until I became rich and successful. I also had letters of recommendation to some people who might help me: Ginny Simms, the singer, who had a weekly radio show featuring talented soldiers; the mastermind agent Irving Lazar; and Variety mugg Jack Pulaski.

After I left the University, I had gone back home to Chicago.

In Chicago I had been hanging around Gibby's, a bar where show people gathered, where a wonderful colored pianist named Sammy played show tunes all night long. I taught Sammy all the songs I had written in college, and every night I'd come in and drink two martinis to get stoned enough to have the courage to sing my songs.

In those days everybody was making jokes about how Eleanor Roosevelt was always traveling all over the world, and one of my songs began:

> *Eleanor, Eleanor, where have you been?*
> *I've been to London to visit the Queen,*
> *I've been to Manchuria*
> *And I can assure ya*
> *I've been to more places than you've ever seen. . . .*

Kitty Carlisle was playing at the Chicago Theatre, and one night she came into Gibby's and heard my Eleanor Roosevelt song, and she paid me $100 for it as a piece of special material, and that was the first money I ever earned for writing. Now I was a professional writer.

A few days later Franklin D. Roosevelt died, and of course the song was worthless, and I gave Miss Carlisle her money back, and became an amateur writer again.

One night at Gibby's I had *three* martinis, and I really outdid myself. I sang for maybe two hours.

Winged Victory, Moss Hart's Air Force show, was playing Chicago then, and many of the stars in it hung out at Gibby's. One of them was Edmond O'Brien.

He came over from the bar and he shook my hand.

"Kid," he said, "you've *got* it."

"What should I do with it?" I asked.

"Go to New York," he advised, "and see my agent, Irving Lazar." And O'Brien gave me a letter to Lazar. Joe Bushkin, the jazz pianist, also told me I had it, and he said I should hustle over to New York because, first of all, I was a veteran and Ginny Simms featured soldiers on her radio program and she'd put me on the radio right away with my songs.

I didn't mention to a soul that I had served only three lousy months in the whole Army and had been discharged because I was allergic to goat dander and Brazil nuts. I let the word leak out that I had participated in the North African landings, the invasion of Italy and the Battle of Normandy. I don't mean that I lied, but I didn't contradict anybody who thought I had been through hell under fire.

So that's how I happened to go to New York, and the first place I went was to Ginny Simms' suite at the Waldorf-Astoria Hotel. Miss Simms and her producer, whose name I remember as Mr. Cool, were neither cool nor calm, but in a state of extreme hysteria. (I later learned that this is perfectly normal for people in radio and television.) What was bothering them that day was that the war in Europe had ended and the sponsor had just called up and informed them that he no longer wanted a radio program featuring soldiers, and the show was canceled.

If Ginny Simms' soldier show was canceled, there was absolutely no point in my being there looking for a job. As a matter of fact, I realized that Miss Simms would now be looking for a job herself. That's show biz.

She was very nice to me. She kissed me because I was a hero home from the wars. Mr. Cool poured me several double martinis. I blushed at their worship, making light of my deeds on the battlefield. I implied, ever so vaguely, that I had been on a few secret missions, which of course could not be discussed, what with the war still going on in Japan. As we said good-bye, Miss Simms kissed me again, and Mr. Cool kissed me on both cheeks, like a French general, and I knew I had a good thing going here with this war-hero business.

On my lapel I wore a button we used to call a "Ruptured Duck." It was given to all veterans so people could tell you had been a G.I. As I left the Waldorf I found I had developed a slight limp in my right leg. A bit of shrapnel, I decided, which I had caught in the Salerno landing. I limped over to the RKO Building to see Richard Rodgers.

My Ruptured Duck got me in to see Mr. Rodgers immediately, and I showed him about a dozen lyrics which I thought represented my best work. (I also wrote music, but I did not feel it would be nice to submit music to Richard Rodgers. There are limits to anybody's gall, including mine.) Mr. Rodgers looked through my songs, and then he spoke into an intercom. He summoned Larry Spier to his office. Spier was the head of the Rodgers music-publishing empire.

"Larry," said Mr. Rodgers, "see what you can do for this young man. He is a veteran. I like him and he writes a nice lyric."

"It was hell on earth in North Africa, Mr. Spier," I said, limping into his office. I left samples of my best lyrics with him.

Then I went to *Variety* to see Jack Pulaski. Pulaski was a giant of a man. He was the only *Variety* mugg (all the *Variety* reporters and editors like to call themselves "muggs") who looked like a real mug. He had the broken nose of an ex-pugilist. He was, as I found out, a heavy drinker, which did not stop him from being a shrewd drama critic. His reputation as a critic had been made because he was the only New York reviewer who predicted that *Abie's Irish Rose* would be a smash hit.

Pulaski was not at his desk upstairs in the 46th Street office of *Variety*. They told me I would find him next door at a bar and grill, where, indeed, I found him drinking rye and ginger ale. Pulaski congratulated me on helping to win the war and bought me a drink and listened to my story and said, "I like you, kid. You're going places, kid. You go over to Famous Music Corporation and tell the bastards Pulaski sent you and I'll kill them if they don't publish your songs, and then—now remember this, soldier boy—then you come right back here and report to me how they treated you. You come right back and give me a full report, see? I wanna make sure they give you the red-carpet treatment. You'll come back, immediately, and give me a report?"

"Yes, sir, Mr. Pulaski, I'll be right back in a few minutes," I said gratefully. I had a violent coughing spell.

"What's the matter, soldier boy?" Pulaski inquired.

"Nothing really," I replied, keeping a stiff upper lip. "Just a touch of poison gas in the lungs. Omaha Beach, y'know. It was —well, hell—I was luckier than a lot of them."

I told the receptionist at Famous Music, "I am a war hero and Jack Pulaski sent me."

I was taken right in to see one of the big wheels and he looked over my material. He was fascinated by a ballad of mine, "Merry Christmas." He said it was a nice lyric, but of course we would have to change the title because there must be a thousand songs with the title "Merry Christmas." So he told his secretary to look into it, and it turned out that there never had been a song in the history of the world called "Merry Christmas." Too obvious. They signed me to a contract and they teamed me with a music writer, Johnny Loeb, to finish up the song.

I was put in a little room with Loeb, and the first afternoon he played me some of his hits, which included "Masquerade" and Arthur Godfrey's theme, "Seems Like Old Times."

Loeb said I should meet him there in the office in two weeks and by then he'd have a melody blocked out and we'd finish *our* song—"Merry Christmas"—which would certainly be on the Lucky Strike *Hit Parade* with Mark Warnow and his Orchestra by next December.

Two weeks later Loeb played me the melody and I loved it.

Loeb asked, "Well, kid, don't you get it?"

I shook my head.

"Don't it sound a little familiar?"

I told him that, though I remembered many popular songs, I did not remember anything that sounded vaguely like the music to *our* "Merry Christmas." He gave me a smile, and then he played the same notes, but slower and changing the rhythm, and, so help me, it was "Silent Night."

The song was published, and I had to join SPA (the Songwriters' Protective Association) and pay the $25 initiation fee. A year later when I got my royalty statement on "Merry Christmas," I saw I had earned $17.84 royalties, which meant that I had lost $7.16 on the song.

I told Dee: "Honey, if I'm gonna lose seven dollars and sixteen cents on each song, then I better find a new business, because I write a lot of songs and I'm not sure we can afford it."

So I gave up songwriting for eighteen years.

But back to V-E Day, or rather V-E night.

The kissing and naked lamppost climbing and drunkenness and general madness had become even rowdier than it had been at noon. It was too much for me, and I ducked into a little bar across the street from the Edison Hotel. I asked for a triple martini, which they gave me on the house because of my war record, and as I drank it I sat there trying to put together all the pieces of this crazy day.

Then I heard a voice from down the bar:

"Hey, Allan—Allan Sherman—come on over, I want you to meet somebody."

It was Henry Slate, of the Slate Brothers, who had been in *Winged Victory* and had seen me singing my songs at Gibby's in Chicago. He was sitting with a good-looking man of a dark complexion who looked worried. Slate introduced me to the man—Lew Parker, who was an up-and-coming comedian.

"Lew," Henry Slate said, "you're looking at one of the most talented writers from Chicago. Your troubles are over."

"Yeah?" Parker said glumly.

"This boy may not look it, but he's got talent."

"Not to mention my great war record," I added.

"Yeah?" Parker said.

"He is the best special-material writer in Chicago today," Slate said, really laying it on.

"Yeah?" said Parker, still in a monotone.

"And I'm a veteran besides," I said, and a tear trickled down my cheek.

"Yeah?" Parker said, throwing me a bored salute.

"No, I mean it, Lew, this is a joke writer that's really a joke writer. He's fresh, he's—"

"Hey, you write jokes?" Lew Parker asked me, suddenly displaying an unexpected vocabulary.

"Yeah," I said, throwing it away so I shouldn't look too eager.

"Good jokes?"

"*All* kinds," I said.

"Go ahead and write me some jokes."

"Now? Like *that?*" I stammered. "Go ahead and write you jokes? Here in the Gaiety Bar?"

"No, not here. Look—I am hiring gagwriters for a new radio comedy show. Half hour. Write me a sample script so I'll see if you got the feel of it. My show takes place in a restaurant. It's like *Duffy's Tavern*, see? Except it's a *restaurant*, not a tavern. You heard the show *Duffy's Tavern*, dincha? Well, write me thirty minutes of jokes like in *Duffy's Tavern*—except different, for a *restaurant*."

I had never written a joke in my life and I didn't even know how to go about writing a joke. I *told* jokes, of course. All my life I had told jokes and made wisecracks—but I couldn't *write* a joke.

I hustled over to a bookstore near the hotel, the Gaiety Bookstore, and I bought every collection of jokes in stock. Then I went back to my hotel room and wrote a script filled with jokes from the book. I brought it to Lew Parker the next day. He immediately hired me at $50 a week.

As soon as I got my first week's salary, I called Dee in St. Louis and said I had achieved success. I had signed a contract to publish a song. I had a job as a gagwriter for a radio comedian. The world was my oyster. Would she please marry me?

She still couldn't picture us as man and wife, but since we were both in love, marriage seemed the logical, if unpicturable, thing to do. So she said Yes she would marry me.

As I write this, Dee and I have been married twenty years and we have two growing children and I still don't know whether she can picture being married to me.

Anyway, I went to Chicago, and Dee met me there, and we went to a lot of parties during which she met most of my crazy relatives. We had an engagement party first, and my mother served a dinner and a cake she had baked, and next to Dee's slice of cake was the beautiful diamond ring which was my engage-ment ring to Dee.

I didn't have any money at all. In fact, I had moved out of the Edison Hotel because I couldn't pay the bill and was living at the Lincoln Hotel, where I couldn't pay the bill either, but it was cheaper.

My mother gave us $300 in cash as a wedding present and Dee's parents gave us $1,000 in War Bonds.

Grandma took Dee aside to give her some domestic family-type advice. I guess Grandma was trying to play the role of a Jewish grandmother. Horserooms, gambling, poker—these were more Grandma's style, but she wanted to make nice on my new wife.

You have to realize that Dee came from De Soto, Missouri—population then 5,129—and hers was the only Jewish family in De Soto, and she had never heard a word of Jewish or dialect in her life. So Grandma took Dee to one side, and in her thick Weber-and-Fields accent she intoned, "Vell, so you gung to New York mit Eln, hah? Listen, something, to me."

"Yes, Grandmother," Dee said dutifully.

"I'm gung give you a piece advice," Grandma said. *"Don't forget the tits."*

Dee looked at the white-haired old lady. Dee's face showed complete shock. "The—the—what?" she asked.

"The *tits*, the *tits*," Grandma repeated, a little annoyed with her granddaughter-in-law, "don't forget the *tits*."

Dee's expression was a symphony of embarrassment. But then she thought it over and figured maybe there's some kind of a family sex perversion we all had and she ought to know about it right away, before the marriage was consummated.

So she finally got up the courage to ask, "What do you mean?"

And Grandma, shaking her head at such stupidity, explained, "Don't forget—make Eln brush the *tits* every morning. Mit *tutpaste*."

June 15, 1945.

Dee's parents gave a fine reception for our friends and families at the Pump Room of the Ambassador East Hotel, which was then the most elegant supper club in town.

My stepfather, Dave Number Two, outdid himself and provided us with a bountiful supply of black-market champagne. (In 1945 his business of the moment was the liquor business.)

Dee and I were hoping to spend our wedding night in a bedroom or a compartment on either the 20th Century Limited or the Broadway Limited to New York. But in 1945 it was almost impossible to get accommodations on any train, and bedrooms or compartments or roomettes were really out of the question.

But Dave Number Two said we shouldn't worry. He had "muscle" with the railroads and he would fix us up.

But Dave's "connection" failed him. All the space had been commandeered for military personnel. There was a great deal of shifting around of soldiers and Air Force officers then because of the war. He couldn't even get us a lower berth. *And this was our wedding night.*

It began to look like Dee and I would be consummating our

marriage in a Greyhound bus. But Uncle Maury rose to the occasion. He said for a case of Scotch he could wangle us the space from Chicago to New York. My stepfather, who was not only a crook but a frugal crook, and usually would not give you even the *wrong* time, had a romantic streak deep down in his black-market heart. He rose to the occasion with great nobility.

In 1945, if there was one thing that was harder to get than Pullman space, it was authentic imported Scotch. Most of the liquor stores only carried a terrible substance called "Scotch-type whiskey." Stores that had Scotch made you buy five bottles of rum with each bottle of Scotch. But Dave Number Two had plenty of Scotch. He gave Uncle Maury a case of Cutty Sark.

Uncle Maury was so busy with his intrigue with the railroads that he almost missed the wedding ceremony, but he finally showed up with a look of triumph. He was waving two long strips of tickets.

"I got it!" he chortled. "I got it—your honeymoon is assured!"

Big deal—he had gotten us *two upper berths.*

And the upper berths were located in two different cars.

"This is terrible," I moaned. "This is ridiculous."

"What kind of a wedding night is this lovely bride and groom going to have, you schnook," Number Two said to Uncle Maury, "with him in an upper berth in one car and she's in an upper berth three cars away?"

Uncle Maury sensed that somehow he had failed us.

"Ain't you ever heard of sex, you stupid *schmuck?*" Dave shouted. "Now you go back to your friend from the railroads and tell him he's got to change the location so the bride and groom will be occupying the same premises. Tell him it's the wedding night. Tell him the whole future of a couple is *hanging.*"

"If you could maybe spare another case of Cutty Sark," Uncle Maury whined, "maybe he'll do it."

Dave Number Two said, "Screw him—*rum* he can have."

Uncle Maury, out of breath, arrived back at the Pump Room several hours later. He was clutching our tickets for a roomette on the Central Railroad of Michigan, connecting up with the Canadian Pacific Railroad of Canada, and linking up—in some way I have never been able to figure out—with the New York, New Haven and Hartford Railroad into Grand Central.

As we pulled into New York, I warned Dee that the situation at the Lincoln Hotel was delicate. I now owed them $380. They were getting impatient with my excuses. I did not believe they would be overjoyed when they learned that *two* of us would now be living in my room—and I wasn't even paying for one. As usual, I sneaked into the hotel from a side entrance to avoid the front desk. I sent Dee up in the elevator. They were used to strange girls in their elevators. I paid a bellboy $5 to smuggle in our suitcases.

The Lincoln Hotel engaged in guerrilla warfare against us. They shut off our supply of toilet paper. This, during the greatest paper shortage America has ever known.

Next, they cut off our towels. After a shower we ran around the room naked, flapping our arms wildly, air-drying ourselves. They cut off our chambermaid service; we made our own beds. They changed the lock on the door; after that, one of us had to remain in the room at all times to let the other in.

It was a hard-fought battle with the Lincoln Hotel, and it took every bit of cleverness and courage I could muster. Eventually I won.

I am still here, and the Lincoln Hotel is gone. Let that be a lesson to all hotels at which I stay henceforth.

I remember our first dinner alone in our love nest in the Lincoln Hotel. I insisted that we have our first meal at home, like married people should. Like a real husband, I sent my wife out to buy dinner. I told her to go to the Gaiety Delicatessen and get two hot corned-beef sandwiches and two salami sandwiches, with a paper cone of mustard, a brace of pickles, a quart of potato salad, Danish pastry, and three bottles of Dr. Brown's Celery Tonic. Like a loyal wife, Dee bravely went out.

I stretched out on the bed. I was king of a castle—even without towels and toilet paper. I drooled as I pictured our first true connubial dinner. Time passed. Twenty minutes, thirty minutes, an hour. No food, no wife.

The phone rang.

"I can't find it." Dee was crying. "Where is it—the Gaiety Delicatessen?"

"Near Broadway."

"Where's that?"

"Broadway is where you'll see all the lights and there's crowds of people and you'll see a big artificial waterfall and a sign saying Times Square and a building with lit-up headlines—the Times Building."

"Is it anywhere near the New York Public Library Main Branch, which is where I am calling from?" she moaned in desperation.

"For Chrissake, no," I said. How she had wandered from the Lincoln at Eighth Avenue and 45th, to the library at Fifth Avenue and 42nd Street, I did not know.

"I've been walking all over looking for a Gaiety Delicatessen. I don't think there is any such place."

The Gaiety is a hole in the wall, eight feet wide. I carefully told her how to retrace her steps, walking west and then north, and told her to look for a Gaiety Bookstore, a Gaiety Music Shop, a Gaiety Tobacco Shop—everything was gay in that block —and then she would know she was on the right track. "And watch out for a Pepsi-Cola sign, Dee. When you see it, make a left turn and you can't miss the Gaiety Delicatessen."

Another twenty minutes elapsed. Dee phoned again. She was sobbing her heart out.

"I can't find any Pepsi-Cola sign," she wept.

"My God!" I said. "The Pepsi-Cola sign is *a whole block long!* It's got millions of little lights dancing around in it, and you'll see hundreds of soldiers inside at the Pepsi-Cola Canteen drinking Pepsi-Cola!"

"Oh! I was looking for a *little* Pepsi-Cola sign in a store window," she said. "Just a minute. Hold the phone. I'll go look if it's there." She returned. "Oh, yeah, *now* I see it!"

It was a delicious dinner, after all.

A few days later I was passing a newsstand and I saw a copy of *Variety*. I suddenly remembered Jack Pulaski. I ran over to the bar on 46th Street. Pulaski was sitting on his regular stool, with the complete composure of a man who is lovably drunk at two in the afternoon and who predicted *Abie's Irish Rose* would be a big hit. I sat down on a stool next to him.

Seven weeks had passed since I'd told him I'd be right back in a few minutes.

"Hello," I said.

"*You're late*," he said.

CHAPTER 6

Seven Years with the Wrong Income

AFTER THE LINCOLN HOTEL PEOPLE showed their true colors by demanding payment, we turned our backs on them. We moved out. It was July. We sublet for the summer a charming old-fashioned furnished railroad apartment at 250 East 60th Street. It belonged to Ruth and Helen Hoffman, twin sisters, both writers. It was furnished mainly with books. Every room, including the kitchen and bathroom, was lined with bookshelves, floor to ceiling, and many of the books were signed by the authors, friends of the Hoffmans. The Hoffman girls were marvelous landlords. They didn't ask for rent in advance. Which was just as well. I was having trouble making ends meet, and my beginnings weren't meeting either.

Lew Parker had promised me a raise to $125 a week. The head writer of the show was named Fat Larry, to distinguish him from another head writer who was called Skinny Larry.

One week I handed in my usual ten pages of jokes. Fat Larry found fault with several of them.

"You can't tell *me* how to write funny," I said indignantly.

Fat Larry thought of a funny answer.

"You're fired," it went.

So began seven years of poverty, squalor, starvation and economic insecurity.

Jack Pulaski sent me over to Willie Weber, an agent for comedians.

Willie Weber handled the careers of several dozen comedians, most of whom were named *Jackie*. Willie, as far as I could tell, had only one single show-business instinct: he was one hundred percent dead certain that the only good name for a comedian is Jackie. You couldn't argue this point, because he was making a fortune. If a Sam, Alvin, Clyde or Montmorency walked into Willie Weber's office and signed a contract, he walked out under the name of Jackie, and somehow Willie kept his Jackies busy working all the time. Willie wasn't too happy when I insisted on remaining Allan, but he figured it would be real good if he could have somebody like me around to supply jokes and funny songs to his stable of Jackies, which included Jack E. Leonard, Jackie Miles, Jackie Winston and Jackie Gleason.

Willie kept me very busy indeed, supplying them with jokes and songs. The only trouble was, Willie neglected to tell me that none of the Jackies were going to pay me for any of those jokes and songs. I had taken this for granted, which was very foolish, and every few weeks, when I'd get up the courage to complain, Willie would throw me $50 or $100 on account. It was kind of an Oliver Twist–Fagin arrangement.

That's how we lived in those days, from hand to mouth, and what we usually put into our mouths was something called Kraft Dinner.

Now, to most people the word "dinner" suggests something like shrimp cocktail, vegetable soup, sirloin steak and fried potatoes, apple pie and coffee. But to us it was some kind of a special spaghetti concoction with cheese which the Kraft Company, with devilish ingenuity, had named Kraft Dinner. This was the staple of our diet.

We were always searching in pockets of suits or looking under cushions for lost change to find the nineteen cents to buy a Kraft Dinner.

Sometimes when the pockets were empty and there were no nickels in the furniture, I went down to the basement and collected old magazines, which I took to a store on Sixth Avenue that bought and sold secondhand magazines. I'd get a dollar for three hundred magazines (as many as Dee and I could carry). Then we'd blow ourselves to a big meal at the Horn & Hardart automat.

This was our way of life.

And we were happy.

We were young and we were in love and we were discovering each other in that first year, and we were discovering New York.

Manhattan—it was like a wonderland to us, like a perpetual World's Fair, a place of unexpected streets and sudden simple delights and happy adventures.

When Dee and I took American Poetry together at Illinois so we could be in the same class, there was a poem, "Recuerdo," by Edna St. Vincent Millay, that both of us loved. And years later, when we were married, in those early struggling years in New York, we remembered it because it said so much that seemed to be about us. It goes like this:

We were very tired, we were very merry—
We had gone back and forth all night on the ferry;
And you ate an apple, and I ate a pear,

From a dozen of each we had bought somewhere;
And the sky went wan, and the wind came cold,
And the sun rose dripping, a bucketful of gold.

We were very tired, we were very merry,
We had gone back and forth all night on the ferry.
We hailed, "Good-morrow, mother!" to a shawl-covered head,
And bought a morning paper, which neither of us read;
And she wept, "God bless you!" for the apples and the pears,
And we gave her all our money but our subway fares.

Dee and I went back and forth on the Staten Island ferry; for a nickel it took you right up close to the Statue of Liberty. And we went to Palisades Amusement Park and rode the roller coaster—the most frightening roller coaster in America. And we rode on top of the open-air double-decker Fifth Avenue busses uptown to the Cathedral of St. John the Divine and downtown to Washington Square Park. And we explored Greenwich Village and took the subway to Chinatown and took another subway to Wall Street and another to Brooklyn, and it ended in Coney Island. And sometimes in the middle of the night we would ride to Coney Island and go to Nathan's on Surf Avenue.

Nathan's is open all night, even in winter, and there is always a crowd there, even at two in the morning in frozen January. And we would eat hot dogs and fried clams and walk along the boardwalk.

We were like two kids at a fantastic, noisy, endless birthday party, and we were allowed to stay up as late as we wanted, even all night, and sometimes we did. We were intoxicated with freedom and love and fun and the sights and sounds and people of New York.

And everything we saw, and everything we did, came out cockeyed and crazy and funny—the museums and concert halls and movie theatres and restaurants and all the lights and excite-

ment. Happy crazy. Lovely crazy.

Near us on Third Avenue, one block apart, there were two restaurants. Both were called Original Joe's. We never found out which was the *original* Original Joe's.

And we tasted our first egg creams, a concoction found only in New York. Egg creams contain neither eggs nor cream; they are chocolate sodas with a dash of milk. Delicious. A little old Jewish lady ran the candy store near our apartment, and she could tell we were new in New York and in love, and one evening there was in her eyes the delight that you feel when you're going to give somebody a wonderful surprise, and she said, "Let me make you something you never tasted before." And she made us two egg creams. And she wouldn't let us pay for them. And we got drunk on egg creams. *It's possible to get drunk on egg creams when you're twenty years old and you're in love.*

On the southeast corner of 59th Street and Third Avenue, under the elevated track, there was a newsstand run by a tough-looking Italian. But he would let us stand there and read all his magazines; and he gave us credit—he let us take home the *Daily News* and the *Mirror* and the *Times* every night. It was only nine cents' worth of papers a night, but the point is he trusted us and he could see we were in love and he knew we would pay him when we got the money. And we did.

Only in New York could we have joined the Lox-and-Bagel-of-the-Week Club, which we did for fifty-five cents a week. The Club delivered to our door every Sunday morning an aluminum foil container stuffed with two bagels and enough smoked salmon and cream cheese to go with it. We were brokenhearted when the Club went out of business. We had never met any of the other members, and yet we had a feeling of *belonging*.

One time a check for $150 had come in the mail and it was on my desk, among my usual litter of papers and letters. Dee is meticulous. She is an ashtray-emptier and a pillow-straightener. After dinner I went to look for the check. It was gone. She had thrown it down the garbage chute after "straightening up" my desk. For a whole weekend we sifted six floors of garbage. We didn't find the check. But all the time we were having fun and we were laughing, and life was hilarious. *We were very merry and we were very young.*

I am a night person, and Dee is a day person. In New York I soon discovered all-night delicatessens, and almost every night, after Dee fell asleep, I would saunter over to the Carnegie Delicatessen and meet my friend Howard Merrill, and we'd talk about crazy things. Like, How could we get even with Bloomingdale's Department Store for not delivering Howard's and Toni's bedroom furniture when they were newlyweds, so they had to sleep on the floor for the first five months? Or, What does a proctologist order for lunch? Or, Why did the postwar Buicks have those three holes?

Howard and I were fascinated by those three holes.

The American public loved those three holes. One season the Buick people eliminated the three holes, and the public was outraged, and not one single Buick was sold that year, so the next year they restored the holes and everything was all better. Well, neither Howard nor I could afford a Buick of our own, but we liked those holes, too, and we went around asking Buick owners why they loved their holes, and they couldn't or wouldn't answer. We'd ask them what the holes were called, and they would shrug their shoulders and say "Who knows?"

Or "Holes? Holes are holes."

Or "Don't bother me with foolish questions."

Some of them blushed when asked this question, and we concluded that those holes were some sort of sex symbol and that people who drove Buicks were getting some kind of jollies that Pontiac and Mercury owners can never really know or feel.

To this day, Buicks still have the three holes, and the bigger, more expensive models have *four* holes. The Buick people have driven their designers crazy redesigning those holes for eighteen years, and they have presented the American public with round holes, square holes, teardrop-shaped holes, oblong holes, rectangular holes, rhomboid holes, parallelogram holes—every kind of hole that engineering science has yet created. But, American know-how and ingenuity being what it is, I'm sure we can look forward to new and more thrilling holes from the Buick people in the years to come. It is all a part of what President Johnson calls "The Great Society."

The other car manufacturers have tried to compete with Buick in many ways. They have put protuberances on their cars —little things that stick out; they have folded and sculpted the sheet metal. But the simple faith of the Buick people in their three holes comes shining through, year after year, and we Americans know a good thing when we see it.

I live in Hollywood, where you see people driving Rolls-Royces and Mark X Jaguars and Dual-Ghias, but when they get out of their $25,000 cars in front of the Beverly Hills Hotel, their faces lack the serenity, the basic animal satisfaction, of the Buick owner, who drives up, gets out of his car, pats it softly on the trunk, sighs, and lights a cigarette as he leaves his beloved three-holed machine and enters the pink hotel.

And so, many years ago when Howard Merrill and I first saw the true meaning and importance of those three holes in the Buick, we wanted to know what the names of those holes were. And we asked Buick owners and Buick dealers, too, but they didn't know. So finally we wrote to General Motors, and after many weeks there came a reply.

The holes are called: "CRUISERLINE VENTIPORTS."

Honest to God, that is their name. I wouldn't make up such a thing.

At five in the morning, after talking all night with Howard, I would return home and take our dog out for a walk in Central Park. We'd walk until dawn came up.

Gertrude Stein said that sunrise is the most beautiful or the ugliest part of the day—depending on which end of the day you're looking at it from.

Both ends were beautiful in 1946.
We were very poor, we were very merry.
Sometimes there was no money in our old clothes—no magazines in the basement to sell.

Those times we were rescued by Jerry Weinstein. (He was the Harvard fellow I played poker with in the Army hospital.) Jerry would invite us to his parents' beautiful Atlantic Beach home for the weekend. His parents liked us, too. They wanted to help us, but they knew we wouldn't accept money directly. So whenever they saw us, Jerry's folks gave us a $25 or $50 gift certificate from Wanamaker's. *To buy something for the house,* they'd say. But they knew what we'd do with it. *We'd go to Wanamaker's, buy something for eighty-four cents and take the rest in cash.*

We were driven out of the East 60th Street apartment by Freddy Martin's orchestra. He had put out a jazzed-up arrangement of a Chopin Polonaise, called "Till the End of Time." The record was sweeping the country. In particular, it was sweeping through East 60th Street because there was a man who lived in the apartment above us and he had this record and he loved it and he played it twenty-four hours a day, day in and day out. I have had no use for Frédéric Chopin since that time.

It was almost impossible to find an apartment in Manhattan. There was a shortage of everything after the war: apartments, private homes, automobiles, Scotch whiskey, tires, nylon stockings, refrigerators—everything except Freddy Martin recordings.

Then a fraternity brother, Billy, came to visit us, and we couldn't talk because Chopin was playing, and Billy asked wasn't it driving us out of our minds? And we said, "Yes."

And he said he had an Uncle Sol who was a real-estate operator; he owned buildings. Billy telephoned his uncle and arranged an appointment for me. In those years you had to be of high moral caliber to even be considered for a new apartment.

Uncle Sol had just built a new apartment house on East 66th Street, a beautiful apartment house with a lobby and two lovely push-button elevators. It was a desirable location, and he had available a nice one-room apartment with kitchenette and closette and toilette and we could have it for the bargain rent-controlled price of $50 a month.

"It sounds very nice, sir," I said, "and we will take it sight unseen, and I'm prepared to give you references and sign—"

"Not so fast, *boychick*," Uncle Sol barked, blowing clouds of cigar smoke into my face. "One hand washes the other."

"I assure you, sir, that my wife and I are *clean*, and we bathe and shower regularly, and I can give you the deposit and sign the—"

"A tit for a tat, I'm referring to, Sherman. I'll do something for you—and you'll do something for me."

Why, he sounded just like a Cole Porter lyric, I thought.

"Sir," I said, wondering if he wanted a little money under the table, though he seemed very rich and prosperous already, "I would do *anything* to get this apartment."

Uncle Sol parked his cigar in an ashtray. He leaned forward and fixed me with his sharp eyes. His voice became confidential and low. I had to lean forward to follow him closely. "My nephew Billy, he tells me you're a big shot in the radio business, no?"

"Very kind of Billy to say that, sir."

"I have a daughter Sylvia. A beautiful girl with a golden voice, like an angel. She needs only a little chance, a little push. You do something for Sylvia and you will have the apartment. Here's what: arrange for her an audition at a radio station."

I assured him that I would move heaven and earth to get an

103

audition for Sylvia, and he presented me with a cigar as I departed, and he waved before my nose a lease already made out to me.

"Listen," I said to Howard Merrill, "I want to set up an audition with one of the networks for a girl. She's a singer."

Merrill smirked. "Some broad you wanna lay, Allan? I didn't know you were the type. I figured you for a faithful type of husband. Well, well, *well*. Who's the broad?"

"Howard—there are more important things in the world than sexual intercourse," I replied.

"Name one."

"An apartment."

He had to agree, in those years, that I was right.

He arranged with a network executive for an audition for Sylvia. Roger Bower, a producer-director, sat in the control room, and Sylvia stood in the studio, and she sang and told jokes and made recitations, all by herself, for thirty minutes. Finally Bower said, "That was fine, Sylvia, we'll call you when we have a program for you."

Sylvia, wherever you are, I apologize, because it was a dead microphone you were singing into. I was desperate for an apartment, but I should not have stooped so low. Yet I must also congratulate you for having gotten out of show business. Your father kept his word and got us the apartment. Maybe I really did you a favor without intending to. Anyway, I hope this finds you healthy and happy. And if you happen to be reading this, let's hear from you sometime. Let bygones be bygones. Make nice.

It was a small apartment indeed.

There was not enough closet space for our clothes and belongings, so we went out and bought Strongbilt closets and Strongbilt chests. There is, or was, a company called the Strongbilt Corporation, which provides the American public with

build-it-yourself fiberboard closets which are the hardest things
to put together, the hardest things to maintain, and the hardest
things to keep from falling apart in existence. They are called
by such names as Strongbilt chests, Strongbilt wardrobes,
Strongbilt closets.

*To this day, the very word Strongbilt can break up me and
my wife into hysterical nervous laughter.* Well, since we didn't
have any storage space—there was only one tiny coat closette in
the apartment—we went out and bought this Strongbilt stuff.
We brought it home, and then Dee and I and the superintend-
ent and some kindly neighbors attempted to put it together, because what it is is cardboard that buckles, with little ill-fitting
wooden corners that you force together, and you have to get *all*
the ill-designed portions together at the *same split second*, or
else it all falls apart, *klunk.*

If you finally do get it put together and you put, say, a paper
napkin on top of it, the weight of the napkin bends the whole
Strongbilt storage chest, and it falls apart again, because that
seems to be its destiny.

*May I say this directly to you, Strongbilt Corporation: Go
ahead and sue me. I have been waiting lo these many years to
get this off my mind. You may have improved your product
since 1946, but, by God, it happened the way I say it happened
twenty years ago, and if you take me to court you'll have to
prove it didn't happen and you can't because I have friends
and relatives who came and saw my rotten squashed-in Strongbilt chests and they will gladly testify, and I will take this to
the Supreme Court if necessary, and Justice will triumph, I
promise you.*

We had to have beds to sleep in. We went to a place called
Avant Garde and their Official Interior Decorator sold us two
Hollywood beds and a corner table, and he drew us a plan of
how they should fit into our one-room apartment. The plan
called for the beds to be at a ninety-degree angle to each other,

each against one wall, with the corner table in the corner. That way, the interior decorator explained, the room would look like a sitting room during the day.

During the *night* he didn't care about, because this interior decorator was a fairy, and *his* nights were considerably different from what Dee and I had in mind.

Only a pansy could devise such an antisocial method of sleeping with your own bride.

Imagine: it's the middle of the night, and you reach out for the warmth of her body, and instead of touching exciting, lovely, warm skin, your fingers wind up in an ashtray or a half-filled cup of cold coffee on the coffee table which the fag interior decorator also sold you to complete his ridiculous arrangement.

In this little apartment there lived me and my wife and Dusty, a miniature collie with a beautiful face. We saw her in a pet-shop window on Third Avenue, and she cost fifteen dollars, which was a lot of money, but we couldn't resist her.

Next door to our building there was a cleaning-and-tailoring store owned by a Morris Bloomberg who was seeking immortality, I guess, because one day when Dee was in his store she told him we had just bought a puppy and we didn't know what to name it.

Morris Bloomberg said, "Name it after me."

"After you?" Dee said. "We can't call it 'Mr. Bloomberg'—it's a girl."

"All right," he said. "So call it '*Morris*.'"

Life on East 66th Street was crazy because of the neighbors. First of all, while there were some elegant old brownstone homes still standing there, and new apartment buildings were beginning to rise, there was also a contingent of juvenile delinquents in the neighborhood (EAST SIDE CARDINALS, it said on their jackets), and that year their favorite sport was slashing the tops of convertibles. We had bought a 1939 Ford convertible, and they at once slashed the top, and we installed a new top and they slashed that, and so we finally said the hell with it.

Then, every Sunday—and I still to this day don't know why—there marched in the backyard a full-scale Scotch bagpipe band. They rehearsed every Sunday afternoon for several hours, marching and blowing and honking, repeating the same numbers over and over. It was terrible—the whole building reverberated with forty bagpipes blowing in unison. We lived there for three years and I never found out what in hell they were rehearsing for.

Directly above us lived a woman who was constantly moving her furniture around. When I say constantly, I don't mean every couple of weeks; I mean daily, I mean *hourly*. Things constantly got moved up there—couches, floor lamps, tables, God knows what. I figured this way: Different people have different hobbies, and this woman's hobby was moving furniture. Maybe somebody once told her it was nice to change furniture around and keep a room looking new and interesting, but she interpreted it to mean *constantly*. She believed furniture should be in perpetual motion. One evening she drove me so crazy moving her furniture that I leaned out into the airshaft and screamed up at her, "Keep it moving, *keep it moving!*"

Somewhere above us was a different family, also facing on our airshaft. These people did not believe in incinerators. They threw their garbage down the airshaft. There was a continuous stream of garbage flying down past our window for an hour after each meal.

We decided to trade in our slashed-top convertible. A used-car dealer on Broadway's automobile row, near Columbus Circle, showed us a magnificent 1941 Mercury convertible. It was a "name" car, because it had once belonged to H. V. Kaltenborn. We traded in our 1939 Ford and gave the dealer $700 out of our $1,000 in War Bonds, which we had been holding for just such a crisis.

We began driving around in the suburbs, looking for a bigger apartment. Our search took us to Flushing, Long Island. A sneaky real-estate agent showed us a two-family house and said he could make a deal for us to rent the lower floor. It had a separate entrance and the use of a garden and the price was reasonable, provided—he added, licking his lips as he studied our H. V. Kaltenborn 1941 Mercury convertible—provided we sold him this car at the "blue book" price. In those days, used cars were selling for twice or even three times their blue-book prices.

Like the two lovable idiots we were, we let him steal our Mercury for $350, and he made the deal for the house. But when the owners of the house found out we were Jewish and, even worse, that we had sold the Mercury to the real-estate agent and not to *them*, they wouldn't let us move in. So now we had no car and we had no home in the country. In order to go apartment-hunting in Westchester and Long Island, we had to have a car.

On Second Avenue, uptown, we saw a nice-looking 1937 black Plymouth coupe in a used-car lot. The price on the windshield was $250 "as is." I didn't know that in the automobile business the phrase "as is" has a special meaning. To me it was just two words. *As is, as was, as will be, as would be, as should be, as is.* Two little words, simple nice little words, sweet harmless little words expressing the present tense. *As is.*

So we paid the man the $250 and drove away in our present-tense car, and we drove not quite four blocks—and the car died. Did you ever see a car die? It's a tragic death. The whole car died—at once. The motor died, the pistons died, the crankshaft perished, the transmission passed away, the brakes succumbed, the clutch kicked the bucket, the horn beeped its final beep. I have never seen anything sadder. Ten minutes before, we had paid $250 for this car, and now it was dead.

I went screaming to the dealer, and he explained to me the true meaning of the phrase "as is." It means that you are buying a very sick automobile, a terminal case, practically in the past tense—not the present tense at all—and the dealer does not guarantee it for twenty-four hours or even twenty-four minutes. The dealer wouldn't even come down the street to look at the dead car, and he wouldn't trade it or give me a nickel for it. He said if I wanted, he would tow it away if I paid *him* $25.

Finally I sold the "as is" Plymouth for junk. A junk dealer paid me $10 for it. He told me it had once been a police car. It had been painted over to disguise its cops-and-robbers background. He showed me bullet holes in the windshield. He looked over the engine and said he guessed that car had run over 500,000 miles.

I decided if I was going to be a success at writing jokes, I should make a scientific study of humor. So, working for many evenings, Dee and I compiled jokes: we stole from radio shows, joke books and old magazines, and we wound up with some of the finest and oldest jokes in the world. We had 20,000 jokes, in three volumes, and all catalogued under subjects like Fat People and Mother-in-law and Money.

Those were the pioneer days of television, and Jerry Lester, the star of *Cavalcade of Stars* on the Dumont network, hired me as a writer. It was a standard variety show, with vaudeville acts, and with everything planned and carefully written in advance.

I thought the best program on television was *Kukla, Fran and Ollie*, a puppet show, with various puppets who talked to an attractive woman, Fran Allison. The puppeteer was an original creative genius, Burr Tillstrom, who fashioned something completely new for television. I believed this program was pure television. It was not theatre, it was not movies, it was not radio. It was television. Unplanned. Unpredictable. Spontaneous. Fresh.

I would beg Jerry Lester to allow me to change the formula of *Cavalcade of Stars*. I wanted to do with human beings what Burr Tillstrom was doing with puppets. Jerry would tell me I was a nut and it was strictly a small-time puppet show for little kids. The late-evening shows that eventually developed in television —the programs of Steve Allen, Jack Paar and Johnny Carson— were the kind of program I had envisioned. It was improvisation; it was like the *commedia dell'arte*. It was really happening before your eyes.

I lasted thirteen weeks on *Cavalcade of Stars*. Then I was one of the writers on *Broadway Open House*. I lasted three weeks. I was having arguments all the time with the other writers on the show and with the various personalities who appeared. I didn't know what the trouble was. It was like arguing with phantoms. I would write a joke about a butter churn, for instance, and it would come out a joke about a Sunbeam Mixmaster; or a joke about a horse came out a joke about a step-down Hudson. All my jokes were being switched around and they weren't coming out so funny. I got tired of arguing and I quit.

After I quit, one of the other writers let me in on the secret of what was going on.

"You're a *schmuck*," he said, "that's what you are."

"Why am I a *schmuck*?"

"Because if you write jokes about butter churns, who's going to give you a free butter churn?"

"And if I wrote about Sunbeam Mixmasters?"

"Come to my house sometime and my wife will whip you up a cake."

That's how it was. In the early days of television, there was lots of what we now call "payola," and I hadn't known about it, so the other writers figured why the hell should they share the loot with me? And that's what all the secrecy was about.

Television commercials cost a lot of money and are very effective in selling products, and any company that could get its product mentioned without buying commercial time was getting off cheap and was delighted to give the writers and/or the star and/or the producer a Mixmaster or a Polaroid camera or a case of Coca-Cola every week for a year and so on up to, for a really important plug, a brand-new car.

But the writers had to *sneak* the name of the product into the script. Nobody dealt directly with the companies involved or with their advertising agencies. There was a strange, creepy breed who handled payola, and they were called "schlockmeisters." They made the deals between the manufacturers and the joke writers without the knowledge of the networks, and they crept around in the shadows of the studios to make sure the names actually got on the air. The going price for a plug in those days was either a gift of the product itself or, since there is a limit to how many Mixmasters any one writer's wife can use, he was given the choice of a $75 gift certificate from any store in town, or a case of liquor.

Once I knew about all this, I thought it was marvelous. The only thing I knew of that had ever topped it was the Natalie-and-Allan Doorknob Game. In fact, it was just another version of the same thing.

The next job I got, I started right off by writing jokes about Cadillacs, Tiffany's jewelry store, Hilton Hotels, the ships of the Cunard White Star Line and so forth.

If any of the above companies are reading this book, we live at 906 Chantilly Road, Los Angeles 24, California. Take the west gate of Bel Air, and turn right off Sunset Boulevard. This applies to any of the above products except the Queen Mary *and the* Queen Elizabeth. *Just park those somewhere near Santa Monica Beach and I'll find them myself.*

* * *

The quiz-show scandals put an end to the payola era. The Federal Government stepped in, and in order to protect themselves, the networks agreed to police their own programs. They instituted a system that requires everyone who appears on a panel or quiz show and everyone who works behind the scenes to sign and initial hundreds of legal documents, riders, loyalty oaths and pledges of honesty and integrity. By now, so many people have signed so many of these legal documents that it is absolutely impossible for another quiz scandal ever to happen. Nobody has become any more honest, you understand. But everybody has become so confused and legally entangled with everybody else, and the amount of paperwork is so overwhelming, that there just simply isn't any time left for plain, good old-fashioned, normal dishonesty.

Furthermore, each network has appointed a Czar in Charge of Honesty; all honesty must go through him, and his job is to reassure the network that everything that is supposed to be honest is as honest as necessary. When things reach this degree of honesty, they are known as "Officially Honest" and may be used on the air.

The most fascinating character in this whole melodrama is the man appointed by one of the networks to be its Supreme Czar in Charge of Honesty. In order to take this job with the network, he had to quit his previous job, which he was glad to give up because things were getting too hot for him anyway.

You see, right up until he became the network's foremost authority on honesty, he was television's foremost schlockmeister.

It was starvation time. When the dinner bell sounded in our house, it was for Kraft Dinner.

Only this time our problem was a little more complicated.

Dee was pregnant.

Dee was pregnant and I was out of work, and we were broke,

so we invented the Darryl Zanuck Game.

We played it for years. Whenever the phone rang in those hungry, funny years, both of us would jump up and yell, "I'll get it—it's Darryl Zanuck!" And we would race for the phone, and the first one there would pick it up and answer, in a very dignified, cool voice, "Mr. Sherman's office." It was a one-room apartment on East 66th Street, Mr. Sherman's office, but every time the phone rang, there was this dream—this imaginary Darryl Zanuck calling to tell me that somewhere he had discovered that I was very talented and he wanted me, he needed me at any price, and soon I would be rich and famous, and the Kraft Dinner years would be over.

I don't think we could have stayed alive without the Darryl Zanuck Game.

This is how Dee became pregnant, in spite of our resolve not to have a child until we could afford one: I had written a musical show, *The Golden Touch*, with a man named Bud Burtson. It was optioned by producer John Wildberg. Burtson and I had to go to Hollywood in connection with the show. We went by train. It was a three-day trip. Bud and I talked about many things. He said I should be ashamed of myself for being married almost five years and not having a child.

"But we can't afford it," I said.

"Money," he lectured me, "has nothing to do with having a baby. A child will enrich your life. It will make your wife happy. It will cement your marriage. It will help your love attain its highest and noblest peaks."

"Honestly?" I asked.

"Go," he commanded me, "go—and procreate."

Upon my return to New York, I shared this great revelation with Dee over a Kraft Dinner.

"Money has absolutely nothing to do with having a baby," I said. "An infant is a noble and enriching experience. So let's enrich our lives. We could start tonight. *Now,* in fact."

"How can you be so sure?" she said.

"Bud Burtson guarantees it," I said with utter conviction.

"Somehow I can't *picture* you as a father," Dee said.

"Are you starting up again?" I asked.

"And I can't picture myself as a mother," she said.

"Are you gonna believe your pictures or Bud Burtson?" I cried.

So we started to have a baby.

Our obstetrician believed in "natural childbirth." He gave us *Childbirth Without Fear,* a book by Dr. Grantly Dick-Read. We both read it.

The whole idea of *Childbirth Without Fear* is that if a husband and wife understand clearly what is going on during pregnancy, from fertilization until the baby is born, if they study carefully the diagrams and pictures of the female internal organs, they will realize that what are usually called "labor pains" are not really pains but, as Dr. Read puts it, just extremely hard work and nothing to fear. (*Dr. Read should worry. Dr. Read is a man.*) Dee and I got violently sick from just looking at those diagrams of cut-away internal organs. We shelved the book; Dee decided she would rather have Childbirth *With* Fear.

Everything went swimmingly. Dee takes everything in stride. We had everything we needed now. A four-and-a-half-room apartment in Jackson Heights. Dr. Read's book. A stopwatch to time the contractions. We were booked into the Le Roy Hospital at 40 East 61st Street, a neighbor of the Colony Restaurant. In fact, patients can have meals sent in from the Colony. And the atmosphere at Le Roy is luxurious. It is a small but very elegant hospital. It is very well set up for any type of hospitalization up to extreme childbirth. Luckily, Dee was not sick —only pregnant.

We ran up a tremendous bill at Le Roy because I went there every night to have dinner with Dee, and it cost twelve dollars and up for dinner. Then one morning when Dee got out of bed, she tripped on a footstool and cut her foot badly. My lawyer arranged for Le Roy to pick up the hospital bill and we agreed not to sue them.

We named our son, who weighed 5 pounds 14 ounces, after the hero of *The Green Years*, Robbie. Even as a baby he showed fantastic studiousness. He would practice a new word by himself for days, and wouldn't utter it except in perfect context.

Once I was drinking beer and he reached out his chubby finger and smiled. He was one year old. I let him have a sip of the beer. He made an awful face.

Then he said: "*Beer.*" He was making a mental note never to drink beer again.

Several times we took Robbie to visit my family in Chicago or Dee's family in St. Louis. We went by plane. For years this sensitive, poetic little boy believed that Chicago and St. Louis were places in the sky. His reasoning was: If you get on a plane in New York, and then you go up in the sky, and then you get *off* the plane in Chicago, then where else is Chicago but in the sky?

Robbie had a baby blanket, one corner of which he chewed constantly. He called it his "bone," because he had seen our dog Dusty chewing on her bone. We were told to wean him from his blanket by cutting it into smaller pieces until there was no more blanket. *We did it, but it always seemed cruel to me.*

I could have used a security blanket myself when I finally became a head writer. I was made the head writer of *The 54th Street Revue*, one of the pioneer variety shows on television. The total writing budget, for me and four junior writers, was $350 a week, and this budget was so microscopic that no other head writer in the business would accept the job. Among the writers were Max Wilk, who has since written novels, plays and films, and George Axelrod, author of the smash comedy *The Seven Year Itch*. There was a long succession of comedians until

Al Bernie became the permanent comedian.

Dee had helped me make that three-volume, indexed collection of jokes, and for years you could throw Dee any subject—Wives, Mothers-in-law, Dogs, Drunks—and she'd give you six jokes on it. The biggest joke on television in the period 1948 to 1949 was: *"Since I've been on television, they've sold a lot of sets —my uncle sold his, my father sold his. . . ." People never seemed to tire of this joke. Every comedian told it. Milton Berle loved it. He told it every week.*

Al Bernie was a one-line comic of the Bob Hope school. He was an open canyon down which a writer had to throw jokes, and you could never hope to fill that yawning canyon. He exhausted my whole three volumes of 20,000 jokes in a few weeks, and I was fired again.

Then I got a phone call from Sid Reznick. Reznick, who was the author of a book on how to write comedy, told me he had just been made head writer of a new Dumont program, *Schoolhouse,* starring Buddy Hackett and Kenny Delmar.

"Al-baby," he said, "I got a job for you, baby, a hundred a week, you go to work tomorrow. You'll be working with a team of writers, Will Glickman and Joe Stein. You go to Room 356 at the Edison Hotel ten A.M. tomorrow, and you get right to work on the show."

"Sid-baby," I replied, "you've made me a very happy man. I feel this will be the beginning of big things."

"You said it, baby," he said.

I hung up the phone and said, "Dee, the days of wine and roses have returned. The nights of milk and honey are come again. No more Kraft Dinners from now on."

We were waltzing on the clouds, dancing in the dark and singing in the rain.

At ten A.M. the following morning I met my co-writers. Reznick was not present at our first writing session. Reznick, as behooved a head writer, was with the studio executives, the advertising agency bigwigs, the brass. They were having their meetings and we were having our meetings.

Stein was a short, muscular, laconic man, and his partner, Glickman, was a thin, nervous fellow with a long, thin mustache. We went right to work, laying out the show, routining the spots, planning the comedy sketches, figuring out jokes for Buddy Hackett and Kenny Delmar.

At 11:30 the phone rang.

Stein answered. "Hello," he said dourly, and then he was suddenly smiling. "Oh, yes, hello, Mr. Abbott." He put his hand on the mouthpiece and whispered to his partner, "Hey, Will, it's *George* Abbott. . . ."

Stein kept nodding and smiling and listening, and finally he said, "Yes, of course. We'll be right over."

"Will," he said to Glickman, "George Abbott is going to direct and produce our play!"

They had written *Mrs. Gibbons' Boys*, a farce comedy. (It ran five performances. Later they wrote *Plain and Fancy* and Stein wrote *Fiddler on the Roof*.)

"Let's go," Glickman said. Then he said to me, "I'm afraid we'll have to quit the program. It's in your hands now."

They walked out, and I was left alone to write the whole show. I was not even sure yet what the show was about, but I wrote like a man possessed—like an expectant father.

I filled forty-five pages with jokes and comical sketches and song specialties—in case we had song specialties. I worked until after seven o'clock. I had finished a good first draft of the script with the music cues and the camera shots, and I got home about eight o'clock with the contented feeling of a man who has fulfilled himself and done a fine piece of work.

"Dee," I said, "I want you to know that I put in a solid day's work. You can be proud of me."

"That's good," she said. "Sidney Reznick called. He wants you to call him back."

I called Reznick to tell him what a fine job I had been doing and he should be proud of me, but he stopped me and said I should be proud of *him*.

"Listen, Al-baby," he said, "we had a big argument with the brass at Dumont this afternoon."

"We did?"

"They wanted us to do certain things and write certain things and agree to certain conditions that we simply could not agree to."

"We couldn't?"

"It was a matter of principle. But we stuck to our guns. And, Al-baby—we quit."

"What do you mean, *we* quit?"

"That's it, Al, we quit—you and I—we both quit. I quit on your behalf. It was a matter of guts and principle."

I hung up the phone with a sick feeling in my heart.

"What did Mr. Reznick want?" Dee asked.

I sighed and said, "Oh, nothing much, honey. He just called to say the A & P has a special on Kraft Dinner."

CHAPTER 7

Not So Nicely-Nicely

I GUESS MOST OVEREATING is psychosomatic. I'm sure that mine is. Just after we were married, during those awful years of unemployment and frustration, I had eaten my way into a size 46 Portly Short suit. A friend of mine suggested a reducing doctor. I will call him Dr. Friedkin.

I went to Dr. Friedkin's office on Park Avenue and sat down for a consultation. When he learned I had just been married, he said, "Well, that explains everything. You were recently married—and overweight is frequently caused by increased sexual activity."

"But, Dr. Friedkin," I said, "my wife weighs ninety-six pounds."

The doctor pondered this for a moment. Then he shrugged and spoke.

"The hell with it," he said. "Let's go out and have a banana split."

After five years of psychosomatic gluttony and squalor and penury and noisy desperation, something happened which, now that I look back at it, must have been a glimmering of the fact that I secretly wanted to be a performer.

In 1950, *Guys and Dolls* opened on Broadway, and within a few months the producers decided to send out a road company.

At the time I was a client of MCA (Music Corporation of America), a theatrical agency which was recently put out of existence by the Federal Government because it controlled almost all of show business. And yet, even with all this monopolistic control, they were unable to get me a job. I used to call the man in charge of writers, and he would say, "Why should I bother with you? I handle Arthur Miller."

Anyway, I read in *Variety* that Feuer and Martin were casting the *Guys and Dolls* road company. There was a character in the show called Nicely-Nicely Johnson who was fat and funny.

I phoned the man in charge of writers at MCA and said, "I realize you can't get me a job writing. In fact, you will be relieved to hear that I am thinking of giving up writing. Perhaps you can switch me to somebody who won't be able to get me a job acting?"

He switched me to Mr. David Susskind, who has since startled America with his *Open End* and other novelties. Mr. Susskind was then the MCA representative for casting Broadway shows, and he arranged an audition for me the following Thursday afternoon at the 46th Street Theatre.

I memorized one of the Frank Loesser songs from the show, "Sit Down, You're Rockin' the Boat." On Thursday afternoon, at the stage door of the 46th Street I joined the fattest group of actors I have ever seen and waited my turn.

There is no experience more frightening to a human being

who has any self-consciousness at all than standing on the bare stage of a Broadway theatre, behind the bare light bulb they call a work light, and staring into a dark, cold theatre lined with empty seats, with the exception of two or three. And in those are seated indistinguishable people who are passing judgment on every move you make, every noise you utter, your looks, your personality, your dress, your bearing, your poise—everything you are ashamed of. Years ago I watched auditions at the Copacabana in New York and I saw the producer stop a girl in the middle of her dance and say, "You're ugly, honey. Go home to Scranton."

Whoever was sitting in the 46th Street Theatre that Thursday afternoon was much kinder to me. When my turn came, I walked up on the stage (my voice was no better then than it is now, and I was just as scared) and I began to sing:

"I dreamed last night I got on the boat to heaven
And by some chance I had brought my dice along. . . ."

The word "along" ends on an extremely high note. I didn't make it. I got close, but I didn't make it.

So I tried again:
". . . along."
Closer.
I tried again.
". . . along."
I was getting closer all the time, and I am sure that after five or six more attempts I would have hit that note perfectly.

Just then a voice from the dark bowels of the theatre said, "Thank you!"

I don't know whether it was the voice of Abe Burrows or Frank Loesser or Cy Feuer or Ernie Martin, all of whom have since become my friends. It might even have been David Susskind, trying to save his career. All I know is that if they had given me just a few more shots at that note, they might have discovered one of the Great Thrilling Singing Stars of Our Time.

For the second time in my life I gave up forever the idea of being a performer.

I devoted my full energies to being unemployed and waiting for a phone call from Darryl Zanuck.

CHAPTER 8

The Disorganization Man,
OR Up Madison Avenue
with Goodson and Todman

ONE MONDAY AFTERNOON in August of 1951, Howard Merrill and I were having coffee at Colbee's on the ground floor of the Columbia Broadcasting System's building. We were both out of work.

"You know what would be good?" Howard asked.

"What?"

"If we owned a show of our own."

The ambition of every writer in television is to create and own a *property*—a television series which goes on the air and becomes a big smash hit and runs five years, and once you've created it and sold it, you don't have to do anything, other people do the writing and producing, and you collect a fat royalty check every week, and you don't have to go through the anguish of writing for television any more, because you're so rich and successful.

"Hey, that *would* be good," I said. "Let's think up a show."

"What kind of show should we think up?" Howard asked.

"Let's think up the most successful type of show there is."

"Good idea."

"Like *What's My Line*, for example."

"Precisely. Now, what is the basic reason for the success of *What's My Line?*"

I had seen *What's My Line* the night before, so I thought about it for a moment. Then I said: "Well—it's dirty."

"Right," Howard agreed. "And the panelists wear tuxedos."

"All the better. That makes it a typical American family show."

I thought back to last night's show. The first contestant had signed in and sat down next to John Daly. After a little chitchat, the contestant's line was revealed to the audience:

SELLS MATTRESSES

The studio audience giggled in delighted anticipation.

The first panelist was a lady. She asked: "Is there a product connected with what you do?"

"'Yes."

"Is this a useful product?"

"Yes, indeed," said the mattress salesman.

"Is it used by members of both sexes?"

The audience howled.

"Yes."

The lady looked dumfounded at the laughter. "May I assume that this is not used primarily during business hours?"

The audience laughed even louder. The innocent lady continued. (She could keep questioning until she got a *no* answer.) "If Bennett Cerf and I had one of these, could we use it together?"

Screams.

"Well, you *could* . . . yes."

"Then is this thing used primarily for entertainment?"

The audience gave out with a deafening roar, and Mr. Daly had to wait almost half a minute before he could say to the innocent lady: "No! That's five dollars down and forty-five dollars to go!"

So it went. The panelists continued to question the mattress salesman, who by this time was himself dissolved in hysterical laughter.

"Think hard." Howard said. "What is even more personal than a person's occupation?"

I gave a hard think.

"*Secrets!*" I said. "Everybody has terrible, guilty secrets that they are ashamed to tell to anybody else."

"Exactly!" Howard shouted. "Now—all we have to do is get these guilt-ridden, shame-filled people to tell these awful secrets to twenty-five million other people every week, and we are rich."

Howard took a sheet of paper, and across the top of it wrote a title and one line of hard-sell:

I KNOW A SECRET
An Exciting New Game Panel Show
Created by Howard Merrill and Allan Sherman

"Now," Howard said, "we need some secrets."

"Oh," I said, "they'll come in the mail. Millions of Americans will unburden themselves and confess everything to us weekly. We might even open up a little blackmail business on the side."

"Don't be funny. I mean we need some examples of secrets in order to sell this thrilling show we have just created."

So we sat there and thought up twenty-five sample secrets. Such as—a man who comes on the show and says, "I *just became the father of quadruplets*"; or a woman who says, "*My husband snores"*; or a celebrity who says, "I *sleep in pajama tops*."

Howard and I tested the game on each other for about an hour, and when we were sure that it would work, we took our sheet of paper and walked across the street to the CBS radio building at 49 East 52nd Street, and went up to the seventh-floor offices of Goodson–Todman Productions to sell our magnificent creation.

We were ushered into Bill Todman's office and we told him about the show. He listened very studiously, leaning back in his chair and playing a game in which he touched the fingertips of each hand to the corresponding fingertips of the other hand. When we were finished, he said, "Just a minute," and he went out of the office.

"What do you think?" Howard asked while Bill was out.

"I think he's got a serious fingertip problem," I replied.

Then Bill came back into the office with Mark Goodson, and we explained the show all over again. Then Mark played the game with us several times. Then he began to shout questions at us, rapid-fire—finding every possible "bug" in the idea, every conceivable problem—and seeing if we had the answers. Some we did and some we didn't. After this third-degree, Goodson said, "Excuse us a moment," and both he and Todman left the office.

Five minutes later Todman returned with a single-spaced typewritten sheet of paper. It was a Letter of Agreement between Goodson–Todman Productions and "The Undersigned," who turned out to be Howard and me. It said that The Undersigned would hereby transfer, assign, sell, rent and give all rights to the television show entitled *I've Got a Secret* (I don't know whether the name got changed by design or by a hasty typist) and that those rights included television and radio broadcast rights, world-wide subsidiary rights, motion-picture rights, dramatic and musical rights, toy-and-souvenir-manufacturing rights, re-broadcast rights and civil rights.

In trade for this, it said that Goodson–Todman agreed to pay The Undersigned the sum of One Dollar ($1.00).

Howard looked at me, and I looked at Howard. We both knew that a contract was something you should show to a lawyer before you let yourself become The Undersigned. But Bill Todman, in his infinite wisdom, knew what was going on in our minds, and he said, "You guys drive a hard bargain. You know, if I didn't need a show right this minute, I wouldn't be able to buy this. For example, if you were to come in an hour from now, it would be no sale."

Howard and I got the message.

Howard, who was the more courageous of the two of us, gulped and said, "I don't know . . . *one* dollar . . ."

I put an end to his doubts.

"What the hell," I said. "We need the money."

And so we signed the Letter of Agreement, which also included a promise that if and when the show went on the air, one of us would be offered the job of Associate Producer at $125 a week, and we would each receive a $125 weekly royalty.

Seven years later, when Goodson–Todman Productions sold I've Got a Secret to CBS for something like three million dollars, I sent them a wire: NICE PROFIT, FELLAS.

All this took place on a Monday in August, 1951. It was eight months before the show was sold to a sponsor, and three more months before our one-page outline was translated into a real television program.

There were constant run-throughs, day after day, and at every one of them Goodson found new bugs. Then there were constant meetings at night to work out the bugs. There were dozens of auditions to find the perfect panelists. There was session after session with Mark Goodson seated at a typewriter and Howard and me pacing Goodson's office, trying to simplify and clarify the rules of the game. The rules of a television game are terribly complex and must be completely precise and exact or else you can get into some ridiculous lawsuits.

When we went on the air on June 19, 1952, the host was Garry Moore. The perfect panel we had chosen consisted of Orson Bean, Louise Allbritton, Laura Z. Hobson and Melville Cooper. This perfect panel lasted one week, and so did the original format of the show. After all those months of taking out the bugs, we had a regular insectorium on our hands.

The public had not yet begun confiding their secrets to us through the mail, so we had to use friends for the contestants. I got my friend Shelly Keller, who had come to New York to be a comedian, to come on, and his secret was "*I am wearing a girdle.*" I got the wife of another friend to come on with the secret "*My husband snores.*" (Dee explained to me that the trouble with this secret was that *everybody's* husband snores.)

I was the Associate Producer. The job had fallen in my lap because, luckily for me, when it came open, Howard Merrill was employed. If he hadn't been, I suppose we would have flipped a coin. I'd have won. Fate. Kismet.

Every good thing that has ever happened to me in my life has happened like that—not by plan or grand design but by some lucky accident.

The show was sponsored by different clients on alternate weeks. One week it was Carter Products—a company that somehow managed to make Carter's Little Liver Pills, Rise Shaving Cream and Esquire Boot Polish and God only knows what else —and on the alternate weeks the sponsor was Prom Home Permanent. The president of Prom Home Permanent was violently opposed to Laura Hobson and later to Nina Foch and Faye Emerson because they had straight hair. In this man's mind there was something basically disgusting about any woman with straight hair. He would rather have had Harpo Marx than

Faye Emerson, because Harpo's wig would have showed the advantages of a Prom Home Permanent.

Thank God the Carter Products people weren't that anxious to show the advantages of their products. We'd have had to hire constipated panelists with beards and dirty shoes.

Anyway, the president of Prom didn't like the show. The morning after the first program he went to CBS and canceled sponsorship of his alternate weeks. So all through the summer *I've Got a Secret* played alternate Thursday nights with a show called *Racket Squad,* a program about a curly-headed investigator. When the summer was over, we somehow survived and *Racket Squad* was gone forever.

I don't know what happened to me. When somebody finally gave me some authority, I became responsible. I worked like a fiend. There were only three of us on the staff: a completely indispensable girl who in television is called the Production Assistant and who does everything, but everything, on the show; and a young boy who opened and stapled the mail (often to his own thumb); and I.

And the mail was prodigious. The first week there were more than four thousand letters. I read every single one. That remark I had made at Colbee's had turned out to be no joke at all. The American people were anxious to confess their secrets, and it wasn't the money—the most you could win was eighty dollars.

There were letters from kooks, and there were letters from college professors; there were printed postcards with the heading Committee of One from people who objected to our morals. There were letters from the Bible Belt (which is everywhere) from people who warned us that Jesus was on his way back and would get our show canceled, or get it renewed.

A man from St. Louis wrote: *"My freckles are green."* A man from Flushing, New York, a Jew: *"I was personal tailor to Heinrich Himmler."* An Air Force sergeant in Florida: *"I parachuted into a nudist colony."* We heard from couples who had been married in a diving bell at the bottom of the Atlantic, married on roller skates on top of a flagpole, and while dancing the Lindy Hop and trying to stay awake during one of those marathon dances in the 1930's. A professional boxer sent in a news clipping to prove that one night he had walked into the ring, removed his bathrobe and discovered, along with the audience, that he was stark naked underneath. There were dozens of survivors of the *Titanic* and, later, of the *Andrea Doria*. There were people with hearts on the right side, livers on the left, and there was one letter from a man with four kidneys.

I didn't want the show to become a carnival sideshow. I wanted it to be wild and crazy and even bawdy, but I wanted it also to reflect the kind of people we are in this country.

The letters, the constant letters, gave me a new look at the vastness of this country and the depth of the loneliness among its individuals. Here is one from a man in Oregon. The original was scrawled in a tortured, barely readable longhand. The spelling and punctuation are exact.

DEAR SIR

I have a secret. I worked shoulder to shoulder with a woman for five years. She exposed part of her breasts and I faced her to write orders every day & I would glance down her neck. She made me think by little things she would say from day to day that my wife didn't appreciate me. Because she didn't help me make money. Finally I couldn't stand it any longer so I started loving her a little at the store. Finally she was so willing that my desire grew & grew and I thot of everything to justify it. Then I took her to a neighboring town to dinner & then intercourse. My wife knows by the little things said & done that only a wife can tell. Her heart is broken but she has no way of making a living or no place to go so she must start another year knowing this. I deny it and I do not want to let the woman go. *My wife would be a different person if I could but the bond is too strong. We are very careful and discreet now because every one is watching us but she understands and there are moments when we can talk or smile and it stimulates me just to have her near. It will be a living hell for my wife but I don't care for I hate her & success and money are now my god. I used to think this other woman was cheap but she gave me what I thot I wanted now she is very lady like & dear to me. I called my daughter up to come to my hotel room for a bluff and after she had gone. We met and I lay with my hand on her breast all night.*

At first I felt guilty and couldn't eat or sleep & lost weight but now I am feeling better and like to think of our times together as I feel I deserved them I hope my god will understand because my wife never will. I even told my wife I hate her looks now. I don't even want her to have new clothes, My new love has had four beautiful coats this year and I smile as I see her wear them. This is my secret.

I read four thousand letters every week and I was thinking up ideas for the show twenty-four hours a day and I was squeezing ideas out of anyone who would be squeezed.

I learned that ideas are everywhere; that you don't have to be an executive or a producer or a writer to think of them. I learned that anyone who opens his mind and isn't inhibited and laughed at by the people around him can come up with ideas.

So I listened. And a secretary from another show would poke her head into the office and say, "Why don't you get the man who figures out Albert Einstein's income tax?" We did. A cameraman said, "Hey, you ought to find somebody who's got a library book that's been overdue for years." We did. My old friend and insurance man David Streger, had a library book *nineteen years* overdue. (At two cents a day, including Leap Year days, his library fine would have been $142.43, and, furthermore,

David Streger was on the board of the New Rochelle Public Library.)

I worked like a madman. The show was never out of my mind. Two or three nights a week I worked so late that I missed the last train home, so I slept on the couch in the Goodson–Todman reception room. In the morning the receptionist would come in and put her coat over me so I could sleep warmer for another hour until the rest of the staff began to arrive.

The Production Assistant's name was Adrianne. I remember making her cry one day. That morning I had heard on the radio that Sir Edmund Hillary had reached the top of Mount Everest. I couldn't wait to get to the office. When I got there, I said: "Adrianne—get Sir Edmund Hillary on the phone."

"*Who?*" she asked.

"Sir Edmund Hillary."

"Where is he?"

"On the top of Mount Everest."

It had never occurred to me that there might not be a telephone booth at the top of Mount Everest.

I'll hand this to Adrianne—she placed the call. And, by God, she did reach someone at the *bottom* of Mount Everest, where there *is* a telephone booth. Then she said to me, "Mr. Hillary is expected down in a month."

"Too late!" I yelled, Goodsonesquely. "Tell them we need him *now!*"

Adrianne started to cry, but she told them through her tears.

Once I called the Air Force Public Relations Office and said, "Why don't you have somebody fly across country and break the jet speed record on a Wednesday, and we'll put him on the air the same night?"

The Public Relations Officer said, "Oh, we couldn't arrange anything like that. We have no control over those things."

A couple of weeks later three Air Force jets flew from Los Angeles to New York in three hours and nineteen minutes *on a*

Wednesday. And somehow we had the pilot of one of the planes on the show that night. Captain John Glenn. He later became the first American to orbit the earth, but that Wednesday night was the first time he had ever appeared on television.

One night the six-o'clock news announced that a young British doctor named Roger Bannister had become the first human to run a mile in less than four minutes.

I called Adrianne at home. "Do me a favor," I said. "Get up at four in the morning—it will be nine o'clock in England then—and call Roger Bannister." By now Adrianne was accustomed to this type of thing. *Only Adrianne didn't get up at four in the morning; she stayed out till then. That's none of my business. I love her.*

Adrianne made contact with Roger Bannister, and later in the day I talked to him and somehow persuaded him to fly to New York incognito the next morning and go on *I've Got a Secret*. I even invented a code name for him, "Richard Belmont," so he could avoid the press and the whole thing could be kept secret. *Ha!* At five o'clock the following morning I drove out to Idlewild for my secret meeting with Richard-Roger Belmont-Bannister. I parked my car and tiptoed into the International Arrival Building. Surprise: there were remote television trucks from NBC, CBS and ABC news, and milling around at that hour in the morning there were no less than 300 reporters. There were 20 representatives of the British Information Service, and the complete staff of the Amateur Athletic Union, and at least 500 autograph-seekers.

I knew almost at once: something had gone wrong. Bannister didn't go on the show—but the fact that he had come to America to be on *I've Got a Secret* was on every news broadcast and every front page in the nation.

* * *

One Wednesday, just before a Labor Day weekend, we discarded the regular show and, against everybody's better judgment, I went out on the farthest tip of the highest limb.

We brought onto the stage the crumpled wreck of an automobile. A man in his early forties came out and sat next to Garry Moore. His secret was *"My son was killed in this automobile."*

We took a picture of our live studio audience of 700 people sitting there, not knowing what to expect. Garry Moore explained: "By the time this weekend is over, this many people will have been killed by auto accidents." As he spoke these words, the picture slowly changed and the 700 seats were empty.

The next morning *The New York Times* ran a headline: PANEL SHOW PERFORMS GENUINE PUBLIC SERVICE.

Within one year we passed What's My Line in the ratings and I won a ten-dollar bet from Mark Goodson. And they changed my title to Producer.

Eventually the big-name celebrities began coming our way, partly because the show became so popular and was the "in" show to do, and partly because Goodson and Todman finally agreed to let me change the format of the celebrity spot.

It had occurred to me before the show went on the air that the celebrities should not have secrets in the same way the regular contestants had them. First of all, a celebrity is someone whose secrets are known to the general public; of course, celebrities have real secrets, but they sure as hell don't get on a television show and reveal them.

Our first celebrity guest was Boris Karloff, and his secret was *"I'm afraid of mice."* This was a lie; we concocted it because it seemed to have some contrast with what we thought was the public image of Karloff the Frankenstein Monster. It was also dull and commonplace and trivial.

In those days I did a lot of talking and philosophizing about honesty in this type of show. Not because I'm so morally righteous; I simply believed, as I still believe, that there is nothing more exciting or interesting on television (or anywhere else) than reality—spontaneous, unpredictable reality.

I kept saying to Mark Goodson and Bill Todman and whoever else would listen that reality was the great secret of their success; that this entire genre of show was successful because it had the fresh smell of actuality—it was *happening* right there before your eyes.

The best things I've ever seen on television—the moments that have remained indelibly in my brain for years, even if they have only flashed across the screen for a few seconds—were *all live*. They all had reality and spontaneity and unpredictability.

I will never forget the Army-McCarthy hearings. I can still see that kindly pixie Joseph Welch, who came from nowhere and cut Senator McCarthy down to human size in front of the American public. I can still see McCarthy and hear him insanely mumbling, over and over again, *"Let me finish—let me finish—let me finish."* I can see the puzzled, hurt-boy faces of Roy Cohn and G. David Schine.

I can see clearly the last ten seconds of the 1947 World Series when Cookie Lavagetto hit a double off the right-field wall (the ball ricocheted off a sign advertising Danny Kaye in *The Secret Life of Walter Mitty*), winning the game for the Dodgers and breaking up Bill Bevins' no-hitter.

I remember distinctly the very first morning the *Today* show was on. There was a split screeen, and on it I saw something no human eye had ever seen before: I sat there in my living room and saw—*live*, at one incredible moment of time—both the Golden Gate Bridge in San Francisco and the George Washington Bridge in New York. And it gave me a totally new sense of the vastness of this country and of the genuine magic of television.

That is what television really is; it is another eye so you can see anywhere; another part of your heart so you can feel and care about things you never felt and cared about before; another ear to hear strange music. No matter how they disguise it and cheapen it—no matter how many situation comedies and Westerns and monster shows they put on, no matter how much the money-counters use it for their own purposes—that is what television is and will always be: the first and only international language, so that we can look at the Russians and the Chinese and the South Africans and they can look at us. And once we've all done that, how is there ever going to be another war? Another eye, which in our lifetimes will show us the dark side of the moon and a close-up of Mars and Venus—and once we've seen that, who will ever again deny that there is a God?

Reality. Life. People. Feelings. Ideas.

Close-up: The hands of Frank Costello fumbling with his glasses while he took the Fifth Amendment in front of the Kefauver Crime Committee.

Audio: The beat of drums—that awful, insistent, monotonous drumbeat that went on forever (and is still in my ears) as they carried President Kennedy's body away.

Wide shot: The formless, unhappy little band of human beings who happened to be Kings and Presidents and Prime Ministers, as they walked down Pennsylvania Avenue behind the body.

Medium-wide shot: Caroline and John-John Kennedy standing by the coffin while their mother knelt and kissed it.

Medium close-up: They are taking Lee Harvey Oswald through the basement of the Dallas police station. A man with a dark hat steps out of the crowd and kills him.

Wide shot, zooming into close-up: The capsule in which Alan Shepard is crouched as we hear the countdown. *"Four . . . three . . . two . . . one . . . lift-off . . ."*

* * *

Goodson and Todman had discovered the importance of reality when television was very young, but when I made my speeches about reality and honesty, they felt I was making a fetish out of it—that I was some kind of maniac on the subject. *You have to exercise control,* they said.

Years later I saw control exercised to its fullest extent on this type of show. I saw men (not Goodson and Todman) arrogate to themselves the privilege of controlling reality. I watched— millions of us watched—as they manipulated the truth. My first suspicion came when they referred on the air to Gino Prado as a "cobbler." Mr. Prado was a shoemaker. The word "cobbler" had gone out of use a half-century before; we remember it only from stories and fairy tales where the cobbler Geppetto is Pinocchio's friend.

Why were they calling him a cobbler?

They were manipulating my sympathies. When I thought of a *cobbler,* I thought of how *poor* he must be, and I wanted him to win the $64,000.

Why did Mr. Van Doren hesitate so and gesticulate so and then, week after week, give the right answer at the very last instant?

Because the Manipulators told him to.

To compete with *Twenty One,* the $64,000 Question people doubled their prize to $128,000. Why did Mr. Van Doren win exactly $129,000?

Because the Fixers figured out exactly how to take something that was really exciting and replace it with synthetic excitement. Because they decided they were omniscient: they knew exactly how many weeks the American public wanted Mr. Van Doren on the air and when the American public wanted him knocked off. They were manipulating, not just him, but you and me.

I saw this with my own eyes.

When the truth came out that the show was rigged—when we

learned, at last, that all those weeks we had been fooled, and *Time* Magazine had been fooled; that our hero was made of clay; that they had manipulated us—forty million puppets, forty million suckers, to be done with as *they* saw fit—I watched Ruth, our colored maid, sit before the television set and cry real tears.

And she asked me, because I was in the television business, *"It's not true, is it, Mr. Sherman?"*

Because all those weeks she had not been watching Charles Van Doren; she had been watching *Ruth*, watching herself there on the screen, getting the big chance, winning the $129,000.

The morning after it all came out, I rode into Grand Central on a commuter train and there was a silence among us. A little angry, but mostly confused. We didn't know what to say to each other, because we had all been damn fools.

We were confused because we, too, spend our lives grubbing money. We couldn't quite understand what was wrong with manipulating human beings for the sole purpose of getting more money.

The lid was blown off the whole thing, the cat was let out of the bag, by a nervous, thin, acne-faced young man named Eddie. Eddie told all because they refused to give him more money to keep quiet. And so the hero was as rotten as the villain. And we Americans, those of us with some remaining dignity and decency—we got a good, close look at ourselves and the way we had been living.

Skinny Eddie had been a contestant on *Dotto*.

Just before the scandal, Dee and I were vacationing in the White Mountains of New Hampshire when I got a call from my agent in New York.

"How would you like to produce *Dotto?*" he asked.

I was out of work. I needed a job, but something kept me from saying yes right away. I told him I'd call him back.

I thought: Dotto *is a successful show. It has a high rating and it's professionally done. I honestly can't think of any way to improve it. What do they need me for?*

I called my agent back. "What do they need me for?"

"The producer is going to Europe," he said.

"I don't know," I said. "I don't think it's right for me. There's nothing new that I can do for the show."

A month later I found out what they had wanted me for. If I had taken the job, the scandal would have been on my head.

It was worth a thousand dollars a week to them to have a scapegoat. Especially one who had made a reputation for himself as an Honest Fool.

On *I've Got a Secret* we kept inventing semihonest secrets for the celebrities until the night Monty Woolley was our guest. For him we concocted "I sleep with my beard under the covers."

After the panel guessed it, Henry Morgan asked, "Now, Mr. Woolley, do you really sleep with your beard under the covers?"

"Of course not, you bloody idiot!" shouted the Yale-professor-turned-actor. "*Some damn fool named Allan Sherman told me to say so.*"

I've Got a Secret was a runaway winner. And my business managers explained to me that, no matter how difficult it was, I must stay with the show because the single most important thing in show business is to ride a winner. To have a smash hit. That's how stars are made. And big producers. And overnight heroes. If you have one big winner, one big hit, you can coast for the rest of your life, if that's what you want.

But that wasn't what I wanted.

There were things going on at Goodson-Todman Productions that were not what I wanted. There were meetings—constant meetings. And memos—immense piles of memos every day. Everything had to be written down in black and white; everything had to run like clockwork; and the closer you came to being an IBM machine rather than an individual human being, the better off you were.

In the 1940's, when their first and only show was *Winner Take All*, Mark Goodson and Bill Todman shared chicken-coop offices in the CBS Radio Building with one secretary and some hand-me-down office furniture. In a corner of the room was a pile of merchandise prizes which they got free from the manufacturers in exchange for plugging them.

Mark told me about a time when they ordered a sandwich from the drugstore downstairs. When the delivery boy came, Mark and Bill between them had just enough cash to pay for the lunch, and not a quarter left for a tip. Mark reached over to the pile of prizes and handed the boy the top box.

"Here," he said. It was a Bulova watch.

Those prizes, together with a few questions and some well-chosen contestants, were the entire stock in trade of the original Goodson-Todman operation. That's all they needed to build a high rating; none of the usual big expenses. They did it without stars or scenery or rehearsals or scripts, and the sponsors begged for more.

In those days Mark and Bill carried the prizes back and forth from their office to the studio. Once they were running to the studio with armfuls of prizes when Todman slipped, and coffee percolators and toasters and steam irons and pressure cookers went clattering to the sidewalk.

Goodman Ace, one of the top comedy writers, happened to be passing by. He yelled, "Hey, Todman, you dropped your script."

Bill Todman was born wealthy in New York. He didn't quite finish medical school at Johns Hopkins. He had an enormous capacity for whiskey; but it never slowed him down. He is a superb, almost hypnotic, salesman. He spoke a fantastic language loaded with big words which I came to call "Todmanese." I would go into his office to ask a little question like: Should we have the tickets printed on green or orange cardboard?

Bill would reply something like this: "Due to the irrevocable differences between the prolixities of program scheduling and the limitations foisted upon us by the dichotomy of network budgetary practice, it is impossible to viably consummate the goals previously ascribed. Nevertheless, we must resolve this dilemma with a solution that will encompass this and other problems, however indefinitely."

Then he'd look at me as though he had said something of earth-shaking importance. *Then I'd run across to Mark Goodson's office to find out what color the Goddam cardboard should be.*

Bill was a maniacal telephoner. He only talked to me in small spurts between phone calls. And his phone calls were impressive. He'd say to his secretary, "Get me Henry Ford."

You're looking for a five-dollar raise and he's calling Henry Ford to have a special Lincoln built to his design.

Bill owned a lot of things made of solid gold. He had a solid-gold toothpick, a solid-gold cigarette lighter, a solid-gold cigarette case, a solid-gold fountain pen and, I have no doubt, solid-gold jockey shorts.

My moment of Uttermost Confusion with Bill Todman came when Goodson-Todman was planning a new panel show and Bill was looking for a new host. He called me into his office.

"*Secret* is going great, isn't it?" he asked.

"Yes," I said.

"Wouldn't you say that Garry Moore is the most human and warm of all the hosts on television?"

"There's no doubt of that," I said.

Bill paused, then leaned forward.

"*Who else do you know that does warmth?*"

* * *

Mark Goodson had a keen, quick mind and, like so many men whose shortness bothers them, a tall ambition.

In his office, among other books, was a copy of Machiavelli's *The Prince*. He often read it as a sort of guidebook to success in modern life—the way J. Pierpont Finch reads *How to Succeed in Business Without Really Trying* in the musical of the same name. He sat at a handsome Empire desk that had once actually belonged to Napoleon. Mark had a long, sharp letter opener, and when he spoke to me he would nervously tap his desk and then suddenly point the letter opener at me like a dagger.

Whatever I did, it wasn't good enough. I always felt I was letting down the team. Mark had ways of talking that made it almost impossible to counter. For instance, he would not say, "Did you remember to call Faye Emerson?" Instead he would ask, "What did Faye Emerson say when you called her?" although he knew damn well that I had not called her. So I wouldn't know what to say.

One night, after a couple of years of this, I went home and Dee proudly showed me the new drapes that had been hung that afternoon. I stood there exploring, and I said, "What did the drapery man say when you told him the cornice was an inch and a half off center?" She began to cry and I realized what I'd done and I never did it again.

There is a game they play on Madison Avenue, a game played for big stakes, a game in which the pawns are people. Mark Goodson was brilliant at it. He was Player-of-the-Year.

The object of the Madison Avenue Game is to grow more powerful, and one of the strategies is to remove anyone who stands in your way.

But you don't *fire* a man. It simply is not done. You humiliate him; you strip off his epaulets in public; you shame him into quitting. You take away his key to the executive toilet and make him pee with the commoners. One morning he walks in, and in his office, where there once was wall-to-wall carpeting, there is now a throw rug. Or he suddenly finds that a nice, middle-aged lady has replaced his sexy blonde secretary. And her electric typewriter has been replaced with a manual machine. And he starts getting memos that are fuzzier and harder to read because they come from behind the last sheet of carbon paper.

Once I understood the Madison Avenue Game, I took great pleasure in trying to defeat it. There was the time Goodson decided to get rid of Frank Satenstein, who was the director of both *I've Got a Secret* and *The Jackie Gleason Show*. Mark had nothing against Frank personally. He wanted to hire a staff director, because that would come out much cheaper for Goodson-Todman.

"I'm having lunch with Frank, Monday," Mark told me. "I'm going to tell him that he must spend a full eight hours a day in our office, with no secretary, and attend all the meetings, and answer all the memos."

"But we don't need him there all that time. Besides, he has the *Gleason Show* on Saturdays."

"I know, I know." Mark winked. "Just my luck—he'll quit, and we'll need a new director."

I went upstairs and called Frank. I gave him the details and we worked out a strategy. On Monday, Mark, Frank and I went to lunch together.

Mark said, "Frank, we're going to have to make some changes."

Frank said, "Oh, really?"

Mark said, "Yes. First of all, we'll be needing you in the office every day from ten till six."

Frank looked at Mark, overjoyed. "Do you *mean* it?" he said. "Isn't that a coincidence! I was just going to ask *you* if I could spend more time in the office. Gee, thanks, Mark!"

Mark hesitated a moment, then he said, "And we won't be able to afford a secretary for you."

"Oh, that's all right, Mark. I type beautifully, you know."
Frank made a little typing gesture on his corned-beef sandwich
with both hands.

Mark said, "And you'll have to come to all the meetings."

Frank said, "Ooh, goodie! I can't wait to see what goes on in
all those meetings. I always felt so *left out*. This is marvelous!"

Mark made one last effort. "But what about the *Gleason
Show?*"

Frank said, "Oh, Jackie won't mind. He thinks I spend too
much time around there anyway. When do I start at Goodson-
Todman?"

"Never mind," said Mark in defeat.

"Really, Mark, I'm very anxious—"

"To hell with it," Mark said. "Eat your corned-beef sandwich."

The playing field for the Madison Avenue Game is the
Conference Room. That's where the endless meetings go
on. That's where everyone has the protection of anonymity, and
decisions are made in committee so that no one man has to
take the responsibility.

Years later I wrote about committees in an album titled *Peter and the Commissar:*

They sit there in committees day after day
And they each put in a color and it comes out gray.
Gray is a nice color, but not if you've ever seen
Orange or red or yellow or blue or green.
And we all have heard the saying, which is true as well as
    witty,
That a camel is a horse that was designed by a committee.
The only reason for committees, people being what they
    are,
Is that everybody wants to be the Big Chief Commissar—

Because you get to wear the uniform, you get to wear the
*   medals,*
And you sit on the handlebar while everybody pedals.
And the people who work under you, they Yes you when
*   they face you,*
But secretly, of course, each one is hoping to replace you.

When you work in a committee, you wind up with what is
left after everybody's fears have been subtracted. You all sit
there jockeying for position, concentrating so hard on the politics of the situation that you damn near forget what the
meeting is about.

That's how the networks choose their new television programs. They have what they call a Program Board, consisting of
all the top executives. In that way, no individual can take the
credit or the blame for what goes on in the network.

I am a silkworm. I spin out my silk alone. I once read in
Lewis Mumford's The Condition of Man *that every idea has its*
beginning inside a single human brain.

I was uncomfortable in Mark Goodson's meetings. I thought
they were a waste of time. I don't like jockeying for power. I
don't like power anyway. The other side of power is fear. You
can't have power unless you make someone afraid.

Mark Goodson was memorandum crazy.

I once went down to his office and said, "At the current rate
of memo writing around here, you will have used up the world's
supply of paper by July 1, 1962."

As the program became more popular and the quantity of
mail (and memos) increased, I needed a secretary desperately.
For some reason, Goodson and Todman did not want to assign
me a secretary.

On January 31, 1955, I dispatched this memo:

```
to:  MARK GOODSON
from:  ALLAN SHERMAN
subject:  I'VE GOT A SECRET secretary
```

As soon as you have some time, I would like to
outline to you the reasons why we could make
profitable use of a secretary in the I'VE GOT
A SECRET office.
May we discuss this further at your earliest
convenience?

I did not get any answer from Mark. I did not get a secretary.
To dramatize the issue, I myself typed the next memo:

```
                     date: XXX Ferb 2, 195555
to: Makr Goodson, biltooDMan¢ GLI Ftem
from:  a;ejt Shermaikye
subject:  sechrotary***we don't nede 1
i agrEE wiht you felloes that we don't need a
secritery here in the IVEG OT ASE CRED offs.
  we canget alonG foNe wihtout one;
                          IdonT mined
ansring the lettrse myslefff½½
  aslo we will save lots of $$$$$ that weigh
%%% iwill aslo take fone cals, openM#le;;;and
mak appointems but pleas donexpetc me to gro a
boss00m.
                    Resp¼@(&fuly,
                    Aln  Shmurnnnnnnnnn
```

This got no results, so I followed it up with more illiterate
memos. For weeks I wrote all my serious memoranda in gibberish. But Goodson and Todman were obstinate. By April 22 I was
getting desperate. Then President Eisenhower declared it was
National Secretary Week. (He really did.)

```
to:  MARK GOODSON, BILL TODMAN
from:  ALLAN SHERMAN
subject:  A SECRETARY FOR "I'VE GOT A SECRET"
```

I know you'll both be pleased to know that
next week has been designated by President
Eisenhower as "National Secretary Week."
To be without a secretary during "National

Secretary Week" is, as we all realize, un-
American.
And so, gentlemen, not for me but for my
Country, can I have a secretary, please?
Thank you very much, and God Bless America.

This appeal to their Americanism at the height of the Mc-
Carthy era scared Goodson and Todman into hiring me a secretary after three years of waiting. And dreaming.

What would she be like? Blonde? Slinky? Curvaceous? Sexy,
throaty voice? Prim? Wild? Blue eyes? Exotic perfumes?

I could hardly wait till Monday.

Then Monday came. And at the stroke of ten my new secretary walked in.

His name was Roger Peterson.

Today the Executive Men's Room in the Park Avenue offices
of Goodson-Todman Productions has walls covered with real
gray flannel. It also has telephones, so that nature's calls won't
interfere with business calls. That's how well-organized things
are at Goodson-Todman.

But I was disorganized. I was a Disorganization Man, playing
a lonesome off-key melody in the Goodson-Todman Symphony
of Organization. I hated all the memos and I hated the endless
meetings and conferences, and I was not an IBM machine. I
am an individual human being and a pretty crazy one to boot—
and at Goodson-Todman that could get you into a lot of trouble.

I wrote my masterpiece of interoffice memo composition in
1957.

For six years I had beheld, with incredulity, the annual
Christmas party in the office. There were bottles of Scotch
whiskey, blended whiskey, gin and vodka. There were paper
cups. There were lukewarm quart-size bottles of ginger ale and
sparkling water. There were soggy hors d'oeuvres. There were

147

men. There were women. Sometime around eleven in the morning the drinking began and then the men would start chasing
the women all around the office. Everybody would be running
around desks and comptometers and water coolers, kissing and
necking and carrying on something terrible.

In a burst of creative frenzy I sat down and wrote the following:

MEMO TO: All Office Personnel
FROM: Allan Sherman
SUBJECT: <u>1957 Office Xmas Party</u>

The Office Party, as most of you know, is
set for next Tuesday, December 24th, at 12
Noon.

Girls who have been present at previous
Office Parties have been, I realize, looking
forward to seeing me at this party next Tuesday.

Due to the unprecedented demand for my serv-
ices this year, and the limitations imposed
on me by nature and time--I must set forth the
following rules and regulations for conduct
at the Office Party:

1.   ALL GIRLS WISHING TO PECK ME POLITELY
ON THE CHEEK, or pinch my cheek and say, "Isn't
he a doll?" will kindly line up at the 29th
floor water cooler. If time allows, I will
appear there late in the party, to accommodate
one and all.

2.   GIRLS WITH NO PREVIOUS SEXUAL EXPE-
RIENCE, OR GIRLS SUFFERING from emotional
trauma, will please report <u>Monday</u> <u>night</u> at
7:30 to my assistant, Mr. Chester Feldman, who
will give you pre-party instructions, a chalk-
talk, and a specially prepared pamphlet from
the National Safety Council.

3.   DOROTHY KRESSLER WILL REPORT DIRECTLY
TO ME IMMEDIATELY ON RECEIPT OF THIS MEMO.
What I have in mind is the same thing as last
year but I'd like to get started a little
earlier.

4. ALL GIRLS WILL TAKE WHATEVER SPECIAL PRECAUTIONS ARE INDICATED. DON'T DEPEND ON ME FOR PRECAUTONS---YOU KNOW WHAT A MAD, IMPETUOUS FOOL I AM.

5. I HAVE NO DESIRE TO REPEAT MY UNFORTUNATE EXPERIENCE OF LAST YEAR'S CHRISTMAS PARTY. Most of you will remember my regrettable case of trench mouth which lasted well into February of this year. I'm not going to name any names. You know who you are.

6. Married girls whose husbands do not understand them: to all those in this classification, a brief note---it would be best if you could keep in mind how messy emotional entanglements can become. What I mean is--- I'll give you the usual few words of sympathy about your husband, we'll drink our little toast to mankind, we'll have our little moment of wild ecstasy and then---LET'S BREAK IT OFF CLEAN. Back to the office Thursday morning, cheerful as ever, as though nothing had happened. No wistful looks, no tears, no regrets. No remorseful blubbering about how I won't look at you any more. We're grown people, all of you and I. Let's remember that.

7. Due to the unprecedented demand, priority will be given this Christmas to those who have done their part during the course of the regular year.

8. A little rack with numbered tags will be placed on the corner of my desk. (I'm sure you've all seen this system used in the bakery.) Girls--please take your number, then line up in an orderly fashion, keeping very quiet so as to allow me to concentrate. To ensure fair treatment, memorize your number, and, when called, be ready to specify exactly what you want.

9. Girls--remember the Golden Rule. Be fair to the other girls. Do unto me only what you would let me do unto you. Take only what you need. Waste not, want not. Remember, a man isn't made of wood, but he isn't made of iron either.

10.   TO THE NEW GIRLS WHO HAVE JOINED THE ORGANIZATION SINCE THE LAST CHRISTMAS PARTY: How I envy you this wonderful experience-- having me for the first time! O, moment of perfect joy--that can come to a woman only once in her lifetime.   I must beg you to control yourselves as much as you can.   Remember-- you are about to fulfill your purpose as a Woman.   For heaven's sake, maintain your dignity if it is at all possible.   And, in years to come, when you tell your friends about it-- and I know you will--please, be kind.

11.   ANY GIRL FOUND TRYING TO "CUT IN" OUT OF TURN, OR CLAWING AT THE OTHER GIRLS, WILL BE DISQUALIFIED AND WILL NOT BE ACCOMMODATED AGAIN UNTIL CHRISTMAS, 1959.

12.   Girls who bring up the subject of Office Politics at critical moments in the procedure will be regarded as blase, and tabled indefinitely.

13.   Lips that touch Howard Todman's* must never touch mine.

14.   Girls who are essentially "rejects," "seconds," "irregulars," or "dogs," will report to my assistant, Mr. Chester Feldman, who is in charge of sub-standard accommodations.

15.   TO ALL MEN IN THE OFFICE: Once I have completed a given girl, I have no objection, as you know, to your taking up with her, if that makes your Christmas a little happier. For your convenience, I will label each girl as completed.   Men, I am very sorry, but this year I will be entirely too busy to compile my usual Guidebook to the Office Girls.   So it's Pot Luck, and may the Devil take the hindmost.

> Merry Xmas,
> Allan Sherman

I handed the memo to Charlie, who ran the mimeograph machine at Goodson-Todman, and asked him to run off a hun-

* Brother of Bill Todman, and office manager.

dred copies so that I could give everybody one before the Christmas party. Then I went back into my office.

Two minutes later Howard Todman tore in. "You can't mimeograph this thing on company time," he said.

"Howard," I said, "it's *Christmas*."

"And what about the paper?" he asked.

"I'll be glad to pay for it," I said.

"I still don't know," he said. "I'll tell you in a while."

So he went back to his office and dictated a memo to his secretary explaining the whole situation, and he sent his memo along with my memo out in triplicate: one to Mark Goodson, one to Bill Todman and one to his own files. And then Mark Goodson dictated an answer to *his* secretary. And then Bill Todman dictated an answer to *his* secretary. And they delivered these answers to Howard Todman, who then came into my office and said, "Okay."

And that is the story of how they almost saved twenty minutes of Charlie the Mimeograph Boy's time by having the two bosses, the office manager and their three secretaries each spend a full hour on the problem.

The Christmas memo became an instant hit. Not only at Goodson-Todman. Within a few days it was bootlegged and reprinted at NBC, at CBS, at Random House book publishers, in advertising agencies. There were thousands of copies floating around New York. Two years ago my Christmas memo showed up, word for word, except for the names, and without any indication that I was the author, in the Christmas issue of *Playboy* Magazine. That was five years after I wrote it.

Why did it persist in staying alive?

Because, I believe, we are all aware, even those of us who play the Madison Avenue Game, that there is something a little nuts about Big Organizations, that there is something subhuman about trying to get human beings to act like clockworks, and that there is something very human indeed about the Christmas party—about the one day in the year when you have a few drinks and the office boy can talk to the boss like one human being to another and the secretary and the vice-president can kiss each other.

I didn't fit.

My gray flannel suit didn't fit and my title didn't fit and I didn't fit in the comfortable womb of Goodson-Todman. Being curled up in the fetal position, however warm and safe, bothered me and stultified me and gave me claustrophobia. I wanted to fly away, but I was afraid to leave the security and the steady salary; and I wanted to do wild, new things, but I remembered all those Kraft Dinners. And now we were eating Steak Dinners and Lobster Dinners and Breast of Chicken Virginie Dinners.

In 1952, when our seven lean years ended and our seven fat years began, we had our second child, Nancy. I brought Dee a box of chocolates in the hospital.

When she opened it, she bit into one of the chocolates and then she burst into terrible tears.

"You don't love me," she said.

"I love you heart and soul," I said.

"If you loved me, you would not have brought me this candy," she said.

"What's wrong with it?"

"You brought me creamies," she said. "You forgot. I *hate* creamies. I love chewies."

I devoured the box of creamies.

In those next years at Goodson-Todman, I did a lot of psychosomatic eating because I didn't fit. Every once in a while in the middle of a double banana split or a triple portion of mashed potatoes I'd think to myself, *You ought to go and have your head examined.*

So I went and had my head examined.

Four times.

CHAPTER 9

The Four Faces of Freud

I DIDN'T DECIDE I was crazy until 1952. That's when I began making a steady salary and could afford to be crazy. Everybody in my new Goodson-Todman social set was on the couch. It was a status symbol. Years ago, if you were a lunatic or you had a crazy aunt or uncle, it was kept a secret. But now people at the cocktail parties I was going to were proud of their insanity, and you were really out of it if you didn't discuss toilet training with your dinner partners. I don't mean your children's toilet training—I mean yours.

My hunger for psychoanalysis coincided with my jump into the gray flannel snake pit of Goodson and Todman. Something in me wanted to adjust and conform and make a steady living and be part of an organization; and something else in me, something much stronger, something I have since learned to follow without question—this other something wanted me to be somewhere else, to be going back and forth on the ferry all night, to be writing crazy Christmas memos, to do not what They wanted me to do but what I wanted to do. I didn't hear this little voice inside me until The Album came out. So I worked out those frustrations by (to use a word I learned in analysis) "sublimating."

Sublimating means doing what you don't want to do, because you don't want to do what you do want to do.

I took up hobbies. Hobbies were my hobby.

My first hobby was building model electric trains. Later on in one of my analyses I was told that this was my poor substitute for the missing trains in the basement.

I had never done anything with my hands before, and I got real pleasure from building the tiny cars and locomotives and laying out the track and the scenery and making the whole thing work. Robbie was not much more than a baby then, but he helped and he did all the electrical wiring (he was born with a complete knowledge of electricity and electronics, don't ask me how). And bit by bit I bought every piece of equipment known to model railroading.

When I was quite sure I had bought all the equipment and all the magazines and all the books and built all the kits, I dropped model railroading like a hot potato. This is known in psychoanalysis as "compulsiveness."

I next compelled myself into photography. I started with a $3 Kodak Brownie. I began to haunt the camera shops and discount houses of New York, and I did what they call "trading up." Trading up means that you bring in your $3 camera and trade it for a $29 camera and they give you a $2 credit, so you only pay $27. It is of no importance that they would sell you the $29 camera for $27 without a trade. The important thing is to keep an endless chain of trades going.

Each hobby has its own vocabulary. Robbie and I would have long discussions about "depth of field" and "depth of focus" (Robbie understands these) and "parallax." Parallax is what has happened when Uncle Charlie shows you his home movies and Aunt Minnie's head is cut off at the top of the picture.

From still photography I plunged myself into motion-picture photography. I made an art film, the stars of which were my own left eye, the Queensboro Bridge, some hot dogs turning on a grill at Nedick's, a train wreck on the Long Island Railroad and a large plate of spaghetti and meatballs. *I was the Ingmar Bergman of Jackson Heights, but the world was not yet ready for this art film.* I showed it to everyone who came over.

Then one night a friend of mine invited us to a party at which he showed us four hours of *his* home movies. Sometime during the second hour I received the message, and that night I said farewell to photography.

My next madness was antiques.

We were furnishing our first home at the time. I had business managers who were husband and wife, Phil and Pauline. Their entire home was furnished with antiques. Nothing made Pauline quite so proud as to take you through her home and display her antiques. She would walk you into the dining room and show you her magnificent ten-foot pine harvest table. You would have to say "What a magnificent harvest table!"

Then she would say "I picked it up for a dollar thirty-five."
"No!"
"Yes," she would say. "Don't you love the way it's *distressed?* And look at that *patina!*"

Dee and I dashed around Westchester County and upstate New York and downstate Connecticut and Cape Cod, gobbling up antiques.

A lot of things have become antiques because there is no longer any use for them. Pauline helped us find a use for them.

She would take those useless things and make them into either lamps or planters.

Dee and Pauline and I would walk into an antique shop, and on a musty shelf we would see what appeared to be a vase.

"My!" Pauline would exclaim. "What an unusual slop-jar." (I don't know the full history of this item, but I presume it was used by the Colonials for the preservation of slop.) Now and then we would find one with some nineteenth-century slop still inside it. "Grab it up!" Pauline would yell. "Quick! Before someone else gets it! It will make a beautiful lamp (planter)!"

There isn't a single lamp in our house that looks like a lamp. One is an old grocery scale. Another is one leg of an old kitchen sink, turned upside down. One is fashioned from four volumes of the collected works of Alfred, Lord Tennyson, with a hole drilled through them for the wires. One is a barber pole. One is a French brass coffeepot. One is an English mailbox. When all of these strange devices are turned on, they shed a lovely light on the crank telephone, the tool bench, the butter churn, the umbrella stand and the bedpan. Those are our planters.

As I got affluenter and affluenter and fatter and fatter, I decided to take up some physical open-air sport. But I didn't want to get *too* physical, so I chose golf.

The words I learned were "divot" and "pronate" and "supinate" and "clubhead" and "overlapping" and "interlocking" and "bunker."

I bought a set of clubs and a lot of balls and tees and every book available, and I played golf every day. I would play nine holes at seven o'clock in the morning and then go into the Goodson-Todman office, where I would practice on the carpet with a putter.

I bought golf shirts with little alligators on them. Those shirts are guaranteed to take four strokes off your game. I bought eyeglasses that made the holes seem larger, hand-warmers for playing in subzero weather, pocket flasks for drinking Scotch while playing in subzero weather. I joined the Vernon Hills Country Club in Tuckahoe, New York. The golf pro told me I would swing better if I didn't have so much stomach out in front of me. In four months I lost fifty-five pounds. I broke 100. Then I broke 90. When I broke 80 in 1960, it was the supreme achievement of my career as a sportsman and I had this yearning to see my wife and children again. So I at once lost interest in golf.

I looked around the country club and saw that all the other players were Jewish. That inspired me to write the following parody of "Seventy-six Trombones":

> *Seventy-six Sol Cohens in the country club,*
> *And a hundred and ten nice men named Levine!*
> *And there's more than a thousand Finks*
> *Who parade around the links—*
> *It's a sight that really must be seen. . . .*

When I quit golf, I resumed writing. I said to myself, *This time I'll do it in style.* I furnished an office in my Rye mansion with Danish modern furniture, a dictating machine, a photocopier, fluorescent lighting, an electric pencil sharpener and the Executive-style IBM electric typewriter.

My first story was about my grandmother and the football. My agent at once sold it to *The Reader's Digest.*

Well, Allan, baby, you're on the track again. You took the wrong fork back there in 1952, but you're on the right road again and now you'll write more funny pieces, like Robert Benchley or James Thurber.

But I couldn't. I developed the worst case of writer's block you ever heard of. I was miserable. Dee said, "Why don't you take up a hobby?"

So I decided to become an art collector. There was only one painting I wanted to collect. I had seen it in the Museum of

Modern Art. It was Edward Hopper's painting of a Victorian house. It was called "House by the Railroad." I asked my secretary to find out how much it would cost. She called the Museum of Modern Art and put me on the phone with the man there. I offered to take Hopper's painting off his hands. "How much?" I asked.

After I convinced him that I was not kidding, he told me that the painting was not for sale and there was no price on it because it was priceless, but he *could* tell me that it was insured for $140,000.

Well, I thought, *if I can't buy that Hopper painting, I will paint it myself*. So I started taking painting lessons. I learned words like "chiaroscuro," "egg tempera" and "don't-mess-up-the-linoleum"—an art term which Dee taught me.

In five weeks I painted a very good imitation of "House by the Railroad." It's so authentic-looking that it fools many people—especially if they're drunk and looking at it from a distance. It is now hanging in my living room in Bel Air. I call it "Mr. Hopper's House." What else should I call it? I can't call it *my* house.

But my hobbies didn't help. I was still a square peg in one of Goodson-Todman's innumerable round holes.

Then there came a day when my Uncle Maury called and told me that my mother had cancer. Even though I had spent so little time with her, she had always been *there*. I loved her and I needed her and the thought that she would suddenly not be there, that she might cease to exist, was impossible to face.

But I had to face it somehow, so I decided to look for psychiatric help.

Four times I looked for psychiatric help, and each time I arrived at the inescapable conclusion that the psychiatrist was crazier than I was. When I say they were crazier than I was, I mean to say that they are human, too, and subject to the same pressures and prejudices and emotions and feelings, and in the end all they can do is get you to help yourself, which is why you went there in the first place. I believe that the most important thing is your decision that you need help. Once you have made this decision, I suggest that you make a list of all the desirable and honorable and worthwhile things about yourself, because chances are that you are a lot better and more beautiful and worthier than you were given to understand by all the people in your childhood who considered it their duty to make you submit to what they thought was right for you and conform to what they thought was social and what they thought was moral. Chances are these people tried to solve a lot of their own personal problems by brutalizing you in one way or another.

I am not against psychoanalysis for people who are really mentally ill. I am against it for people who are indulging themselves, as I did four times, in a popular new hobby where the words are "compulsion" and "psychogenic" and "schizophrenic."

Dr. A started our relationship by lecturing me about my obesity and warning me that if I didn't go on a strict diet it was because I *wanted* to be fat, to build a wall of fat around myself, to devour food instead of the love I had never been offered by my rotten parents. This would have been much easier to swallow if Dr. A had not been an inch shorter than I and weighed fifty pounds more. Not only that: he was growing a beard. That is something which, crazy as I may have been, I had never done. (I have done it since, in times of extreme anxiety.)

Dr. A kept sucking on a briar pipe, and it kept going out. Every now and then he would take out a big lighter and strike it, and an immense flame would shoot out, and I would stop talking to watch and see if he could manage to ignite the tobacco. He would chew viciously on the mouthpiece. I diagnosed

him as a man with a serious oral problem. Finally he would give
up, and then he would look at me savagely and say, "Go on, go
on!"

Dr. A advised me not to take things personally. If someone
walked up to me and said, "You are an ugly fat slob," I was supposed to think, *This person had a bad breakfast this morning.*
He said I should learn how to say no.

All the time he was advising me not to go crazy his beard
grew longer. It was a pointy beard, and to me people with
pointy beards are the craziest of all.

*I do not care what religion you belong to or what is the color
of your skin. But I do have two prejudices. I think people with
pointy beards are crazy, and I am suspicious of people with
protruding bellybuttons. You know as well as I do that a bellybutton is supposed to be indented.*

During the early stages of Dr. A's beard I was telling him what
I considered the terrible, guilty, shameful episodes of my life—
like wetting the bed until I was fourteen, masturbating, and all
about Shmoozie in Humboldt Park and the whores of San Berdoo, and he didn't look interested.

I began to worry about boring him. So the night before a session, I would concoct terrible sexual perversions to say I had
practiced, which I had not practiced but had looked up in
Krafft-Ebing's book. The name of this book is *Psychopathia
Sexualis*. It's a real nifty book, all about people who fall in love
with shoes and whips and exciting things like that.

*Which reminds me of a friend at college. He was on the staff
of the* Daily Illini *with me. He was in love with celery. He had
some kind of a sex thing about celery. He used to grab me in
the middle of the night and say, in a strange, faraway voice, "Get
me celery. Please get me a stalk of celery." At first I would.*

*Then I became emotionally involved with this fellow's prob-
lem. I wanted to help him, yet I didn't want to get mixed up in
this sordid celery business. One night I made up my mind to go*

straight. *When he grabbed me with tears in his eyes, I turned to him coldly and said, "No more celery. I'm no pimp!"*

Lately I have been feeling guilty about this. Ken, if you are reading this, I hope all is going well for you and that you now own a chain of vegetable markets.

It's a marvelous thing how some people can fall in love with a stalk of celery or with a pair of ladies' shoes. As I grow older I get more tolerant of things like this. You want to fall in love with a shoe, go ahead. A shoe can't love you back, but, on the other hand, a shoe can't hurt you too deeply either. And there are so many nice-looking shoes.

When I began recounting my adventures with shoes and whips, Dr. A began sitting up, alert, and there was a gleam in his eyes and he began taking notes, and when he lit his pipe it actually lighted and he puffed on it furiously throughout our sessions.

He sent me to a psychological tester whose office was in a terrible dingy apartment on the West Side. She was a tall woman with straight, severe hair. She wore a tailored suit. She was to give me several tests which evaluate personality. She gave me the Rorschach test and the Szondi test.

When she showed me the Rorschach cards and asked me what I saw, I could not say, "This looks like an inkblot." To me the Rorschach test looks like inkblots. In fact, it *is* inkblots. But I had to give her something to work on, because, after all, I was paying $50 for the psychological tests.

"Over here," I said, "is a little gazelle running through the forest. And here I see a jukebox, and on top are a man and a woman dancing the cha-cha. On this card it looks like two men are fighting over that unicorn over there. On this card I see a woman sleeping, and a man is trying to murder her. Oh, here's the jukebox again. This looks like three children playing a game of jump rope. And this card—by God, there's the jukebox again!"

She glared at me. "You are the first patient who has ever seen a jukebox," she said.

"Is that bad?" I asked.

"I'm not allowed to tell you," she said. And no one ever did.

Then she gave me the Szondi test, invented by a Hungarian psychoanalyst. In this test they show you sets of ten close-up photographs of people, and from each set you pick the person you like most and the person you like least.

The tester put the first set of photographs on the table in front of me.

I looked at the pictures.

What kept going through my mind was that this poor Dr. Szondi lived in a back alley somewhere in the slums of Budapest and he had one of these old box cameras. Whenever some poor vagrant wandered by, Szondi would run out into the dark alley with his inadequate box camera and snap a picture of the poor soul, because these were people who would pose for anything for a pfennig. At least fifty years have passed since Szondi took those terrible brown pictures of those wretched individuals, and it has not yet occurred to anyone to take a new set of pictures with people with whom a present-day patient might be able to relate.

The lady put the ten poor souls on the table in front of me and said, "Which one do you like the most?"

I said, "Madam, I like them all. I feel sorry for them. I am sorry they have all that dirt on their faces and the stubble, I am sorry they cannot afford a comb, and I am sorry they have so many teeth missing, and I am sorry about all those warts. But, madam, I warn you, I may be prejudiced. You must realize that I have just come to you from the Madison Avenue office of Goodson-Todman Productions, where everyone is garbed in either the latest Paris modes and coiffures or Italian silk suits, and both Messrs. Goodson and Todman are thoroughly manicured, shaved, and powdered every morning, and anoint themselves with rare colognes, and, search though I might, I have never found a wart on any exposed portion of anybody at Goodson-

Todman Productions."

"Never mind," said the testy lady. "Which one do you like the most?"

I studied the ten poor souls. One of them, whom I shall call Herr Stubblewartz, had no shirt on. I was smart enough to know I shouldn't like him the most, because if I pick him, he's naked, and right away I'm a fairy, so him I didn't pick.

I started to pick up all the photographs. What I had in mind was to put Mr. Stubblewartz aside, shuffle the other nine, and then cut the deck and be crazy about whoever showed up on top. But the lady wouldn't let me. It was a hard choice to make. All ten pictures were of men. No girls, no women. *I guess they assume you are a homosexual already or you wouldn't even be taking the Szondi test. To them the only question is, What kind of homosexual are you?*

Then it hit me. I have had lots of cameras, and I have taken pictures of girls, women, old ladies, babies, my own left eye, the Queensboro Bridge—whatever showed up in front of the camera. But what kind of a man would take pictures of men only? *Dr. Szondi was a fag!* He flunked the Sherman test. So did Dr. A.

When I got back to his office, I looked him straight in the pointy beard and said, "Doctor, I have just learned how to say no."

Dr. B was a woman. She was recommended by Pauline, the lamp-and-planter lady, who had sent her young boy to Dr. B when he was emotionally upset. When I went for my first session, I learned that Dr. B was primarily a child analyst.

Each time I went, I had to wait in the outer office with kids aged eight or nine; the oldest was maybe twelve. I would sit there with my black Mark Cross briefcase full of important Goodson-Todman memos, and around me were those boys and girls, reading comic books, chewing bubble gum, and now and then shooting a water pistol or a spitwad at me. I felt ridiculous. I, who in two hours would be giving orders to Faye Emerson and having a conference with Hubbell Robinson, Vice-president in Charge of Television for CBS. Here I was in an office with little kids giving me hotfoots or hotfeet and slobbering on me, wiping their noses on my custom-made Italian-style black suit. It was humiliating.

Dr. B was an elderly woman, very strong, very handsome, with long, graying hair combed into a bun. She looked like a New England mother figure in a Grant Wood painting. I hated to say anything to her that might in some way offend her. I could never bring myself to say a swear word in her presence, and I would never embarrass this fine lady by telling her about Natalie and the Doorknob.

I would lie down on Dr. B's couch, and there were a teddy bear and a blanket to chew on, but I didn't use them. There really wasn't a hell of a lot to talk to her about, but she managed to make an awful lot of notes on a yellow pad. After about three months I had said nothing much more than "Hello, Dr. B" and "Good-bye, Dr. B," but she had twelve yellow pads full. One day she brought them all in to the session.

"I have been looking over your case history," she said. "We are not making enough progress. I think you should go to Dr. C. He specializes in brilliant people who are blocked writers. Oh, yes, there's just one thing," she warned. "He charges like anything."

"How much?" I ask

"For a forty-minute hour—fifty dollars."

I chewed on the blanket a little.

Dr. C was a famous psychoanalyst. He had written nineteen books on everything from writing to gambling to women to frigidity to homosexuality. He had worked with Dr. Freud in Vienna. Dr. C was the inventor of masochism. He preferred to call himself the "Discoverer of Masochism," but I think he invented it because he had a use for it. Dr. C was a sadist. At our first session I asked if I should lie down on the couch.

"I don't care if you stand on your head," he said.

During our first week I ran into Abe Burrows at a party, and he asked me what was new. I told him I had started treatments with Dr. C. "That rotten, no-good charlatan and quack?" Burrows said.

"Abe," I moaned, "what have you done to me?"

I knew I couldn't face Dr. C without confessing that Burrows' comment had shaken my confidence in him. It took me seven sessions ($350) to clear the air of Abe's remarks. I figure Abe Burrows owes me $350.

Dr. C refuted Abe Burrows by saying Abe was a charlatan and a quack.

Dr. C spoke with an unbelievably thick Viennese accent. His fee came to $1.25 a minute. If you were late by three minutes, it became a thirty-seven-minute hour, because he didn't give you three minutes at the other end of the hour.

It was almost impossible to understand what he was saying, and he talked through the whole forty minutes. He used fancy big words and phrases. I remember one: "architectonic predilection." When he first quoted this, I said "*Gesundheit.*" Not to be funny. I was sure he had sneezed. When it dawned on me that he had spoken some words, I asked him to repeat them. It took about two minutes, or $2.50 worth of repeating, until I had the words straight. Then I made the mistake of asking what he meant by "architectonic predilection." The explanation took roughly nine minutes, or $11.25.

It wasn't long before all the problems I came in with disappeared.

The big problem of my life became: *How can I afford this analysis?*

Then came July 1st. At the end of the session Dr. C said, "I vill see you next September?"

"You will see me Wednesday," I replied.

"Oh, no," he said, "I go away for zee summer. I always do ziss in zee summer. I ride books. I am ziss summer riding a book on ugly fat writers who do not so good understand zee English."

I didn't know psychiatrists went away for the whole summer. It hit me with a big shock. You can go crazy in summer just as easily as in winter. But he seemed quite willing to let me go crazy for the whole summer while he was up there in Putney, Vermont, enjoying the mountain breezes and turning me into a case history.

I told him maybe I was a masochist, but there were limits to masochism and I would have to take my neuroses to somebody else.

"It's your funeral," he said. "Close zee door on your way out."

Dr. D was recommended by Josephine Plummer, the wife of my friend Stewart. Josephine told me that Dr. D had saved their marriage and turned it into a peaceful heaven of goodwill and happiness.

"Dr. D brought us peace and abiding true love," Josephine said, "and gave our marriage a firm foundation of mutual trust and tenderness."

We were having this discussion on the patio of my home in Bronxville. Josephine continued. "I'm sure that Dr. D can bring to your life the same warm glow he has—"

"Now, just a minute!" Stewart shouted. Stewart had taken from Dr. D, too. "God damn it, Josephine, you know as well as I do that he's a no-good quack."

"That's not so," Josephine said as her eyes filled with tears.

"That son of a bitch!" Stewart exclaimed. "He will turn Allan into an even worse lunatic than he is already."

"You are despicable, Stewart!" Josephine said.

Dee was ready with the Kleenex, and when Josephine finished drying her eyes, she and Stewart had the Goddamnedest argument I have ever heard between two married people, especially two married people who have a life filled with mutual trust and tenderness and who have such a warm glow for each other.

Dr. D took notes. He had a large spiral notebook which he balanced on his folded legs. I lay on his couch and talked, and he made notes and hummed softly under his breath. After I spent $3,500 with Dr. D, I found out what he was humming and what he was writing. His hobby was playing the piano with an amateur symphony orchestra in Westchester.

One day he was called out of his office by some emergency, and I was left alone, so I took a peek into his notebook. I discovered that he was writing down the names of famous classical compositions and a few lines of melody from different piano concertos. Then I began to listen to what he was humming. Snatches of Beethoven's "Moonlight" Sonata, here and there a Chopin Etude, and occasionally a little Brahms Piano Concerto No. 2.

I left him in a fit of indignation.

So that is how I cured myself of insanity—by realizing that the rest of the world and the psychiatrists in it were as crazy as I was, if not crazier. I remained fat. But I remembered what the English essayist Cyril Connolly said: "Inside of every fat man there is a thin man trying to get out."

I only let mine out on special occasions.

CHAPTER 10

The Compleat Fun Person:
Funny Songs, Cocktail Parties, Suburbia, and Other Noisy Symptoms of Desperation

Roots.

That's what I always thought I never had. Roots. I guess that's why I went to all those psychoanalysts—to unearth some roots in my life. Garry Moore used to kid me about buying all those Early American antiques so I would have roots. I had spent my whole life being uprooted from one place after another. And now, hard as I tried, I wasn't taking root on Madison Avenue. Even the steady salary and the successful show and the golf club didn't satisfy me.

Without knowing why, I began to write songs again.

As I look back through those lyrics, I can see that each one took me closer to where my real roots are. Henry Morgan once played a game with me where you ask the other person, three times in a row, "Who are you?" When we played the game, I was thirty years old. Here, as I recall, is how it went:

"Who are you?"

"Me."

"Who are you?"

"A nice boy."

"Who are you?"

"The producer of *I've Got a Secret.*"

Henry excoriated me for calling myself a boy at the age of thirty. At the time my feelings were hurt, but now I know he was right. Now I have taken a look at my roots, which *do* exist and are just as real as yours or anybody else's.

Ask me again:

Who are you?

I am Allan Sherman.

I am a human being.

I am a man.

I am a husband.

I am a father.

I am an American.

I am a Jew.

I am a person with a gift of laughter.

I am a serious person.

I am as good as I know how to be.

I am as bad as I allow myself to be.

That's who I am.

There was a time when I couldn't find roots because I was ashamed to look where they were. When you are Running Around Madison Avenue, when you are Lunching at Louis & Armand's or Michael's Pub, you carefully avoid mentioning your Grandfather, the Ladies' Coat Presser, and your Grandmother, the Poker Player. When you are Golfing at the Club, even though everybody around you is Jewish, you act gentile, and nobody in the foursome brings up his Uncle, the Junk Dealer. When you're at a cocktail party in the Waldorf Towers and they pass you the goose-liver pâté, you very carefully neglect to point out that Lindy's chopped chicken liver tastes a lot better to you. You cover up the old roots because something in your own upbringing has convinced you that they are weeds, and you try to transplant yourself in the Westchester suburbs or on Long Island or in Shaker Heights or Beverly Hills.

The little voice inside me—the same one that sang me "Seventy-six Sol Cohens in the Country Club"—is a rebel. It's who I really am. And it will not tolerate any fancy posturing from me. And when it feels me getting fancy, it makes fun of me. It tells me jokes and sings me songs.

Here's a song it sang to me in 1953, to the melody of "How Are Things in Glocca Morra?"

> *How are things with Uncle Morris?*
> *Does he still work in the candy store?*
> *Does he still run like he always did*
> *To get some kid a nickel* halvah?*
>
> *Is Aunt Bea with Uncle Morris?*
> *Do they still live on the second floor?*
> *Do they still live in the same old flat?*
> *Is she still fat?*
> *And does he walk around in his* gatkes** *there*
> *Eating* latkes*** *there?*
>
> *Since I moved away to Scarsdale*
> *And joined a country club*
> *I've lost touch with them*
> *And they've lost touch with me . . .*
> *How are things with Uncle Morris and Aunt Bea?*

* Turkish-Jewish candy
** Long woolen underwear
*** Pancakes

Okay, *smart-Allan*, it said, *don't get fancy just because you joined a country club. Don't forget your grandfather and your uncle, and don't forget who you are yourself.* And sometimes it said to me, *Too Jewish is no good either. Too much anything is no good.* And it sang me the entire score of *My Fair Lady*, which I wrote and put on at the country club.

The way I wrote my own *My Fair Lady*, it's about a girl trying to sell flowers on the lower East Side of New York, and nobody can understand her because she speaks English too well. So this Jewish speech professor makes a bet with his friend that he can take her under his wing and within six months she will be elected President of Hadassah.

First he tries to teach her about Jewish food:

> *A piece of rye bread isn't very tasty.*
> *A slice of onion isn't such a treat.*
> *A slab of cream cheese tastes a little pasty, but—*
> *With a little bit of lox, with a little bit of lox,*
> *You got something very good to eat!*

Then she asks him, where do Jewish people live? And he sings:

> *We have often walked*
> *West End Avenue*
> *And you'll find us on a Parkway known as Mosholu*
> *Living gaily there*
> *Like Israeli there.*
> *Oh, it's grand on the streets where we live.*
>
> *We've got Scarsdale men,*
> *We've got Great Neck men,*
> *And just lately we've been sneaking into Darien.*
> *Strange new noses there,*
> *Friends of Moses there,*
> *Near the goys on the streets where they live.*

To be too Jewish is too much. To live where everybody is a Jew, whether on a Parkway of the Bronx or in a Fancy Suburb, is too much. And a city without Jews—like Darien, Connecticut—that's too much, too.

For Jewish people to exclude someone because he or she is not Jewish is no good either. In my play the Professor gives Liza a mink stole and sends her away because he has been ostracized for associating with someone who isn't Jewish. He tells her it has ruined the business in his candy store:

> *I've got the customers to face.*
> *They used to flock into the place,*
> *But when they heard the things you say*
> *They turned and ran away.*
> *Where did they go?*
> *Where's Jake? Where's Mo?*
> *They saw a shickse* and they ran.*
> *That's how the Exodus began. . . .*

I kept writing those songs and singing them at parties at my house, at the golf club—wherever anybody would let me. I knew people would get tired of hearing the same songs too often, so I kept writing new songs. Dozens. Maybe hundreds. They poured out of me, and each one seemed to spring from those roots I had buried for so long. Each one made it clearer to me who I am.

My grandfather did not go unsung. I disguised him as a cutter instead of a presser, and changed his name, but here he is:

I'm singing you the ballad of a great man of the cloth.
His name was Harry Lewis and he worked for Irving Roth.
He died while cutting velvet on a hot July the Fourth,
But his cloth goes shining on!

* A girl who isn't Jewish.

172

> Glory glory Harry Lewis.
> Glory glory Harry Lewis.
> Glory glory Harry Lewis,
> His cloth goes shining on!

Oh, Harry Lewis perished in the service of his Lord.
He was trampling through the warehouse where the drapes
    of Roth are stored.
He had the finest funeral the union could afford,
But his cloth goes shining on. . . .

My Voice reminded me of my own boyhood. The lyric reads
like this:

> The party's over.
> The whole bar mitzvah is through.
> I had such naches* and joy
> From our little boy.
> Did you?
>
> He looked so grown-up,
> So tall and cute.
> I'm glad we bought him
> That Ivy League-type suit.
>
> His speech was lovely;
> It made the relatives smile.
> And did you notice he had
> A little of Adlai Stevenson's style?
>
> Someday he may be
> The President,
> Our little baby—

* Unpronounceable but very good word, with no English equivalent. It's
the joy you get from the joy of others.

> *His party's over.*
> *The guests who came here*
> *Have went.*

Robbie was only four or five, and Nancy was just a baby, and we had gone through all the books and pamphlets about what to name the baby. The voice kept saying to me, *Please do me a favor—don't get fancy like a lot of Jewish people. There are a lot of boys who are twelve or fifteen years old now who will have to walk around for the rest of their lives with the name Craig Lipshitz or Lanny Feigenholz or Clark Mendelbaum or Carlyle Lefkowitz.* There is a whole generation of Jewish boys now in their middle teens who are named Barry, so I wrote this to George M. Cohan's "Mary":

> *We'll call him Barry, Barry.*
> *That'll be the baby's name.*
> *We thought of Lance or Josh,*
> *But oh my gosh,*
> *They're not the same—*
> *But if it's Barry, Barry,*
> *That's a name with style and grace.*
> *And if he's not a he*
> *It still could be*
> *Like in Barrie Chase.*

Dee has the same little voice, and it has also told her not to get fancy with too much jewelry. And her voice told her to tell me to write this to the tune of "Golden Earrings":

> *There's a gypsy,*
> *The strangest one I've seen.*
> *She wears a pair of Goldman's earrings—*
> *Her ears are turning green.*

Once we were visiting Dee's brother, Alex, in St. Louis. He was then a traveling salesman with a line of ladies' coats, and he was unhappy because that year all he had to sell was what he called "dogs." The designer for his company had copied the wrong fashions. In the Needle Trades even the big companies are perched so precariously that one bad year can put them out of business. I wrote:

> *Rosen's designing for Picardy—*
> *Ladies Sportswear and Missy Frocks, too.*
> *Wining and Dining for Picardy*
> *Whenever the buyers come through!*
> *Last year he did it for Melnick Modes—*
> *The results I don't have to tell you.*
> *Rosen's designing for Picardy—*
> *So this year they'll go bankrupt, too.*

Singing my songs at parties became the most important thing in the world to me, and I realized that we needed our own house. Eventually I said, "Dee, we should move out of this four-room apartment in Jackson Heights."

"Why?" she asked.

"Well," I said, in my best Todmanese, "Robbie is getting bigger, and the schools here are not as progressive as in Westchester; moreover, a growing boy needs to blossom in an atmosphere of Little Leagues and superior friends and the New Math and stately trees and important flowers and—"

"Flowers? Since when do you like flowers?"

"I *love* flowers. I have often secretly thought of having a rose garden—not a formal garden, just a casual place with perhaps a winding flagstone path. . . ."

"How can we buy a house without money?"

There she had me. We never had money. Poverty was chronic in my life, even when I was making money as a television producer, because I have always lived beyond my means. I am still trying to live beyond my means, but it is getting harder all the time. I am very rich. I don't know exactly how much money I have, but I have what they call "untold wealth." This means that nobody has told me how much. But it *must* be more than I used to have.

We bought our first house shortly before Christmas 1954. We had gone forth in the car, Dee and I, to buy stocking-fillers for the children. (I'm not *that* Jewish. I wouldn't cheat my kids, or Dee or me, out of a Christmas tree for anything.) We parked in front of a Woolworth store in Yonkers. Then we realized suddenly that neither of us had any money. And we didn't have any money at home either. We were, as usual, flat broke. And we didn't have any secondhand magazines to sell on Sixth Avenue.

So as not to waste an afternoon, we drove to the nearest real-estate agent, and I said "Let's go look at houses."

And this agent showed us three houses, and we liked the third one, which was on a curving lane full of stately trees and important flowers and was in the amusing suburb of Bronxville, New York.

A home of your own is a part of the American dream or the American nightmare. It is a labyrinth of problems beginning with how to buy it and ending with how to get rid of it.

My mother once told me how to buy a house. She learned it from my Stepfather the Real Estate Manipulator, Dave Number Two.

"Find out why they want to sell. If you can find some people who have to sell their house because they are in some kind of trouble and have to get out in a hurry, then they'll sell you the house real cheap and meet all your conditions."

I thought the sellers in Bronxville looked very glum, morose, miserable, full of distress and anxious to sell, as though they had to leave the country in a hurry.

They were asking $26,500.

I cagily said, "You look like very unhappy people. People in distress."

They said, "Oh, no! We're very happy!" They smiled, trying to fool me.

"Are you sure?" I asked suspiciously.

They looked at each other like I was crazy. "Sure, we're sure," they replied, smiling gaily. "We've had some very happy times in this house, and we are sure that you will also."

"Not at these prices," I said. "Are you sure there isn't something you want to tell me? Some secret? Some terrible, sad story of personal shame and humiliation?"

They shook their heads.

I whispered to Dee, "They're in distress. It's a distress house and we'll buy it for a distress price."

We paid $26,500 for the house, and then *we* were in distress.

That's how I became a landowner. With a $1,500 down payment and a series of overlapping mortgages I had bought myself a little piece of America. A house in the suburbs. Years later I wrote about it in a lyric to the melody of Percy Grainger's "Country Gardens." It's a dialogue between a suburban husband and his wife:

HE: *Here's to the crabgrass,*
       Here's to the mortgage,
       In fact, here's to suburbia!

SHE: Lay down your briefcase
       Far from the rat race
       Where nothing can disturb ya!

HE: *Uncomplicated,*
       It's what we waited
       For so long in this city—
       Come, let us go there,
       Live like Thoreau there—
       A life of sweet simplicity!

SHE: Did you see the thermostat?

HE: *No, I don't know where it's at.*

SHE: Tuesday the Cub Scouts meet again!

HE: *Walk the dog and cut the grass . . .*

SHE: Take the kids to dancing class . . .

HE: *Jim's Little League got beat again!*

SHE: Can't keep a maid here
       No matter what they're paid here—

HE: *The place has bad publicity—*

SHE: Why did we move here?

HE: *Don't you remember?*

BOTH: To live in sweet simplicity!

HE: *Here's to mosquitoes,*
       Clam dip and Fritos—
       To golf and bridge and scuba there . . .
       Men wearing knee pants,
       Women in Capri pants,
       Discussing what's with Cuba there . . .

SHE: Each big appliance
       Treats you with defiance
       Until it finally falls apart.
       Call the repairman,
       In a week he's there, man,
       To knock your kitchen walls apart!

SHE: *Tommy's got a bloody nose.*

HE: Gotta fix the garden hose.

SHE: *Book-of-the-Month Club came today!*

HE: Didn't read the last one yet.

SHE: *Yes, you did, but you forget.*

HE: Oh, well, they're all the same today!

SHE: *Here's Mrs. Ritter, she's the baby-sitter.*

HE: Tonight we're going joyously
       Back to the city, where life is gay and witty—

SHE: *Back to the noise there that everyone enjoys there—*
HE: Back to the crush there, hurry, let us rush there—
SHE: *Back to the rat race, don't forget your briefcase!*
HE: Back in the groove there; say, why don't we move there?
BOTH: *Away from all of this—*
      Sweet simpliss—i—ty!

Now we had not only a tremendous living room and a beautiful patio but a magnificent dining room and a lawn full of flowers. In fact, one of the things that the miserable previous owners had been miserable about was leaving their magnificent garden, which included three hundred tulip bulbs.

Dee said, "Go ahead, country gentleman, show me some fancy gardening." I did.

When the great history of horticulture is written I will be listed among the absent. When it comes to tulip bulbs, I am of one mind with my late Uncle Maury. Both he and I could think of better things to do on a fine morning than crawling around, sticking tulip bulbs into holes in the ground.

When Maury and Edith first moved to New York, they lived in a garden apartment development, and next door to them there lived a man who was a Putterer. Each garden apartment had a little 4 x 8 patch of lawn. Uncle Maury covered his with the top of a ping-pong table. This is greener than the average grass and doesn't get your shoes all muddy if you happen to step on it.

The Putterer, however, was another story. He planted his tulip bulbs in an elaborate pattern, and every evening at six o'clock he was out with his watering can, watering and tamping the dirt, looking for even one infinitesimal sign that the Goddam tulips were emerging. Uncle Maury watched for weeks. The Putterer saw nothing growing, but remained optimistic.

One night Uncle Maury suggested to the Putterer that perhaps he had planted the bulbs upside down and would have to go to China to see his tulips.

"*Hrrmff*," said the Putterer, which was as close as he ever got to conversation.

A glorious idea came to Uncle Maury. He betook himself to downtown Yonkers, went into a dime store and bought 100 plastic tulips—all colors. Waiting until two A.M., to make sure the Putterer would be fast asleep, Uncle Maury then tiptoed out into the little garden with a flashlight in hand and did his splendid deed.

When the Putterer walked out to his car pool the next morning, he stood agape at what he saw. There, in *his* garden, were 100 full-grown tulips in glorious living color and in an elaborate pattern that spelled out:

SCHMUCK!

With the possibility in mind that this might happen to me with my real tulips, I did the only sensible thing. It was winter when we bought the house, and the tulips were in the garage in their little woolen stockings. I gave them away. And the irises, too. Then I had a man come and cover the garden with flagstones, so that any leftover tulips or irises would be prevented from complicating my life.

This was our first taste of true suburban living, and now, after having had it for some years, I must report that the best description of suburban living I ever heard was a simple three-word sentence uttered by my friend Carl Reiner, the fine actor-writer and mastermind of the *Dick Van Dyke Show*. He had just bought a house, his first, in New Rochelle. And he had called to invite us to a party. I congratulated him on buying a house.

"I have been living in the suburbs three weeks now. You want the world's shortest description of it?" he asked. "Twenty-three Sparrowfart Lane."

Thus did he manage to encapsulate in three words all the trials and tribulations, all the deep longings for the soil, the car pools, the crabgrass, the Little League, the green stamps, the bridge club, the bowling, the commuting trains—the whole ridiculous whirligig of life in the suburbs.

That summer of 1958 turned out to be the summer of my discontent. *I've Got a Secret* was riding high. For almost six years it had been in the top ten and it showed no signs of dropping out. Goodson-Todman offered me a job on their staff, with extra money and a title. (I don't mean Duke or Baron or anything that fancy. It might have been Vice-President. There is no end to the number of Vice-Presidents you are allowed to have. CBS even has four or five *Presidents*.) But I turned down the Goodson-Todman offer because I had to remain free to do what I wanted.

And in early 1958 the kind of thing I wanted began to come my way. Victor Borge hired me to produce and be head writer of his CBS-TV special. The reviews said it was a "distinguished, marvelously funny show."

In one sequence, while Victor played a George Gershwin medley with a forty-seven-piece orchestra, I put ten live cameras in places all over New York and we dissolved from one sparkling February snow scene of live New York to the next. I hope you saw it and got the same thrill I did hearing that beautiful Gershwin music and looking at the Hudson River and the George Washington Bridge, lit up like a big necklace, and at the traffic in Times Square, and at Central Park in winter white, and at the beautiful mink-wrapped girl who rode up to the entrance of the Plaza Hotel in a hansom cab.

A month later Phil Silvers hired me to be producer and head writer of his first CBS-TV special. The reviews called it "hilarious and refreshing."

I was on top of the world and nothing could stop me now. Or so I thought. All this time I had continued to produce *I've*

Got a Secret. The quality of my memos from Mark Goodson was deteriorating rapidly. They were stern and cold and dogmatic, those 1958 memos, and sometimes they made impossible demands. Meetings were called at exactly the same time as my Phil Silvers rehearsals, so I would have to be in two places at once. Nobody is *that* well organized.

The Phil Silvers show was on a Tuesday night. The next night *I've Got a Secret* was on. Henry Morgan had replaced Garry Moore, who was off on his sailboat for a week (and therefore unreachable by telephone or letter). It was a terrible show. Awful. We ran out of program with seven minutes left. Seven minutes of empty airtime is seven lifetimes of catastrophe, and Henry chose this night to forget that he is one of the best ad-libbers in the world, and instead devoted the seven minutes to hollering at me in public on the air for leaving him with seven minutes. This was just what I needed.

Thursday morning my business manager, Phil, called me and said: "I got a call from Mark Goodson. He said they are very unhappy about last night's show. They do not like your spreading yourself so thin. They think you are ruining their program by taking outside shows to produce. They won't renew the contract for a year. They'll give you thirteen weeks."

There goes my wall-to-wall carpeting, I thought.

I did not accept the offer.

So I was fired.

Almost seven years of my life had been poured into this program, and now all I had was a pitiful little stack of memos that I had saved. I had no place to be and no place to go.

It's a long fall from the top of the world. And it's awfully hard to pick yourself up.

After a few tries to get work, I lost heart. I was ashamed to be seen near Madison Avenue. I got a frightened feeling in my stomach when I walked by the building where the Goodson-

Todman offices were—afraid somebody I knew would pop out and see me. I felt that I had done something sinful and was being punished. But what? What?

I withdrew to the golf club and played golf all day every day and I didn't even ask my agent to look for a job for me.

I felt ashamed and scared and very alone. It was time to give a party.

So I went out and bought a mansion located in Rye, New York. It cost $50,000. It boasted a brick terrace of truly tremendous proportions and a beautiful fountain, and if it rained there was space indoors to give parties for 150 people, and if the weather was nice you could easily handle 300.

We had hardly moved in when we gave the first 300-people party. It was on a Sunday afternoon and I had told everyone to come dressed in casual clothes. They arrived in blue jeans and Bermuda shorts and Capri pants and sport shirts, and as each one arrived I answered the door dressed in my tuxedo.

The magnificent fountain never spurted water. I decided that was because it was clogged up with dirt. So I cleaned it out before the party. Robbie and I poured a liquid detergent called Joy down each of the four fountain sprays.

We set out the table for the barbecued hamburgers and frankfurters near the fountain. When the guests had all sat down, I said, with a flourish, "Now you'll see a beautiful sight you'll never forget. I have fixed the fountain. Sit back, relax and enjoy yourselves."

It was getting dark. I lit the many-colored Japanese lanterns we had strung over the terrace. I commanded my son: "Robbie—turn on the water."

He did.

Water began gushing through the pipes and combining with the detergent, and up spurted bubbles—thousands of bubbles, millions of bubbles—all over the hamburgers and hot dogs and rolls and buns and ice cubes and girls' blue jeans and my tuxedo. The terrace became a monster bubble bath, the Joy was unrestrained.

People said, "Allan thinks up such original stunts for his parties."

One day I played golf with Sol Leon, who was my agent at William Morris, and a man named Nick Keeseley, an executive of Lennen & Newell, the advertising agency that handles Kent cigarettes. After the game we had a drink and Sol told me he could get me a job producing *Masquerade Party*.

I said "Phooey. I don't like the show." It seemed stodgy and fake to me, and I guess secretly it was such a terrible comedown from the lofty heights I had just inhabited that I was ashamed to express any interest.

Sol told me the show only had four weeks to run. It was sponsored by Kent cigarettes, and Nick Keeseley said that unless there was a decided improvement in the next two weeks he would have to cancel.

Sol said, "Why the hell don't you take it? If you're really ashamed, don't put your name on it. But it's not as big a shame as playing golf all day, like a bum."

I took the job.

Masquerade Party was packaged by Ed Wolf Associates, and its executive producer was Ed Wolf's son, Herbert.

Ed Wolf Associates was about as different from Goodson-Todman as it is possible to get. It was a family organization and it went along in a loose, casual, family way.

For them I was *too* organized.

The switchboard was run by Ed Wolf's sister; there were three associate producers, all nephews; the one secretary in the office was a niece.

My first day I called her in, to dictate a memo.

She said, "What's a memo?"

I couldn't help loving her for that. In fact, I learned to love the whole nutty bunch of them.

There was only one bathroom on the floor in the old Madison Avenue building where Ed Wolf Associates was. Men and women used the same bathroom. This was simple enough before I showed up, when it was all a family affair, but I did show up and I soon hired a secretary who was not from the family because they had run out of nieces who took shorthand. And so to maintain some semblance of decency, the Wolf office got together and invented a system wherein if a woman was occupying the bathroom, she put a towel around the outside doorknob, and if a man was in there, he put nothing on the doorknob. This system just plain did not work because people are sometimes in a big hurry to go to the bathroom and it is against all natural laws to run in to a bathroom when you have to go real bad and try to remember to grab a towel and run out and hang it on the doorknob and then run in again. By this time the game may be over.

So sometimes a woman would go in and forget to put the towel on the doorknob. Other women who wanted in would look at the towelless doorknob and decide to hold themselves, because they were sure there was a man in there. You can only hold yourself so long—so eventually the holding ladies would get tired of holding and they would send a man in to find out what was taking the man inside such an eternity. This man would charge into the bathroom, only to find the lady who had forgotten the towel sitting there.

He also found, occasionally, that there was no one in the bathroom at all, because the system did not cover this possibility.

I worked hard and I did my best, and the show ran, not four weeks, but two years, and I saw it rise into the Top Ten, where it had never been before, and I saw it pass *I've Got a Secret* in the ratings, and when that happened I asked to have my name put on the show as Producer.

Then my friend Ray Charles called me and asked if I would like to be head writer of the Perry Como summer show. Ray was producing the show. It was called *Perry Presents,* and it starred Tony Bennett, Teresa Brewer and the Four Lads.

For the opening show I wrote a parody of Gilbert and Sullivan's "When I Was a Lad." It said some of the things I was thinking about television. It was my first parody to be sung on television. *Madison Avenue* Magazine liked it so much they reprinted it:

When I was a lad, I went to Yale
And I knew then that I could never fail.
For I studied very hard and furthermore
I polished up the apple for the pro-fess-or.

I polished up the apple so frequently
That soon I had a Phi Beta Kappa key.

On Graduation Day I made a stop
At a very exclusive clothing shop.
I opened up a charge account and asked them for
The best gray flannel in the clothing store.

That suit was part of a great intrigue,
For it proved I was a member of the Ivy League.

Then I got a crewcut and a sincere tie
And for my first job I did apply.
'Twas a job in an advertising agency,
Sharpening the pencils of a big V.P.

Funny Songs, Cocktail Parties, Suburbia

> *I sharpened all the pencils so pointedly*
> *That now I am a partner in the agency.*
>
> *I kept my ears open and my big mouth shut*
> *And I learned all the agency scuttlebutt.*
> *I learned who was going out with whom*
> *And who had the keys to the powder room.*
>
> *For the key to the powder room, you see,*
> *Is the key to the structure of the agency.*
>
> *I worked real hard for the dear old firm*
> *And learned most every advertising term.*
> *I said to the men in the dark gray suits,*
> *"Let's run it up the flagpole and see who salutes."*
>
> *I ran it up the flagpole perfectly,*
> *So now I am a partner in the agency.*
>
> *Now I have a big office at the end of the hall*
> *With expensive carpeting from wall to wall.*
> *Now I keep my mouth open and I keep my ears shut*
> *And I've got a little palace in Connecticut.*
>
> *So I thank old Yale and I thank the Lord—*
> *And I also thank my father who is Chairman of the Board!*

I love to sing. I sing lousy, but I can't help it, I love to sing. During the *Perry Presents* meetings I actually had the nerve to sing songs for Tony Bennett and Teresa Brewer and Ray Charles, and I went around the office singing all the time, and after two or three weeks Ray Charles had a big sign painted and put up in the Conference Room: ALLAN MUST NOT SING

* * *

My mother would have been proud, had she lived until 1959, because she would have lived to see her son become a doctor.

All of a sudden I was getting calls from everywhere to doctor sick television shows. In addition to being a doctor, I was also a priest, because to some of these shows I administered last rites.

One of these was *The Charley Weaver Show*, an impossible tangle of confusion with a very nice and funny man as its star. God knows I tried, and so did Cliff Arquette, who plays Charley Weaver. Everybody tried—but the show was a terminal case. Another failure: *The Herb Shriner Show*. I got fired after three weeks, and Herb got fired five weeks later.

There was an unbelievable mishmash of a show called *You're in the Picture*. It was a panel show. Jackie Gleason was the master of ceremonies. Each of the four panelists put his head into a cutout. There were four painted figures in a tableau. Gleason threw them hints, and they had to guess what the painted bodies that went with their heads represented. It opened and the critics hated it. The public hated it. Gleason hated it. Call the doctor.

I was hired, at a handsome salary, to perform surgery on this monstrosity.

The conferences on this show went on forever, hour after hour, with Gleason drinking bottles of his special red wine, which can only be procured at the Four Seasons restaurant. (*Once he ran out of wine and he sent a CBS vice-president out to the Four Seasons to get another bottle. The man went, like an errand boy. You don't argue with a star.*)

During our first conference Gleason heard me breathing loudly. I always breathe loudly. I have had asthma since childhood.

Gleason said, "I'll cure you in five minutes."

"How?" I asked.

"I'll hypnotize you so you'll breathe normally," he said.

"It's impossible," I said.

All the executives were watching us. "Do what he says," they told me.

So Jackie began hypnotizing me. "You're in deep sleep. The only sound you can hear is the sound of my voice. You're getting tired. Your legs are getting heavy. Your arms are getting heavy. You want to sleep. Sleep . . . *sleep* . . . *s-l-e-e-p.*"

I was wide awake, but I pretended to be hypnotized. I was getting $1,250 a week. At those prices, you hypnotize easy. While I was in this trance Gleason said that when he awakened me I would no longer suffer from asthma and I would breathe quietly the rest of my life.

Then he counted three and snapped his fingers.

I slowly came awake. I rubbed my eyes sleepily.

Now I knew I had to breathe quietly.

If I made one loud breath, I would be fired. So until the meeting broke up I forced myself to breathe without wheezing. I almost suffocated, but I did it.

To this day, Gleason is convinced he hypnotized me successfully, and whenever I run into him I have to force myself to breathe like a normal human being.

Soon I was officiating at the birth of a new game show, *Your Surprise Package,* which I invented with an affable hedonist named Allie Singer. It was a daytime show, across the board, five times a week. *Daytime!* I felt like a department-store executive who has been demoted to selling notions in the basement.

Then CBS President Jim Aubrey decided that *Your Surprise Package* was to be produced live from Los Angeles. I was to tear up my roots and move, bag and baggage and parodies, to California. Just like that.

What would become of my parties now? Would I ever sing parodies again? What did California have waiting for me?

A fire.

A flood.

A public humiliation.

Unemployment Compensation.

Thrilling success.

And Florida oranges, which are the only kind you can buy in California.

CHAPTER 11

And Now, As I Sink Slowly
in the West . . .

THEY WERE BULLDOZING snow off the runways at Idlewild
the morning in February of 1961 when Allie Singer and I
took off for Los Angeles. New York was buried under more than
four feet of snow. Five hours later we arrived in Los Angeles at
International Airport and the sun was shining and it was 92 de-
grees in the shade.

When I left in 1941, Los Angeles was a city made of stucco,
no more than two stories high, with drive-in restaurants on every
other corner and doughnut shops shaped like tremendous
doughnuts, and Brown Derby restaurants shaped like real Brown
Derbies, and chili restaurants shaped like chili bowls, and oil
wells disguised as charming Dutch windmills. There were other

windmills that turned out to be bakeries. Everything looked like something else.

Twenty years later you could see the beginnings of what they call the Southern California "megalopolis," because very soon now Los Angeles will be the most populous city in the world and it will stretch from Santa Barbara, one hundred miles to the north, to the Mexican border, one hundred miles to the south. Now when you drive up Wilshire Boulevard you see those brand-new high-rise office buildings and apartment houses that look even taller than they are, and there are stretches of Wilshire that are more stylish than Fifth Avenue, and the Sunset Strip is getting tall, and Universal Studios has built a skyscraper in the Valley, and you get the impression—which is true—that Los Angeles is not a city but twenty-four shopping centers in search of a city.

They have scarred the lovely mountainsides; they have notched them with gashes to build roads and cantilevered houses. They have uprooted the beautiful symmetrical orange groves that were everywhere; they have slashed freeways through the valleys. But still, wherever you look, you see palm trees and ivy and flowers of every blazing color, and it dawns on you that anything or anyone can take root and thrive in this wild, disorganized place.

Allie and I were met at the airport by a CBS Junior Executive who drove us to the Sunset Tower West, a resplendent motel on the Sunset Strip, and we parked our luggage in suites furnished in Early Conrad Hilton.

When we got to CBS, they showed us around the Executive Offices, and there were all those beautiful big-busted secretaries, typing a very slow hunt-and-peck, and in this warm, tropical, lazy atmosphere you could understand it. Executives do not live by television alone.

From the Senior Executive Offices you could look through the plate-glass walls and see the Hollywood mountains. The whole city gives you the impression of impermanence. You have the feeling that one day someone is going to yell "Cut! Strike it!" and then the stagehands will scurry out and remove the mountains, the movie-star homes, the Hollywood Bowl—everything.

Then they showed us *our* offices and *our* secretaries. I gathered from this that Allie and I were very small executives, because our secretaries were long on shorthand and short on bosoms; and our offices, instead of plate-glass window walls, had no windows at all. What they had was one wall covered with drapery, so that it looked like you did have a window but you enjoyed sitting there in the dark. (This goes back to the old Los Angeles tradition of having everything look like something else.)

One of the writers on the show, a brilliant and dissolute soul named David Vern, took advantage of the bare wall behind the drapery in his office. He would arrive every morning and lock himself in, and we would hear him humming and singing and busily occupied inside. He never let anyone else into his office for months, and we all wondered what the hell he was doing in there.

I would yell in to Dave that we needed the script, and pages would keep sliding out from under the door. But never, never would he let me or anyone else in that office.

A year later, when the show went off the air, I found out what he'd been doing in there.

Dave is a very literate man, and in his youth was a fine illustrator. He was fascinated, not only by his bare wall, but by the question: "How long will it be until someone finally opens these draperies?" From his childhood, Dave remembered reading "The Cask of Amontillado," Edgar Allan Poe's horror classic about a man who seals his enemy into a brick wall. And so for one solid year Dave had labored in that locked office, and on the day we left he called me in to show me his masterwork.

"Behold!" Dave exclaimed, and he pulled the drapes open. The entire wall had been painted in oils and appeared to be

an exact replica of a freshly laid brick wall. You could feel the
wet mortar between the bricks. And near the bottom, in the
scrawl of an obviously suffocating man, was the message:
FOR THE LOVE OF GOD, MONTRESOR!

Back to that first day at CBS. The Legal Department informed
us that we could not call our program *Surprise Package* because
that title had already been registered.

"What else should we call it?" Singer and I asked.

The lawyers said it would be all right to change the name to
Your Surprise Package. Lawyers are very clever at this type of
thing. NBC recently had a daytime show called *First Impressions.*
It turned out that this title was registered, too, so an NBC lawyer
got the idea of changing it to *Your First Impressions,* and the
original title-holders didn't have a legal leg to stand on. As I understand it, the idea is to call it "*Your* Whatever It Happens To
Be." For instance, nobody can stop you if you want to put on a
television program called *Your Beverly Hillbillies* or *Your
Huntley-Brinkley.*

So it became *Your Surprise Package,* and we chose George Fenneman as the host, and we went on the air five times a week,
thirty minutes a program, at eleven o'clock in the morning, opposite *Concentration,* the most popular daytime show in television. I was making a living and looking around for a house to
rent so I could bring Dee and Robbie and Nancy and our dog,
Jackson B. Sherman, to Los Angeles.

Meanwhile, every night, come nine or ten o'clock, you could
find me in P.J.'s on Santa Monica Boulevard, singing my little
songs, telling my stories and girl-watching. For this delightful
sport there is no place exactly like P.J.'s in all the world. *I haven't
been in all the world, but I know I must be right.*

P.J.'s swings, or so they say.

It opened the same night Allie Singer and I arrived in Hollywood, and we were there for the gala festivities. It is a dimly lit bar and grill where the music in both the front and back rooms is so loud you can't hear anything else. And because it is the only place open till four in the morning, you will find there all the better class of insomniacs from New York and Chicago and all over. P.J.'s was full of people who could not sleep and also people who were anxious to sleep but were looking for the right person with whom to sleep.

Los Angeles has more beautiful girls than any other city in the country. It is astounding. The first time I really was aware of it was when, after having lived in Los Angeles for two years, I took the family to the Seattle World's Fair. The girls of Seattle looked like girls anywhere—fine, upstanding girls, some plain, some pretty. They looked like real girls, like Chicago girls, New York girls, Miami, Houston, Boston, Philadelphia and Terre Haute girls, but still girls, human-being girls. But they were not to be compared with the Los Angeles girls, who are rare and beautiful creatures.

I suddenly realized that for a long time there has been a most peculiar situation in Los Angeles. For the last forty years, practically every girl who was voted most beautiful in her high school anywhere in America came to Los Angeles to get into the movies and, since 1950, to get into television. And today you have the daughters and the granddaughters of those beautiful girls, whose mothers married the handsome sons of the beautiful girls who came from all over, and the result is that it makes a tremendous number of beautiful and stunning girls of every imaginable type. They are unfortunately the worst-dressed girls in the world and the worst made up and the worst coiffed.

The boys in P.J.'s all look alike. They have the same haircuts and the same clothes, and they all look like those actors who play the lead in television Westerns, where you can't tell one from another.

I would sit in P.J.'s, which was to me like a great and fascinating zoo of human animals, myself included, and I would think, *Hollywood has more sexual freedom and open promiscuity than any place in the world, but something is wrong—something is definitely wrong.*

I feel sorry for *swingers.*

Swingers are not very happy people. They lead lonely and selfish lives. Every swinger I've ever known gets no kicks out of what he or she is doing for kicks. They are deeply afraid of being attached or connected or involved with other people, so they plug their skin into another person's skin and they think they are making a connection. I am in favor of a more abundant sex life for humanity, but not the way the swingers go about achieving it. A swinger's only desire is never to get involved, never, not with anybody; to avoid *caring* for anyone else. And they have their own language, the "hip" talk. They speak it because they are afraid to use ordinary words, and with this weird language they hope to prove they are beyond the human race and don't have to communicate with other people. They even have a special laugh of their own—a hard and ungenuine laugh which means *"I dig you, but the squares don't."* When I hear this laugh during my act, it makes me sick.

I also feel sorry for another large segment of the Los Angeles population. They are the Do-Gooders, the morals people who have taken it upon themselves to join fancy, crazy new religions and to protect the rest of us—the ones who are normal— from what they think might degrade us.

I will do my own deteriorating, thank you. I will read what I want and say what I want and do what I want, and as long as I don't hurt anybody else, I think I am entitled to that much by virtue of having been born on the earth. I think you are entitled, too. I respect your right to be a Goddam moralist or a Goddam swinger, as long as you don't mix into my life.

* * *

In Hollywood I learned to accept the idea of the Unemployment Clubs which abound in the swinging hills.

I found out about the Unemployment Clubs when we were hiring secretarial personnel for *Your Surprise Package*. From the CBS Personnel Department, there walked into our office a tall, well-stacked nymph. Did you ever see a dream walking? *Well, I did.* Did you ever see a *Playboy* Magazine centerfold nude except with clothes on walking? *Well, I did.* Allie Singer and I looked at her and we looked at each other and we were two minds with but a single thought: *She doesn't have to type so well and her shorthand doesn't have to be too perfect. We will hire her. Anyway. Just to give us inspiration. Just to put us in a good mood.*

Miss Abercrombie had a friendly smile and a come-into-my-bedroom look in her big black eyes with long black eyelashes, and her dark hair was stacked up in a beehive coiffure.

"Miss Abercrombie," I said, "I am going to give you a secretarial test. Take this pad and concentrate very hard, because Mr. Singer and I run a tight ship."

She smiled lazily. She unfolded the notebook and crossed her shapely legs and revealed just a suggestion of gloriously tanned thigh.

I dictated slowly because I wanted to give her every chance:
"*See the dog. His name is Spot. Run, Spot, run.*"

There was a moment's pause.

"Go on," she said as she recrossed her legs in a wide arcing movement.

"That's all," I said. "Of course if it's too difficult—"

"No, it's all right," she said. "I think I can make it out."

Then Miss Abercrombie went to the outer office and she came back an hour and a half later and showed me the results. She was hopeless. She was impossible. I hated to tell her the bad news. She had been out of work almost two months, she had told me. I begged her to try again, but she said, "No thanks."

"Miss Abercrombie," I said, "I hate to tell you this, but you type like a rabbit. We don't have very high standards of stenography and typing in our little organization, but, Miss Abercrombie, as low as our standards are, I am sorry to inform you that you have fallen short."

"How sad," she said.

"Yes," I agreed. "You would have made a good soldier in our little army."

"I'm sorry," she said, and she started to leave.

"Oh, yes, Miss Abercrombie—a word of advice. There's only one g in dog."

She smiled. In fact, she looked downright happy. She gave me a slip of paper to sign that stated she had applied for work and been rejected. She had to show this to the California State Unemployment Office in order to prove that she had looked for work. Otherwise she wouldn't receive her $55 a week Unemployment Compensation checks. I signed the paper and she walked to the door. Then suddenly she turned around.

"Mr. Sherman, you look like a nice man, so I am going to tell you. I belong to an Unemployment Club. In shorthand I'm like Wow!—a hundred and twenty words a minute. And as far as my typing is concerned . . ." She sat at the typewriter, put in a piece of paper and typed out the entire California State Unemployment Act in three and a half minutes. From memory.

Tears filled my eyes. "Miss Abercrombie," I said, "why did you fail our little test?"

"Because I'm in this Unemployment Club I was telling you about. It's cool. I've been in the club two months, and I've got four months to go until my Unemployment checks run out, and then I'll come back and show you some cool shorthand and typing, sir. But now I don't want any jobs. You won't tell anybody, I know. You're a kind-looking man."

I asked her what an Unemployment Club was. She explained that it was a group of six boys and six girls, and there were Unemployment Clubs all over Hollywood. They were all collecting Unemployment Benefits. By merging their individual $55 payments they had a total of $660 a week, $2,800 a month. They lived in a rented sprawling ranch house in the Hollywood Hills. They had a swimming pool. They were able to rent one convertible car, which was shared among them. They cooked their meals together. They swam in the nude together. They made love to one another, whoever was home. They lived in the sun all day, listening to transistor radios by the swimming pool. And they went on picnics on weekends. They played dirty-word Scrabble. And all they had to do was look for work and make sure they were not hired. There was only one sad aspect. After six months they had to leave the club, and a new member was taken in.

Miss Abercrombie told me there would be a vacancy in her Unemployment Club the following month. She urged me to give up the dull, boring life of the bourgeoisie and join the club. She said I was a jolly, nice-looking man with a good sense of humor, and she thought I would definitely be an asset to her Unemployment Club. They could use somebody my shape. I said I loved my wife and loved my children and did not want to be unemployed. And she looked at me as if I was very square, and she sighed over my wasted life, and then she smiled again and said good-bye. She tenderly squeezed my hand as she left.

I found out that Hollywood was even a sexy place for a dog. Jackson B. Sherman loved it. He went Hollywood as soon as we uncrated him at the airport.

We had bought Jackson in New York, after Dusty died. Jackson was a used beagle, two years old, with a very impressive pedigree. His maternal grandfather has his picture in the *Encyclopaedia Britannica* as an example of the perfect beagle. Jackson's manners were impeccable until he cased us and found out that he was the boss. At once he began to jump on the furniture and pee on the rugs, and we resigned ourselves because we loved Jackson. Robbie said we should give him the full name of Jackson Sherman.

Then one day Nancy said, "You know Jackson's really full name? It's Jackson B. Sherman."

"What's the B for?" I asked, smiling proudly at my eight-year-old daughter.

"Balls," she replied nonchalantly.

"*Balls?*" I shrieked.

There is a moment in a father's life when he knows that his sweet little daughter is growing up. *This,* I reasoned, *is it.* After all, dogs don't wear any clothes. Dee was embarrassed and so was I.

I was trying to think of a nice way to explain to Nancy the whole reproductive process when she continued: "It's because Jackson likes to chase balls."

Jackson is a veritable Richard Burton of a dog. He likes girl dogs and they like him, and he frequently disappeared for two or three days and then he'd return looking smug. But one thing was that he always had a terrible smell when he returned from those romantic sojourns. We tracked him to the local dump, which we found out was the romantic rendezvous for the dogs of Rye.

In May, 1961, I finally rented a house in Brentwood, and Dee packed up our belongings, and the children were taken out of school, and she was all ready to leave for the airport one morning when she saw that Jackson was not in the house. She went up and down the streets, calling "Jackson . . . Jackson!" Robbie and Nancy and their friends fanned out in separate searching parties, seeking Jackson. Jackson was not to be found. Dee was desperate. She was on the point of canceling the trip. She would not leave without Jackson. She called me long distance to explain her plight.

"I wouldn't be surprised if Jackson was with his girl friend,"

I told Dee. *"Cherchez la femme.* Find Jackson's true love—and you'll find Jackson not far away."

Dee at once drove to the city dump, and there, sure enough, was Jackson's girl friend, Cynthia, an Irish setter, being made love to by Jackson. Dee told the kids to look the other way, and then she grabbed up Jackson and they all went to the airport.

Jackson Balls Sherman took to Hollywood because the girl dogs of Hollywood are as free and easy as the girl girls of Hollywood.

His favorite haunt is a kennel where we leave him when we have to go on a trip. Usually a dog hates to be dragged to a kennel; he will shiver on his way, and he will moan and cry when his master leaves him there. But not at this kennel, which is in West Los Angeles.

Each dog who is taken there to be boarded is given a separate shed and has a private run. But the best part is that the two little old ladies who operate the kennel see to it that each dog has a companion of the opposite sex. It's sort of like a whorehouse for dogs. When we get within three blocks, Jackson smells the kennel and realizes he's going to be spending a swinging weekend. So, instead of crying and moaning, he actually pulls at the leash, dragging us toward the kennel.

"Faster, faster, faster!" he seems to be saying. *"Let me in there, you fool! What do you know of love?"*

Status symbols are very important in Southern California. Everybody there has a rented Rolls-Royce or a rented mansion, and during the first weeks I was out there it struck me it would be a good idea if someone opened up a Hertz Rent-a-Friend.

The cheapest status symbol you can have is an unlisted telephone number. (You can get the same effect even cheaper by having no phone at all.) Beverly Hills, the name of which is in itself a status symbol, is an incorporated city, an upper-middle-brow island surrounded by low-brow Los Angeles. Everybody in

Beverly Hills has an unlisted telephone number. My plumber has an unlisted telephone number, the Fire Department has an unlisted telephone number, the Police Department, the Information Operator. The Beverly Hills telephone book consists of a back cover and a front cover, and in between there is one page that says CONSULT YOUR YELLOW PAGES. One of the reasons there isn't more contact between people in Beverly Hills is that people do not know each other's telephone numbers. My Beverly Hills friends were shocked when I listed my telephone number. I have always listed it. I believe I am entitled to a listed phone number. Years ago when I was unemployed, I wanted to take out a full-page advertisement in the Yellow Pages and be the first comedy writer who could be looked up there, but the cooler heads of my managers prevailed.

When you look for a house in Beverly Hills the real-estate lady drives you down each block and points to houses and says "Danny Thomas lives there" or "Rosemary Clooney lives there" and the price of the house is in direct proportion to how close you are to Rosemary Clooney. The result of this is that a lot of clothing manufacturers who retired from cold New York and moved to Beverly Hills have bought up all the houses next door to Rosemary Clooney. And before long they will buy Rosemary Clooney's house and Danny Thomas' house and they will discover that they are living next door to a lot of other clothing manufacturers, and the prices will fall out from under them.

In Beverly Hills and Hollywood everybody plays the House Game. The object of the game is to have a bigger and more expensive house than your friends or your enemies. They trade-in houses out there the way normal people trade-in cars. And as soon as you outdo your friends, they go house-hunting, because they can't stand it. It is of the utmost importance to have a view of the city lights, and so everybody has the same view.

The House Game has recently been embellished by the addition of the Bathroom Ploy. Nowhere in the world are there such magnificent toilets as in Hollywood. It all began with wall-to-wall carpeting. Then someone thought up the idea of Mr.-and-Mrs. sinks. It was a simple step from there to the Greek or sunken bathtub. Then came Mr.-and-Mrs. potty chairs. Then came solid-gold water faucets shaped like dolphins or sea horses. Then came the Bathroom with a View, from which one could sit and survey the poorer sections of Southern California. *It just occurred to me that the poorer people of Southern California can sit in their bathrooms and look up at the homes of the rich in the hills. Maybe this is how the world will end—with everybody sitting in their bathrooms, stubbornly viewing everybody else.* The latest vogue is that Mr. and Mrs. should have two separate bathrooms with an intercom.

Of course everybody in Southern California has a swimming pool. These pools are heated and filtered and Shaped Like Something. Liberace's is shaped like a piano. Jayne Mansfield's is shaped like a Valentine heart. Mine is shaped like a human kidney. I suppose, to be really chic and physiologically accurate, I should build another pool shaped like the other kidney.

Crazy David Vern has an idea to alleviate the Freeway Traffic Problem. He says there are thousands of bodies of water in Los Angeles called swimming pools. He thinks everybody should get busy right away and dig three-feet-wide canals from everybody's pool to everybody else's pool.

Equally crazy Howard Merrill has another swimming-pool idea that Sounds Fun. He is working on the invention of a chemical. You put this chemical in your pool, and whenever anyone urinates in the pool, the whole pool immediately turns yellow.

I have been getting ahead of myself. CBS had renewed *Your Surprise Package* for another thirteen weeks, and I was looking for a house to rent so Dee and the kids could join me. I read the houses-for-sale advertisements. Some of the secret abbreviated language of real-estate advertising I already knew from looking around in Westchester. If the ad says the house is *"qnt,"* it means it is very old. If it says the house is *"chrmg,"* it means it is not only old but has a peculiar shape. If it says the house is *"intrstg,"* don't even look. In Hollywood I encountered the new abbreviation. *"Wt. Br."* This turns out to mean Wet Bar, which turns out to mean that the house has a bar which has a sink and a faucet in it and can therefore be made wet when the occasion demands. The house we bought has no Wet Bar. We are ashamed.

On Fridays the show-business trade papers, *Daily Variety* and *Hollywood Reporter*, feature real-estate sections with the wildest house advertisements I have ever read. For instance, one in the *Hollywood Reporter* was for a "showplace" in a fancy section of Beverly Hills—Trousdale Estates. Among the features of this house—which had been built by a producer in 1956 at a cost of $600,000—were the following: a 60-foot indoor-*and*-outdoor combination swimming pool with sliding glass walls; a 20-foot waterfall, a main gate with a pair of 18-foot-high nude statues guarding it; a 40-foot living-and-dining-room with *hand-molded murals*; a 200-foot bomb-shelter tunnel with *wine cellar*; and finally—the supreme achievement—a *"harem-den with round raised platform bed for eight."* All this for only $5,000 a month.

I went around with real-estate agents.

This could be very embarrassing in Los Angeles, because the real-estate agents are beautiful-looking dames dressed in the latest fashion, and they are driving Ferraris and Cadillac convertibles and Lincoln Continentals. If you ask to see a cheaper house than the one they are showing you, they throw you a look that makes you shrivel up inside.

One real-estate lady showed me a $1,000-a-month house on North Saltair Drive in Brentwood. It was on the old Milton Sills estate. Milton Sills was a famous silent-movie hero, very big in 1922. The place still had the original Milton Sills pool and cabana, but the house was modern—a breathtaking Hawaiian modern "showplace" of glass walls and staggering levels.

"And the most unique feature of this showplace," the real-estate lady told me, "is this tree."

It was a low-slung, sprawling tree that spread its tropical-leaved branches far outward.

"This is the second largest rubber tree in the Western Hemisphere. There's only one down in Paraguay that's bigger," she said.

"Do you absolutely guarantee," I asked, "that in all the Western Hemisphere this is the second largest rubber tree?"

She placed her hand on her heart. "By my mother, my father and the National Association of Real Estate Boards, by all that is holy, this is *indeed* the largest rubber tree but one in the Western Hemisphere," she intoned.

"I'll take the house," I said, reaching for a fountain pen.

"You'll never regret it," she said. "It's a *working* rubber tree, you know."

And it really was, it really was. During the rubber-dripping season our tree would drop thousands of little clots of genuine rubber on the ground and into the Milton Sills swimming pool. And the clots would become larger as the season went into full swing, and then the clots would become rubber balls, and Jackson Balls Sherman, living up to his middle name, loved to play with those balls and chew them up and swallow them. He also buried a bagel in the backyard.

When we had a party, I would seat my guests in the living room. There was a glass wall which looked out on my rubber tree and the tree was spectacularly lighted. I would say, "Ladies and Gentlemen, you are about to see a magnificent sight. Behold!"

Then I would press a button which controlled a motor which

opened the draperies. The draperies would *whoosh* apart. Then I'd press another button, and suddenly, outside, the lights would blaze on. The rubber tree would be resplendent in all its glory.

"You are now looking at the second largest rubber tree in the Western Hemisphere," I would say.

On June 12, 1961, I mailed out the following mimeographed invitations to our first soiree in Los Angeles:

```
You are invited to a Semi-Hollywood Party.
It will take place Saturday, June 17, be-
ginning at 3 p.m. at my palatial rented home
in Brentwood.
In the event you wish to swim, bring a bath-
ing suit and a towel. Luckily, we have a pool.
You may bring a date. For appearances, try
to make it someone of the opposite sex.
You may also bring a good piano player if
you know one. I have a rented piano, too.
The address is 307 North Saltair and the
phone number is GRanite 2-6485.
DIRECTIONS: Drive your car all the way,
till you get to our house. Then park, get out
of your car, and come in the house. The party
will not take place in your car. What you do
in your car before getting there or after leav-
ing is your business. What you do in my house,
because it is rented, fills me with apprehen-
sion.
NOTE: A delicious barbecue dinner will be
prepared on my rented spit. Don't be a hog--
there's plenty for everybody. I can't stand
vulgar displays of greed, especially from my
so-called friends. Being the host, I eat
first.
                         Your beloved host,
                         Allan Sherman
```

Dee and I began to notice that angels were playing music outside our bedroom window early in the morning. From somewhere, we didn't know where, came the sound of a harp. Every morning we woke up smiling at our angel music. And then one day, over the tall fence flew a badminton shuttlecock. And I went next door to return it.

The man who answered the door was Harpo Marx. He had rented the house next door for the summer.

I told Harpo about my rubber tree. He came over one afternoon to admire it and to pick up a few free samples of raw rubber. We became friends at once. Harpo knew me only as the owner of the rubber plantation next door. He had no idea that I was also a thrilling singer of hilarious parodies. He came to our first party. When I began singing my songs, he went completely crazy with laughter.

A week later Harpo and his wife, Susan, invited us to drop over to dinner. "Just dress casually," he said.

On the night of the dinner Dee and I were walking next door to Harpo's house. An enormous white Cadillac drew up alongside of me. It stopped. The driver said, "Excuse me, boy. Is this the Marx party?"

The speaker was Jack Benny. Beside him was Mary Livingstone. In the back were George Burns and Gracie Allen.

"Yes, Mr. Benny," I replied, "it's that house right there."

"Should I leave the keys in the car, boy?" Jack Benny said.

"Why not?" I said.

"You'll take care of it?"

"Sure, Mr. Benny."

He gave me a dollar tip and I parked it in an empty space I found three blocks away.

Then I walked back to North Saltair Drive and entered Harpo's house. I went to the bar and got a drink and mingled with the celebrities. Mary Livingstone did a big take when she saw me. "Look," she told Jack, "there's the parking boy."

"It's all right, Mary," Jack explained, "Harpo is a very democratic person."

At this party were all five Marx Brothers and Milton Berle and many of the leading comedians in Hollywood.

They were stunned when Harpo asked me to sing some of my parodies. I sang, I remember, "My Fair Lady" and "Glory, Glory, Harry Lewis" and "How Are Things with Uncle Morris?" Jack Benny went positively ape over those ditties. He gave a scream, lunged toward the floor and began wildly pounding on the carpet and laughing hysterically. For a minute I thought Mr. Benny was having some kind of convulsions, some attack, an epileptic fit—who knows? I couldn't believe it was *me* he was enthusing about. (I later found out that Jack Benny is the best audience a comedian can have.)

As I was leaving, Gracie Allen said to me, "With all your talent, you shouldn't have to park cars for a living, young man."

Harpo kept giving parties, and I was the singing star of them. He introduced me to everybody who was anybody in Hollywood, and I became very famous as a home entertainer, but in real life I was still only the producer of a daytime audience-participation show, *Your Surprise Package*—a thing which has only slightly less prestige in Hollywood circles than parking cars.

Naturally, we gave our own parties as well. Dee likes to give intimate parties—a dozen couples at most for a sit-down dinner and amiable conversation. That's how all our parties start. Me, I like large, uproarious parties. I'm gregarious by nature and I'm always worried that a party should not have "gaps" in it, so my solution is to invite so many different kinds of people that there is always somebody for everyone to talk to.

We always start out with Dee's type of party, and in Hollywood we would begin with our personal friends—like Everett Sloane (the great character actor) and his wife, Lovey; Jim Backus (the voice of Mr. Magoo) and his wife, Henny; Lou Quinn (my old friend and now a leading television writer) and his wife, Christine Nelson (who later sang "Sarah Jackman" with me on "that" record); Ernest Lehman (the screenwriter) and his wife, Jackie; and Steve Allen and his wife, Jayne Meadows.

You see, people *do* come to Hollywood parties with wives. Not always their own wives. But wives.

Marriage is a very strange institution in Hollywood, California. For one thing, adultery—which is the only grounds for divorce in New York—is not grounds for divorce in California. As a matter of fact, adultery in Southern California is grounds for *marriage*. Furthermore, they have something out there called "mental cruelty," which means you can get rid of your wife or husband by just hating her or him. This is a typical convenience of Southern California—something like all those drive-ins.

So when you go to a party in Southern California, you often find a lot of extremely interesting marital relations. There are always at least three couples, each man of whom has been married to all three women. There are also people in their early twenties who have at least two sets of fathers or mothers at the party. In addition, there are several individuals who are having love affairs with each other and soon will break away from their current spouses and get married and complicate the whole thing even further. It's kind of fascinating, once you get used to it.

Our best Hollywood party that first season was our housecooling party, which I gave as an answer to housewarming parties, because we were about to leave our rented house with North America's largest rubber tree because our lease was up and we would have to live in an apartment until we could sell our humble abode in Rye, New York, and use the equity therefrom to leverage ourselves into a mansion somewhere in Los Angeles.

The mimeographed invitation read as follows:

```
YOU ARE INVITED TO A HOUSECOOLING PARTY
  It will take place Sunday, August 27th, at
7 P.M. at the lavish residence which I have
rented through Labor Day.
  Please come to this party so that you may
see me in this setting of magnificent splen-
```

dor, because after Labor Day I will live in a
humble rented apartment. You don't want to
see me like that.

Dress will be informal. Try not to look better than I do. This will be easy for you, since
I have deliberately limited my guest list to
people who are something less than beautiful
—of whom you are one of the uppermost.

A modest dinner will be served. An hour
later you will be hungry again. At which time
another modest dinner will be served.

Don't worry about making brilliant conversation. Most of the guests will be no smarter
than you.

Our address is 307 North Saltair. Attached
you will find a Hollywood Movie Star Map, and
you will notice that we live in the very heart
of Hollywood's bustling movie colony.

Your gracious host,
Allan Sherman

My movie-star map was a parody of the actual movie-colony
maps sold in the souvenir shops of Hollywood and peddled by
those curious fat ladies in mumus and sunglasses who sit under
umbrellas on Sunset Boulevard. They sell maps and will drive
you in your car on a guided tour and point out the residences of
ancient and modern movie stars—very often inventing houses
and making up who lives where. But the small-town tourist gets
a big thrill out of seeing a ramshackle Spanish-type villa which
he is told was once inhabited by Douglas Fairbanks or Mary
Miles Minter.

At our housecooling party, wonderful people were milling
around, including Steve Allen, Meredith Willson, Shecky
Greene, Jack Oakie, novelist Howard Fast, Sir Cedric Hardwicke, Earl Wilson and Bullets Durgom.

Fate brought Bullets Durgom to my party. Fate, for twenty
years, had been hinting to me that I was a performer, but I had
refused to pay any attention to fate and had insisted on being
a television producer. So fate decided to take a hand in my life.

Durgom, a short, cherubic gentleman, looks like a Disney character who would be called "Bullets." He is a sweet and lovable and considerably insane man who is a personal manager of entertainers. For years he had guided Jackie Gleason's career, and I had known him in New York. Bullets shows up everywhere. He was now living on the coast.

When he received my invitation and the road map, he telephoned me and said, "I will come, providing you will reserve for me a parking place smack at your front door, no matter what time I come, because I have just purchased the first Jaguar XKE in the United States and I want everybody to see it."

Which we did.

The Jaguar XKE was the star of the party—next to Bullets. The high point was when he took off his clothes and got into a small plastic rowboat and paddled around the pool while we were having dinner.

Later I sang my songs. Bullets had never heard me sing my songs before. He went wild over them. In his brain there was already beginning the turning of little wheels. But he said nothing to me. Fate had told Bullets to keep his big mouth shut because it was necessary for me to suffer a lot more before I was ready to become famous; fate had to move a few more pieces into position.

The next piece was Lou Busch. Jim Backus gave a New Year's Eve party and invited Lou, not only because he liked Lou but because Lou could, as they used to say, tickle the ivories. As an arranger, conductor and jazz pianist, Lou has been successful for years. He has made lots of hit recordings of ragtime-style, barrelhouse, honky-tonk piano under the pseudonym "Joe 'Fingers' Carr, World's Greatest Ragtime Pianist." He was for many years A&R man for Capitol Records. (A&R means "Artists and Repertoire," and the A&R man is the executive who selects the songs

to be recorded and decides what artist will record what numbers.)

For three years Lou was a genius by mistake. He says the only
way to be a genius in the music business is by mistake. And once
you have the genius label, it sticks on you for at least three years.
How Lou Busch got to be a genius was while he was Capitol's
A&R man: Capitol had the late Nat King Cole under contract.
Cole had never had a hit record. One day Lou found a new
rhythm-and-blues number titled, "The Greatest Inventor Of
Them All." Nat King Cole loved the tune and the arrangement,
and he recorded it as a single. But records have two sides, so Lou
told Cole to sing a ballad for the flip side, the B side—any mild,
harmless little ballad. They picked one that had been sung in a
movie, *Captain Carey*, *U.S.A.* The movie had not been popular
and the song was unknown. When the record was released, nobody wanted to hear "The Greatest Inventor." But the flip side,
the ballad they were just wasting, sold three million copies. It
was called "Mona Lisa."

A few days after our housecooling party I got a call from Bullets Durgom. He told me a man named Jim Conkling was retiring as President of Warner Brothers Records and they were
giving him a big stag party at the Beverly Hills Hotel. The whole
recording industry and a lot of composers and recording artists
would be there. Would I do Bullets a favor and quick write a
parody about Jim Conkling, whom I had never heard of? Bullets
suggested I use a current hit record called "Big Bad John" and
call it "Big Bad Jim" and write a real dirty song about this nice
man to whom everybody was paying such great and glorious
tribute.

So I went to a studio with Bullets and on little pieces of paper
I wrote the dirtiest, most evil-minded song you have ever heard
in your life about this perfect stranger. And I recorded it, and
Bullets played it at the farewell banquet, and all of Jim Conk-

ling's loyal and beloved friends were delighted to hear all those dirty, nasty things about him, and the song was the sensation of the banquet. They insisted on hearing it over and over. Bullets introduced me as the author and I took a bow and apologized to Mr. Conkling, who by then was not talking to me, although we had never spoken to each other before. And then everybody forgot the whole thing—except Bullets.

To me, this was just another party and another parody. But Bullets was scheming his Machiavellian schemes. Still, he didn't say anything to me.

He wasn't ready.

And fate wasn't either. Fate wanted me to go through a fire and a flood first.

CHAPTER 12

One Fire and One Flood, and Go Easy on the Pestilence

W̱E BOUGHT A HOUSE at the bottom of a canyon on Chantilly Road in the poor section of Bel Air. The house was nine years old, which, for California, is a middle-aged house. We were the fourth owners. (In Beverly Hills, people buy a house for $95,000 and then have the house torn down because all they wanted was the lot anyway.) I knew the house was nine years old because the real-estate lady told me how to tell the age of a house. You ask to use the bathroom. Then you look inside the toilet tank. By law, all toilet tanks must be dated.

Warning: Do not attempt this except with toilet tanks that have a removable lid. If the tank is attached to the ceiling and has a chain hanging from it, don't even waste your time.

The price was $64,500, and the Savings and Loan Association loaned us $56,000 of it. *The Savings and Loan Association giveth, and the Savings and Loan Association taketh away.* I promised to spend $12,000 putting in a new kitchen and a *lanai*.

Lanai is the name of one of the Hawaiian Islands. It has been borrowed as a name for a room which is in every house in Southern California. As a matter of fact, this room is in every house in America, and it has an interesting evolution. It was originally called the Basement. In the early years of the affluent society it became the Rumpus Room. Then it was discovered that the Basement Rumpus Room was on the wrong floor, so it was moved upstairs and called the Playroom. Not long after that, somebody who had a lot of extra knotty-pine paneling he didn't know what to do with nailed it to the walls of the Playroom and it became the Den. This later became the Family Room. Then somebody put in gorgeous sliding glass walls, and it became the Lanai.

I designed our kitchen myself. Everything is very thoroughly built in, so that you need a blueprint to find out where anything is. There is a built-in oven, a built-in food mixer, can opener, knife sharpener, dishwasher, intercom AM-FM radio, high-fidelity speakers, breadboard, and an automatic bread box.

Also built into this kitchen for eleven months were a number of workmen who seemed never to get tired of remodeling and seemed never to be able to finish the job, which we had been told would take six weeks.

Dee began to refer to those workmen as the Cast of Characters. They would appear at seven o'clock every morning. That is, *almost* every morning. Mornings when it was absolutely essential they be there—for example, when the city building inspector was to meet them—they didn't show up.

The contractor's name was Marty. He would sit and look at the blueprints of the new kitchen knowingly for hours while Dee made him cup after cup of coffee. Then he would turn the blueprints around because they had been upside down.

A featured player in the Cast of Characters was Ignatz, our

sleep-in painter. He had no place else to go, so he painted by daylight and all night long by the gleam of a flood lamp he brought with him. The reason he had to paint so much was that what he painted in the daytime always turned out to be a slightly different color from what he had painted at night. He also put up some wallpaper. He had a novel system. He believed wallpaper should not be butted edge to edge but overlapped so that you get a nice lumpy effect every two feet or so along the wall.

Marty provided us with an electrical genius named Harold to do the wiring of the intercom and the stereo. Every time you started to play a record in my house, the front-door chimes rang. After Harold left the premises, when there was no chance of hurting his feelings, I had Robbie fix it.

Then there was George, a suntanned Greek God of a man. George was the only one who ever did any work, and his work largely consisted of undoing the damage the others had done. George could do everything: plastering, painting, sawing, cabinetwork, plumbing, electrical wiring.

During those eleven months we got so used to living with those characters—so used to feeding them, so used to having them sympathize with our problems, share in our joys, play with our children—that when the day finally came when the last one was gone, we actually missed them.

We moved into the house on Chantilly Road in mid-October. Our furniture arrived from New York the next week, and with it a moving bill for almost $3,000. *Your Surprise Package* was still on the air, but I knew it was doomed to cancellation in a matter of weeks, so I was making the rounds, talking to whatever television executives I could, looking for my next job.

One night in early November I made an appointment to see Hugh Benson, head of TV at Warner Brothers, the next morning.

There was a high, warm wind that night—the wind they call the *santana*. It comes up from Mexico and it blows away the smog and it whistles through the canyons and it has a kind of exciting violence to it.

The next morning was lovely and crisp and sunny. I got up at eight o'clock. I kissed Dee. I patted Jackson B. Sherman. I got into the Thunderbird. I adjusted the power seat for Fat Stomach. I drove over the mountains to the freeway and then to the Warner Brothers Studios in Burbank.

Hugh Benson was in charge of 77 *Sunset Strip*, and I was hoping to get an assignment to write an episode. I walked into Benson's office, and he had his television set turned on and was looking at it in fascination. I couldn't imagine what could be on so early in the morning that would hold Benson spellbound like that.

"Hello, Hugh," I said. "What's on?"

"A fire," he replied, not taking his eyes off the screen. "A very big fire."

I looked. "*Hmm,*" I said, "very realistic, too. Good special-effects job."

"It's real" he said. "It's going on right now in Bel Air. Say—isn't that *your* neighborhood?"

The fire on the television screen was on Stone Canyon Road, half a mile away from our house. "Jesus!" I said. "Can I use your phone?"

I called home.

"Now, Dee," I said, "I don't want you to get nervous or anything—but look around and see if the house is on fire."

"What are you talking about?"

"Put on the television set and you'll see, and, whatever happens—don't panic."

"I'll call you back," Dee said. But she didn't call. I waited in Hugh Benson's office for two hours and she never called. Then Hal Cooper, the Director of *Your Surprise Package*, called. He had a message from Dee. She had taken Jackson B. Sherman—when the fire was racing down Chantilly Road and had almost reached our house—and she had driven to Bellaggio Road School to find Nancy. Later she would pick up Robbie, and when she had found a place to stay, she would get in touch with me.

The only place I could go was to the CBS office. I no sooner walked in than my insurance man called.

"Your house is gone," he said.

"How do you know?" I asked.

"I've got a big map with pins. The center of the whole fire (it's like the eye of a hurricane) is on the corner of Chalon Road and Chantilly Road, fifty feet from your house. I just stuck a pin where your house used to be."

We had moved in twenty-two days before.

About four o'clock in the afternoon Dee called from the Del Capri Motel on Wilshire Boulevard in Westwood. I drove out there. The sky over the Santa Monica Mountains, in which Bel Air nestles, was the color of dried blood.

The motel was full of displaced families from Bel Air. We milled around and didn't quite know what to say to each other. The police had a cordon around the Bel Air gate until the worst part of the fire was over. It was nine o'clock at night when they let us drive in. There was an eerie glow in the sky, and all over the hills there were little patches of flame.

It hadn't rained for two years, and the brush on the hills was dry and filled with natural oils. The santana—that same wind that had made the sky so beautifully clear that morning—had carried the first spark from one hill to another and the brush seemed to explode. The fire leaped a hundred yards at a time. At one point it jumped across Sepulveda Boulevard and the San Diego Freeway. When the flaming chips landed on the roof of a house, the house would implode. There would be a house there, and then the fire would hit the roof, and ten minutes later nothing would be standing but the stone fireplace and part of the chrome support for the diving board. The fire jumped around like crazy, as though it had an appointment with one house and wasn't allowed to go near another. Chantilly Road was where it did the most damage. Of the ninety-seven houses on our street, ninety-one were burned to the ground.

But our house was still there.

The fire had stopped in our backyard, eight feet behind the swimming pool. What stopped it was the sprinkler system, which had been turned on and left running by George, the man who could do everything. Later the neighbors told us that George had stayed there until almost dark, soaking our roof with the garden hose.

We drove up Chantilly Road that awful night. Here were the ashes of a house that had belonged to a UCLA professor. His wife had run out of the house that morning, taking only her mink coat and his Nobel Prize. Another woman, who owned a collection of Picassos, forgot the paintings in her hysteria and took only *her* mink coat and sixteen books of trading stamps. Burt Lancaster and Joe E. Brown and Arnold Stang lost not only their homes but all their papers, their clippings, their scrapbooks —the precious relics of an actor's life.

I will never forget one man I saw that night. He was standing in the street. All that was left of his house was the brick chimney and the fireplace and the metal mailbox out in front. He was standing by the mailbox, opening and closing it, and he was crying.

We moved back into our house the next day.

Two days later it began to rain . . . and rain and rain and rain. And now there was no foliage left on the mountains, and the rain turned the earth into mud, and soon there were millions of tons of water, rapids, pushing mud down the naked hills. And the mud pushed houses off their foundations, and one morning at three A.M. there was a sound like the sound of a waterfall that woke us all up, and we looked out the front windows and it was Chantilly Road. Chantilly Road was a raging river three feet deep, and pieces of houses were floating down the street, and furniture and books and automobiles.

Our house remained on its foundation, but the terrace and the swimming pool were filled with mud. When the rain finally ended, we had the swimming-pool man come and drain the water from the pool.

The only thing that keeps a swimming pool from bursting is the pressure of the water inside it.

So when we removed the water from the pool, the pool burst. It cost us $1,800 to build a new pool inside the old one. And more money to install sprinklers all the way up our mountain. And more money to plant rye grass to cover the bare hillside.

What lesson could I learn from this almost Biblical curse of fire and flood?

What else could possibly happen?

Dee said, "Cheer up. Things could get worse."

So I cheered up. And, sure enough, things got worse.

CHAPTER 13

You Can't Be Sure If It's Westinghouse*

L ET US REVIEW:
There we were, living in a heavily mortgaged house in Bel
Air that was worth about half what we had paid for it because
ninety-one of the ninety-seven houses on the street had burned
to the ground. Bel Air looked like the Rich Man's Hiroshima,
and every day, especially weekends, cars and sightseeing buses
full of tourists went driving up the street to look at the ruins.
And sometimes they stopped in front of our house and pointed
to us, the survivors, and sadly shook their heads and went "*Tsk,
tsk, tsk.*"

Not only that, but day and night, truckloads of debris roared

* The title of this chapter does not refer to the products of the Westinghouse *Electric* Corporation; it is meant to describe my bewildering encounter with the Westinghouse *Broadcasting* Corporation. But who knows,
maybe this kind of thing goes on in all big corporations. I hope not.

down the street, and there were wretched little groups of people —families—standing in front of the ashes of houses they used to live in, and crying, and wondering what to do now.

Not only that, but our swimming pool was bent, and one wall of the house was open to the elements, and every morning at seven o'clock the Cast of Characters arrived at our house and started hammering and banging and tearing up the walls, each of them pausing for a moment as they walked in to look at Dee and/or me and mutter *"Tsk, tsk, tsk."*

Not only that, but because of the fire and the flood, we had to install an expensive sprinkler system all the way up to the top of the hill, and a costly drainage tunnel out to the street. And no matter how many times we tried to seal up the cracks in the swimming pool, it kept leaking several thousand gallons of water a day.

Not only that, but my CBS show had been canceled, and I was out of work, and of course in Hollywood, when you are out of work, no one will talk to you.

You'll never believe this, but what you have just read is the happiest *part of this chapter.*

I didn't know how well off I was. I thought I was in the doldrums of the worst depression of my life.

During all those years on an emotional roller-coaster, living my whole life as a yo-yo, I had developed my own solution for great emotional depression:

Self-pity.

I go in for enormous orgies of self-pity, during which I am very nice to myself because the world has treated me so badly.

I doubled and tripled my consumption of calories; I found escape in coconut-cream pies, chocolate malted milks, corned-beef sandwiches and spareribs. I found absolution in mashed potatoes.

I found my way into P.J.'s almost every night, and the five owners of the place, God bless them, kept me on the cuff, letting my tab grow higher and higher, although they knew, as I did, that I was a leper and would never get work again.

And before I knew it, the coconut-cream pie and the mashed potatoes and the Scotch at P.J.'s all added up on my waistline and my clothes didn't fit me, and in the middle of all this poverty I had to buy new suits and shirts and shorts, because if you don't *look* prosperous, then you will *really* never get a job in show business.

So for the first time in my life I went on Unemployment— something I had always been ashamed to do. *I was brought up to think you should never take charity. Even after the war I didn't join the 52–20 club and take the $20-a-week-for-a-year that veterans were entitled to.*

But by now one shame was piling on top of another so fast— the guilt and the fear were so enormous inside me, having a family and a mortgage and all those ridiculous expenses and no future at all, none whatsoever—that the California State Unemployment Service called to me like Bali Ha'i. That was where I belonged, so I went.

Maybe you're wondering why I didn't go out and look for a job. In show business, if you are what they call "talent," it's not possible to go ask people for a job. You don't just go to someone and say, "I'm very talented. Give me a job." It's beneath your dignity.

So you sign up with an agent, and *he's* supposed to ask people to give you a job. And for that you give him ten percent of your income. My agents (I had new ones) were the Frank Cooper Agency. They handled a lot of important Hollywood writers and producers. But in Hollywood an agent will not ask anyone to give you a job, because it's beneath *his* dignity, too.

There is a lot of dignity going on in Hollywood, beneath which nobody wants to get if they can help it.

* * *

One morning I was on my seventh or eighth cup of coffee and my dozenth Danish pastry in the lanai when there was a tapping on the gorgeous sliding-glass door. It was one of the Cast of Characters, a big colored man named Chick. He had been wheeling wheelbarrows of wet concrete up our hill to the place where Marty the Contractor was trying to build a retaining wall to hold the mud back in case there was another flood. When I opened the sliding-glass door, Chick said, "Could I use your phone?" I said sure, and he picked up the phone and called the William Morris Agency and asked for the movie department. While he waited he mopped the sweat and some blobs of concrete from his brow, and they fell on our new carpeting. Then he said into the phone, "Hello, Max, this is Chick. What the hell's new with my screenplay, man?"

That was when I realized that everybody in Hollywood, *everybody*, is really in show business. The retaining-wall people are really screenplay writers, and the garbage man is a character actor, and the plumber happens to have a few unpublished songs which he will walk right into the bathroom and sing for you if you don't watch out.

If Chick can call his agent, why can't I? I said to myself.

I picked up the phone and dialed the Frank Cooper Agency. I got Bob Hibbard.

"Hi there, Bob," I said. "Any jobs today?"

There was a brief silence, then he spoke. "Allan-baby, how can you ask such a thing? It's beneath your dignity."

I hung up, ashamed.

In Hollywood there are two little daily newspapers called the "Trades." Their real names are the *Hollywood Reporter* and *Daily Variety*, but nobody calls them that. They are called the Trades. Everybody reads the Trades to see what everybody else is doing and who's in what kind of trouble and with whom. That morning I read in the Trades that Steve Allen was about to do a new late-hour show for the Westinghouse Broadcasting Company.

"You should give Steve Allen a ring," Dee said, "and suggest that he hire you as the producer of the show."

"I can't," I said.

"Why not? He's a personal friend of yours, isn't he? His wife is a personal friend of yours, isn't she? So go ahead and call Steve and ask him for the job."

"I can't!"

"Why not?"

"Because it's *beneath my dignity*," I explained.

"Well, is there anything wrong with calling Steve and saying hello?"

I mulled over this suggestion. It certainly wasn't beneath my dignity to say hello. Who would suspect I was financially desperate and out of work if I just called and said "Hello, how are you, what's new?" And I wouldn't breathe a word about Steve's new television show. Just a friendly call.

My hands were shaking as I made the friendly call.

Jayne answered the phone.

I said, "Hello."

She sounded happy to hear my voice. "Allan! What a coincidence that you should call!"

I said, "How are you?"

"Fine," she said. "Steve and I were just talking about you. You know this new show Steve's going to do?"

I said, "What's new?"

Jayne said, "Steve was wondering if you would be interested in producing the show?"

I said, "How's the family?"

Jayne said, "Fine. Allan—are you all right?"

I said, "Sure. This is just a friendly call."

"But what about producing Steve's show?"

"Well, I would have to think about it."

"Of course."

"Okay."

"Okay, Allan dear, go ahead and think about it and call us as soon as—"

"I mean, okay, I'll produce it. I just *thought* about it."

"Wonderful!" said Jayne, and she put Steve on the phone.

We talked about the show for a few minutes, and we congratulated each other, and we were both very excited because we felt we would be a perfect combination. Steve and I had the same tastes in music and comedy, and the same interests, and the same ideas about what makes good television. Steve arranged for me to meet an executive from Westinghouse for lunch the next day.

I will call this executive David Thrilling. Mr. Thrilling was living in a $90-a-day suite at the Beverly Hills Hotel, and the first thing he did was explain to me that the show was on a very tight budget and They could not pay me my proper salary. He said Steve Allen had suggested my name as Producer several days before, and They had been checking into my past and could not find anything that disqualified me.

I should have known right then. I should have known the first time he mentioned They that I was in the biggest trouble of my life.

Whenever there is a They, catastrophe looms nearby. In every big organization there is a They, and the word is spoken with a certain tone of holiness, and you get an uncontrollable urge to take off your hat and hold it over your heart because you are in the Sanctified Presence—or, rather, the Sanctified Absence—of They. No one ever tells you who They are. You never meet They or see They; but then you've never met or seen God, have you?

They make the Immutable Policies. They hand down Great Decisions. They tell you what can be done and what can not be done.

They are not to be argued with. They are not to be challenged. They are not to be disobeyed, or They will punish you. And you often find out that you have disobeyed one of Their rules, for They are allowed to make up rules as They go along.

So when Mr. Thrilling tells you in hushed reverence about They, he can look at you with compassion and love and pity, and he can say, "It is not *I* who am doing all this, it is *They*."

I should have known. I was out of work and desperate and had two children and a wife and a house with a fancy mortgage, but *still* I should have known, and I should have said right then and there, "Sorry, Mr. Thrilling. Wrong number."

But I was determined to keep this job, no matter what. *Allan, you stupid son of a bitch,* I said to myself, *all your life you have been difficult to get along with, dogmatic, stubborn, obstinate. All your life you have insisted on having things your own way; you've been a troublemaker. Just this once you will learn how to get along with people—how to see Their viewpoint. How to win friends and influence* They.

This time, Allan, baby, you will play the game. For the good of hearth, home, family, dog and the Establishment—you will Adjust.

And so I invented the Sherman Continuous Adjustment Plan. One day the world would know me as Allan the Great Compromiser, Friend To Those Who Need A Friend—Easy To Get Along With, Amiable Al, a real Fun Person.

I took the job with the low-budget salary, and all of a sudden I had friends again in Hollywood, and people were calling *me* up saying, "Hello, how are you, what's new?" Friendly calls.

The Producer of a television show is supposed to hire the people who work for him. I was not allowed to do this. They hired people left and right, and then presented them to me as a *fait accompli*. It was one damn *fait accompli* after another.

They, not I, hired the Associate Producer, the Director, the Production Assistants, the secretaries. The effect of this, of course, was that all those people felt responsible to They, and not to me. I would keep making plans and giving orders, but I wasn't able to get anything done. I wanted a fourth camera. *My own secretary* turned to me and said sternly, "They say you can't have it." And, by God, that was *that*. After a while I was able to Adjust to taking orders from my built-in secretary, but just as I was getting Adjusted to her, she quit. At least, I think she quit. All I'm sure of is that she disappeared, and I was allowed to hire her successor.

We had a suite of three rooms in a long, low building on the Goldwyn Studios lot. I remember my first morning. I sat down at my desk and tried to figure out some way to bring this heterogeneous bunch of people together with the kind of spirit and enthusiasm we would need if we were going to put on a ninety-minute show five times a week.

I called my secretary in and dictated the following memo, which will be known henceforth as Mistake Number 1:

```
            THE STEVE ALLEN SHOW
               1041 N. Formosa
            Hollywood 38, California

TO:       All Concerned
FROM:     Allan Sherman
SUBJECT:  FREEDOM OF THOUGHT

   Everyone on this show can make a contribu-
tion far greater than that for which he or she
was hired.
   My point is---feel free: free to make sug-
gestions; free to think up and express ideas
no matter how wacky they may seem to you; free
to express your opinions, and if you feel
deeply what you are saying, to state your case
in good faith to anyone else who works on this
program, no matter how fancy his or her title
may be.
   If someone were to ask me (and no one has)
what are the Ten Commandments for doing a show
```

like this one, I would say they are something
like this:

1. Thou Shalt Have An Open Mind.
2. Thou Shalt Not Take Anything For
    Granted. (Thou Shalt Check Up and
    Make Damn Sure.)
3. Thou Shalt Have A Good Time and Thy
    Work Shall Be Fun and The Fruits Of
    Thy Labor Shall Be Fun For The Audi-
    ence.
4. Thou Shalt Respect The Intelligence
    Of Thy Audience, and Love Them As
    Thyself.
5. Thou Shalt Not Gather In Small and
    Divisive Groups, and Do Violence
    One Upon The Other.
6. Thou Shalt Fear No One: Yet Thou
    Shalt Fear and Despise Sloth and
    Dullness and Tastelessness and Gut-
    lessness, for These Will Surely
    Bring Down Upon Thy House The Wrath
    Of Neilsen and The Curse of Arbitron.
7. Thou Shalt Walk In Dignity With Thy
    Head Held High, and Thou Shalt Help
    Those Around You To Do Likewise.
8. Thou Shalt Not Commit Adultery On
    Company Time Or Furniture.
9. Thou Shalt Not Panic, and Thou Shalt
    Admit Thy Mistakes, for They Shall
    Be Forgiven.
10. Thou Shalt Adjust. When Everything
    Around Thee Whirleth and Screameth
    and Seemeth To Falleth Apart, Thou
    Shalt Adjust, and Say To Thyself
    Calmly, "This Too Shall Pass."

                              Amen.
                              Allan Sherman

It was several days before I made my next mistake. During
those days I sat quietly at my desk and observed the Westinghouse sea around me.

The Westinghouse people had brought Their own scenic

designer from Cleveland, and he brought with him a model of a set which had already been completely designed and which They had approved. This scenery was covered with little things, about one foot in diameter, which looked something like great big asterisks.

"Why all the asterisks?" I asked. "Are we going to have footnotes on this show?"

"Those aren't asterisks," the designer said.

"Then what are they?"

"Those are Elements of Design," he said.

And, boy, was he disgusted with me for not knowing so.

Well, the set was built and those Elements of Design were painstakingly cut from inch-thick wood—thousands of them—and even more painstakingly attached to the scenery.

I began to call them Bippees. Sue me. To me they looked like Bippees.

Each day I would walk into the theatre to see how things were going, and the pile of Bippees on stage would have mounted higher and higher until they eventually obscured the carpenters who were busily at work, like elves. Half of them were attaching Bippees to the set, and half of them were making more Bippees so that the supply of Bippees would never run out.

I had better explain that television scenery, especially on a show of this type, should not be complex or baroque or fancy.

The idea of the show (I thought) was that people would want to look at Steve Allen, not at the scenery behind him. Furthermore, if there are strange lines or Bippee-shapes behind the person on the screen, they sometimes seem to be growing out of his head and create a bizarre picture.

But They had decided on Bippees, and by now They had a tremendous investment in Bippees. They had more Bippees than any other corporation in the world, and, by God, they were going to use their Bippees and I was going to like it.

So I Adjusted. A *man can adjust to Bippees if his family and his home are at stake.* I began to think of creative ideas for the use of Bippees on the show. I had several of them attached to the set on loose axles, so that they could be spun like pinwheels. I had one made into a sort of combination lock, so that when Steve twirled it to the right three times and to the left twice, a secret panel opened. I had one fashioned to work like a steering wheel, so Steve could play bus driver or U-boat captain if he felt like it.

Perhaps this is a sign of how well I was Adjusting: *I was beginning to like Bippees.*

They hired a motion-picture lighting expert who was accustomed to taking two days to light a scene, but of course we were doing a live television show where the lighting man is lucky if he has thirty seconds to do the job.

They bought all brand-new studio equipment—lights, cameras, dollies, everything. I have worked in television since it began, and in every studio I had ever been in, the equipment had been beat-up and cruddy. I had never seen that much shiny new equipment before.

But there were gaping holes in the ceiling of the theatre, and many of the seats were bent and broken, and the paint on the walls was old and dingy, and altogether it was a cold, unpleasant place for an audience to come and see a comedy show. But when I asked if They could paint it and make it pleasanter for the audience, They said, "No, that isn't in the budget."

We began putting the show together, and there were executive meetings and conferences and memoranda and long-distance calls to They, wherever They were. I was used to writing memos and receiving memos—from the old Goodson-Todman days—but this was different. I wasn't receiving any memos. I was being by-passed. But I Adjusted. Lord, how I Adjusted.

There were two girls on the staff who liked me, Nita Archambeau, Steve Allen's secretary, and Judy Smith, my new secretary. I noticed that every once in a while when they passed my desk they would pause and look at me, and their eyes would fill with tears, as though they knew I had some incurable disease, and they had to keep me from finding out.

One day I cornered Judy and said "What the hell is going on?" She confessed that people were holding meetings without me and making decisions without me, and I realized that I was rushing around in a dream world thinking I was Producer of the show and actually having the title, but everybody knew he or she wasn't supposed to listen to me, and if I gave any orders, he or she was not supposed to obey them but to report immediately to They.

I couldn't understand what was happening. I had the sense of walking through a foggy nightmare where everything was even more unreal than usual. People were *humoring* me, and there is nothing more aggravating than being humored, if you are not crazy.

It was two years after I left the show when I finally learned why people were humoring me (and don't ask me who I learned it from—he could still get fired). It was because of Mistakes Numbers AA1 and AA2.

I made both of those serious blunders without knowing I had done so and years before I had ever met anyone from Westinghouse. But they were supermistakes. And I eventually had to pay for them.

AA1, to my eternal shame, was that I was a friend of Steve Allen's and he was a friend of mine. And They had proof: Wasn't I the only one on the staff Steve himself had hired? This is unforgivable. No big corporation can tolerate such a conspiracy. If They disagreed with Steve, where would my loyalty lead me? Would I side with Steve? Traitor! Spy! Infidel!

AA2, may God forgive me, was that while checking my history before hiring me They had heard from reliable sources that

I was Disorganized. Anarchist! Anticorporationist! Confuser Of The Files! Desk Messer-Upper!

I always, as a producer, sit in the orchestra pit during the show so I can watch the live action on the stage. I have a telephone connecting me with the Director in the control room, so I can tell him what is happening on the stage which he might not see from his glass cage. I also have an applause button near me which I can push, because I do have an unerring sense of when applause should start and when it should stop.

Of course, applause is best when it's spontaneous—when one brave soul in the audience decides to applaud, and then everybody else joins in. But in live television, between the audience and performer there is a forest of technical equipment and stagehands and cameramen, and sometimes the audience can't see the action clearly, so you have a sign that lights up when you push the button, and it reads: APPLAUSE.

I am very proud of the fact that when I was producing the Victor Borge special I invented the word "please." The Borge show was on CBS and they had had no applause signs up till then. When I ordered the sign, I insisted—even though it cost an extra $75—that it should read: PLEASE APPLAUD. That sign is still there, in Studio 50 on Broadway, where Ed Sullivan does his show. And to this day, every time they flash it, it is a monument to my great invention of the word "please." The NBC and ABC signs just read: APPLAUSE.

Well, Westinghouse gave me a telephone and an applause button, just like I wanted. During rehearsals I noticed that the telephone was not connected to the control room, and the applause button wasn't wired to the sign. *What I had was a toy telephone and a toy button, because, Goddamit, they were humoring me.* I told the Associate Producer to get those things hooked up right away, but by now the Associate Producer no longer felt it was necessary to associate with the Producer. So he did nothing about it, and I Adjusted. *Once you get the hang of it, Adjusting gets easier and easier.*

I was Captain Bligh, and the whole Goddam thing was a mutiny. But I hung on for dear life. I kept Adjusting, hoping that once we got on the air and Steve Allen took over his natural position as star of the show, Things Would Get Better.

During the dress rehearsal, before the taping of the first show, Steve asked for a small monitor television set on a dolly, so he could watch himself and see what the show was going to look like. By now *nobody* was listening to me except Nita and Judy, and all they would do when I said something was burst into tears and softly mutter "Poor, sweet Allan" and turn away to keep me from knowing how it pained them to See Me Like This. I ran around the theatre, asking everybody to get Steve a monitor on a dolly—but they were all gathered in little groups, having meetings to which I was not invited.

This was Steve's first rehearsal, and his first look at me as a Big Fancy Producer.

I was aware of this, but I was also Adjusting to the fact that nobody was listening to me. So I had to invent the Sherman Pre-followed Command System: If I saw them moving Camera 3 to the left, I would shout, very snappily, *"Move camera three to the left!"* When I saw them stop moving it, I quickly shouted, *"That's it, leave 'er there!"* I pointed to the little groups of mutineers and yelled, so Steve could hear, *"Okay! You guys meet in little groups!"*

Steve was impressed. I was obviously in full command of my troops.

During the rehearsal Steve said something, I don't remember what, but it was something so ridiculously funny that I literally doubled up laughing. I not only doubled up, but I experienced a muscle spasm—kind of a charley horse in my stomach—and when I was finished laughing, I couldn't undouble myself.

Well, there I was, bent over, unable to move, and after about ten or fifteen minutes people began saying to me, "Why don't you straighten up, pally-bird?" I guess They thought I *wanted* to be doubled up like that, and it was very hard to convince them otherwise. Nita and Judy cried, and one of them called my doctor, and he came to the theatre and gave me a shot of something that unbent me.

I don't know what caused the muscle spasm. It might have been nerves, and it might have been my conscience getting even with me for doing all that Adjusting. Anyway, we taped the show and I kept on Adjusting and we kept on taping shows for two weeks.

The show was to go on the air the next Monday night.

I thought it would be a good idea to make nice on everybody —to try one last time to bring about some semblance of that *esprit de corps* which you must have if a show is going to have any success.

Saturday night was June 15th—Dee and I were going to celebrate our seventeenth wedding anniversary.

So I invited everybody to a party at our house Saturday night. I invited the production staff, the cameramen, the crew, the Little Groups, Nita and Judy and Steve and Jayne. Saturday night at eight o'clock sharp.

Saturday night came, and we put out the clam dip and the potato chips, and the bartender we hired had the bar set up real nice, and the house was shiny clean. I had the stereo playing soft background music, and everything was perfect.

It was close to 8:30 when Judy (sniffling) and her boyfriend arrived. She said hello to Dee, the dog and the kids, but when she turned to me she fell apart completely, bawling like a baby.

Dee looked at Judy. "Is something wrong?" she asked.

"No," I jumped in, "Judy cries all the time."

We passed around cocktails and hors d'oeuvres, and then it

was nine o'clock. And soon it was 9:30. And then it was ten o'clock.

Our house is in a canyon toward the back of Bel Air, reached by confusing, winding, badly lit roads, and I thought, *Everybody has gotten lost.*

But I should have known.

The phone rang. It was Jayne Meadows Allen.

"Allan, darling, is the party still going on?"

"Yes."

"Steve and I will be a little late," she said.

"Okay," I said. "We'll be waiting."

We waited. We waited and drank cocktails and ate hors d'oeuvres. The beef Stroganoff congealed and the noodles sagged.

Nobody ever came. Nobody. Not Steve, not Jayne, not the cameramen or the director or the Westinghouse people. Nobody.

Once again, I should have known, but it never occurred to me. On second thought, how could I have known that the reason they didn't come to my party was that they were all having a meeting and the subject of that meeting was *me?*

About two o'clock in the morning Judy's boyfriend took her, weeping, from the house, and I, having finished all the cocktails that had been prepared for thirty people, went to bed.

It was about 7:30 that morning—Sunday—when the phone rang. I picked it up.

The operator said, "Mr. Allan Sherman, New York is calling."

I said, "*Grrbssh,*" and tried to shake myself awake.

The voice on the other end said, "Allan, this is George Wonderful." That is not his real name. He was one of the Westinghouse Junior Executives. "Did I wake you up?" he asked.

"*Skrplshom,*" I said.

"Good," he said. "Listen, Allan, They are very unhappy about your shows."

"Who?"

"*They*," he said, and he underlined it mournfully.

"Oh, *Them*," I said.

"Yes. Now you've got it," he said. "They're not happy, Allan."

"But the show hasn't been on the air yet. Why aren't they happy?"

"They don't want to go into details."

"What *do* they want?"

"They want you to resign. It'll be better all around if you resign."

"I think it'll be *worse* if I resign."

"Their minds are made up," he said. "This is firm."

"But I don't *want* to resign," I said.

"You'll resign tomorrow morning, for reasons of ill health."

"But I'm not in ill health. I'm a regular Mickey Hargitay."

"You doubled over last Monday, didn't you? That's very ill health."

"Look, George," I said. "I've been doing a lot of Adjusting, but *this* I will not Adjust to. I will not resign for reasons of ill health, because, first, I am in excellent health and, second, I don't want to tell the entire television industry that I am sick when I am *not* sick, or that I am incapable of working when I *am* capable of working."

"You're being difficult," he said. "They won't like it."

"You want to fire me, go ahead and fire me. I can't stop you."

"It's not *me*, Allan-baby."

"I know. It's *Them*."

"*They*," he said.

"*Thou*," I countered.

Now he was pleading with me. "They say you're a very sick man, so please resign for reasons of ill health, and we'll all be friends."

"I don't *want* to be friends," I said.

"What *do* you want?"

"My job," I said.

"I'm afraid that's impossible. Dwayne Marvelous will fly out to talk to you tomorrow. One o'clock, at the Polo Lounge."

"Splendid," I said, and hung up.

It was Sunday and it was eight o'clock in the morning and there was nobody I could reach to talk to or get advice from. And I sure as hell couldn't go back to sleep.

I went into the kitchen and found the automatic coffee-maker and made myself eight cups of automatic coffee.

I took out a pad of paper and wrote at the top of it: *"Positive Things I Can Do in a Situation Like This."* Then I wrote *"Number One."* In fact, I numbered the whole left side of the page. But I couldn't think of a thing.

About 9:30 I called up Perry Leff, of the Frank Cooper office, who lived near me in Bel Air. "I've gotta talk to you," I said.

"Come on over," he said.

I went. Perry was shocked at my news. He had thought everything was going along fine.

"Now, we've gotta act, and act fast," Perry said. "Here's what we do." He took out a pad of paper and numbered the left side.

"I already did that," I said, and I showed him my pad.

"Oh. Well, there must be something else we can do," Perry said. "Let's think hard."

We sat there thinking hard.

I thought of calling Nita. I got her on the phone and she was crying, but she managed to blubber out, "Allan, it's just terrible. They had a meeting last night at Steve's house. Steve was on your side. He wanted to keep you, but they wouldn't let him."

"I'll be right over," I said.

I drove out to Nita's house in the Valley. And she told me about the meetings that had been going on for weeks and how Steve had been staving off my execution as long as he could until finally they boxed him into a corner Saturday night during my party. At the time Jayne had called me, she still had hopes that Steve would win and they would be able to come to the party. But he lost.

"I better go over and talk to Steve," I said.

Jayne and Steve lived in a beautiful mountaintop house in the Valley, not far from Nita's place. I drove there.

But Steve wasn't home. All day.

The next morning I got hold of Frank Cooper, and he joined me in the Polo Lounge for lunch. Dwayne Marvelous came in at exactly one o'clock.

Frank wanted to do the talking, and I let him. Through the conversation I just sat there between them and looked from side to side, like an idiot at a ping-pong tournament.

Frank Cooper said, "Mr. Marvelous, my client feels that perhaps your decision was a bit hasty, and he would like you to reconsider."

"I'm afraid that's impossible," said Dwayne Marvelous. "This is not *my* decision."

Frank understood. He had dealt with dozens of Theys in his time.

Frank said, "There is no possibility of reconciling your differences?"

"None," said Dwayne Marvelous. "None whatsoever."

"I see," said Frank Cooper, and I could tell that Frank had given up all hope of talking me back into the job. "Of course, Allan's contract has ten weeks to run. Firm."

Marvelous said, "We are prepared to make a settlement. We are willing to pay Allan four weeks' salary as severance pay."

"Perhaps you didn't hear me," said Frank. "I said ten weeks."

"And I said *four* weeks."

Frank said, "My client feels he's been sorely damaged by your actions. He feels he was never given a chance to really produce the show. He feels he was undermined at every turn. And he tells me that your assistant, George Wonderful, asked him to resign *because of ill health*. Allan is entitled to ten weeks' pay, and that's what he's going to get."

Dwayne Marvelous picked at his lobster salad for a moment. "We will make a full settlement of ten weeks' pay," he said, "*on one condition*."

He waited for Frank to ask *what* condition, but Frank picked at his own lobster salad. The suspense was awful. All I could think of to do was pick at *my* lobster salad.

Frank Cooper and I turned out to be better lobster-salad pickers than Dwayne Marvelous. At last he spoke.

"This is the condition: that neither you nor Allan will release anything to the press about this until we have another meeting tomorrow and decide on a mutually agreeable release."

Cooper turned to me. "Is that all right with you, Allan?"

"Sure," I said, and the lunch was over.

Now, you have to understand that in our business, or in any big business, when you get fired, there is a gentlemen's agreement between you and the company that fired you that they will try to help you save face.

You write up some kind of story for the trade papers, and it doesn't say you got fired—it says you resigned to go into business by yourself, or that you are considering several other offers, or writing a novel, or *something*. That way, you aren't humiliated, and the Company Image seems less cold and brutal, and in general the whole thing is very chummy.

That's the way it's done, *always*.

So when Dwayne Marvelous asked me to promise not to release a story, he was protecting the Company Image from any nasty things I might say. And when he suggested we mutually agree on a press release, I was glad to promise him that, because I knew my face would be saved, and my face was one of the things I have been saving since birth—with the exception of the part of my nose that I gave to Dr. Becker.

So I promised, and I waited until morning.

I was on my ninth cup of black coffee in the morning when the mail came. On the front page of the *Hollywood Reporter* there was a box about two inches high and one column wide, and the headline at the top read:

SHERMAN AXED
AS PRODUCER OF ALLEN SHOW

My phone began to ring and it rang all morning. Friends of mine, people who had been in the business all their lives, were calling up to ask me how such a damaging, humiliating story could have been released and who had released it.

I didn't know who had released it. All I knew was that I was keeping my promise to wait until They and I could work out a mutually agreeable statement, but meanwhile—last night— somebody had released this.

I called Dwayne Marvelous and asked him who had released it.

He said, "I didn't release it, and neither did anyone else around here."

"But who else knew about it?"

"I haven't the vaguest idea."

"Have you tried to find out?"

"Look, Allan," he said, "we're very busy putting on a show. I haven't got time to make like a detective."

"Jesus, Dwayne—don't you know what this item will *do* to me? Don't you care?"

"I've got a long-distance call waiting," he said. "Sorry, kid."

And that was the end of it.

I had reached the bottom of the bottom of the bottom.

Reality stinks. It never was any good, I thought, *and nobody cares. Nobody gives a damn if you live or die, and every time I touch something tangible, somebody takes it away from me.*

Where are those goddam electric trains, anyway?

I hung up the phone on Dwayne Marvelous, and I went down to Sepulveda Boulevard, and I bought a new red Buick convertible with air-conditioning, power windows, power steering and white sidewall tires. On time payments.

CHAPTER 14

Pluck and Luck,

OR Welcome Home, Horatio Alger

I WAS STANDING on the beach with Dee and Robbie and Nancy and Jackson B. Sherman, and the tide was out. The tide was so far out we were sure it would never come in again.

This time I didn't play golf. This time I didn't do anything. The phone didn't ring. There was nothing in the mail but bills. I just sat there. We all just sat there.

There is a kind of rock-steadiness about Dee and Robbie and Nancy. None of them has ever asked for anything, none of them is selfish, and they all believe in me. They all know that I'm disorganized, and they don't care. They love me anyway. And that's how I feel about them. That made it even worse. Because there they were and they loved me and I loved them, and there was nothing I could do for them. Nothing.

Don't worry, kids. Daddy will take care of you. Daddy knows lots of ways of making money:

For Sale, cheap: Bel Air mansion, by family in distress.

Auction Today: Priceless Early American antiques, incl. lamps made from barber pole, kitchen-sink leg, grocery scale, English mailbox, works of Alfred, Lord Tennyson.

Or Daddy could go down to Bel Air Camera and trade *down.*

Or Daddy could search through the backyards of Beverly Hills for used magazines. Or look in the crack of the sofa for lost coins.

You kids have never tasted Kraft Dinner, have you?

That's all I had left. That, and three more months of $55 unemployment checks, and then what?

Think hard, Allan-baby. Scrounge around and see if there's anything else.

I had some crazy songs.

There was a college fraternity brother, Skippy, who was now working in the legal department at Capitol Records. I sent him my songs, and he turned them over to the Capitol A&R man. A week later I got this note:

DEAR ALLAN:
Thanks for submitting your parodies. They're very funny, but I regret to say that we don't think there's a market for this type of thing. Sorry.

I called my friend Louis Quinn and asked if he knew of anything I could do with the songs. He said he'd think.

A few days later Louis called and said, "Come out to Warner Brothers tomorrow, kid. I want you to sing your songs for the record company."

I drove out and sang "My Fair Lady" and a lot of the other things. For Mike Maitland, Joe Smith and Jimmy Hilliard. Lou Busch played the piano.

They thought the songs were funny. Mike said if it didn't cost too much, the company might take a shot with an album.

I called Bullets Durgom and told him Warner Brothers was willing to make an album and asked him if he'd talk to Mike Maitland and make the deal for me. He said okay.

He made a deal to get me a $1,500 advance. That would leave me $1,350 after I paid Bullets his 10 percent. *Whee!*

Maitland suggested that I write parodies on folk songs for the album, rather than on Broadway show tunes, because folk songs are in the public domain and so we wouldn't have any copyright problems.

I wrote day and night. I wrote in the shower and I wrote in bed and I wrote in the car on the way to the Unemployment Office.

One day I was driving home with my $55 check in my pocket and a whole song came to me in a few seconds:

> *Sarah Jackman, Sarah Jackman,*
> *How's by you? How's by you?*
> *How's by you the family?*
> *How's your sister Em'ly?*
> *She's nice, too—*
> *She's nice, too.*

> *How's your brother Bernie?*
> He's a big attorney.
> *How's your sister Doris?*
> Still with William Morris.

> *How's your Uncle Nathan?*
> Him I got no faith in.
> *How's your Cousin Ida?*
> She's a Freedom Rider.

How's your brother Bentley?
Feeling better ment'lly.
How's your cousin Seymour?
Seymour joined the Peace Corps.

I knew very well that Seymour does not rhyme with Peace Corps. But I was not writing by craftsmanship or by technical knowledge. I was writing by *feel.* And it felt good—Seymour joining the Peace Corps. It felt good to me, the way it feels good when you're standing at the crap table in Las Vegas and you know the luck is with you—you know you can't lose. I was *swinging.* Rhymes were coming into my head faster than I could write them down.

Long before you make an album, you make the album cover. The cover is a four-color printing job, and it takes much longer to process than a record does. I called the most beautiful blonde I knew, Linda Bennett, who was then married to Bill Dougherty (one of the five owners of P.J.'s), and I asked her if she would pose for the cover with me.

She said, "What do I have to do?"

I said, "You'll be flicking a chicken."

Linda said, "Don't talk dirty, Allan." Linda isn't Jewish.

I told her that "flicking" means the same as "plucking," and we took the picture.

During the last week Lou Busch came over every day and rehearsed me. On the Saturday night before we made the record we invited about twenty-five people to a dress rehearsal. They went crazy laughing. Dick Gehman, the writer, was there. He said it was the funniest thing he ever heard in his life. He asked me if he could write the liner notes. The next day he sent them over, and in them he said I was a comic genius.

On Monday night I recorded The Album.

Thursday morning I met Jimmy Hilliard and Lou Busch at Radio Recorders to do the editing. We worked in a little room less than eight feet square, filled with tape-recording machines and other electronic monsters.

That was the first time I had ever heard myself sing on a record.

God, I'm a lousy singer. Sour notes. High notes I reached for but couldn't make. Not enough breath.

But Lou Busch said it sounded alive, it sounded human, and it was funny. This was the first time he had realized that it was funny. During the month of making the arrangements, Lou had concentrated so hard on the music that he hadn't once noticed the words.

A week later we "mastered" the tape. You decide how loud the orchestra should be, how loud the singers should be, the audience and the soloist; you decide what parts of the record should have an echo sound.

After the tape is edited and mastered, they cut a disc called the "master." Then they pour melted silver over the master and make a reverse impression of each side, and those inside-out impressions of the grooves and the land—the hills between the grooves—are known as "mothers."

They went through this whole process twice, once for monaural and once for stereo. Then they sent the mothers to the manufacturing plants in Bridgeport, Indianapolis and Los Angeles.

While this was going on, Bullets Durgom called me and asked me to come down to his office. "Before the album comes out," he said, "let's decide on how much you're going to pay me, and get a contract signed."

"Sure," I said. What did he mean, decide?

"Well, you've got no agent on this deal. That would have cost you ten percent. So you just pay me his ten percent, plus my ten percent—that makes twenty percent—and everything will be nice."

There goes $300 of my $1,500, I thought.

"*How* much?" I asked.

"Twenty percent. That's all."

"Bullets, ain't you got no shame?"

If he had any, it wasn't showing. I told him I'd have to sleep on it, and I went home but I didn't sleep.

Bullets called me constantly for three or four days to get me to sign the contract. I avoided his calls whenever I could. He finally got me at nine o'clock one night and told me to meet him at the home of movie producer Joe Pasternak, about a half a mile from my house, and sign the contract immediately or the whole deal was off.

My friend Everett Sloane went with me to Pasternak's house, but before we went I typed out a single sheet of paper.

When we got there, Everett, Bullets and I sat down in Pasternak's library for a half an hour and I tried to get up the courage to tell Bullets that I thought he was asking too much money. I never did get up the courage.

Once again I became The Undersigned.

But before I signed, I handed Bullets the single sheet of paper I had typed out at my house. "You sign this first," I said. The paper had just one line written on it:

```
This will certify that I am a greedy bastard.
                                   Bullets Durgom
```

Bullets signed it with a flourish.

Warner Brothers made what they call a "reference dub" of the album. They played it for the girls in their office and the girls got hysterical. Bob Summers, their Sales Manager, took the reference dub to Chicago and played it for some people there. Dan Sorkin, the Chicago disc jockey who almost single-handedly made a star out of Bob Newhart by playing his first album over and over, listened to *My Son, the Folk Singer* and told Summers he would keep playing it until it sold a million albums.

I was so totally unknown to the record-buying public that I figured it would be a good idea to have some well-known names on the album liner. So I took a copy of the reference dub and I played it for Harpo Marx, Jack Benny, Jerry Lewis and Steve Allen. They all loved it and gave me quotes I could use on the liner. Steve liked it so much, and was so anxious to do something nice for me after the Westinghouse catastrophe, that he walked right over to his typewriter and wrote me a whole 1,000-word essay on the subject of what a thrilling humorist I was. All I wanted was a 10-word quote. I didn't have the heart to tell Steve I already had a 1,000-word essay from Dick Gehman.

I went to Ken Kim, Warner Brother's Art Director, and said, "You'll have to make the print smaller. I have *two* 1,000-word essays." Ken figured out a design that would encompass all the quotes and essays I had. In one of his typography books I found a funny little picture of a laughing bear. I told Ken to put seven of the little laughing bears on the jacket liner. Every album I have ever made shows those seven laughing bears. For luck.

I wanted to say somewhere on the liner that it was a live record made in front of a real audience. I have never used any fake laughter or applause. Robbie suggested this line: RECORDED LIVE AT A BIG EXPENSIVE HOLLYWOOD PARTY.

After that, I waited.

There is nothing you can do but wait until the record is released and you find out what people think of it.

I was standing on the beach with Dee and Robbie and Nancy and Jackson B. Sherman and the tide was out. The tide was so far out we were sure it would never come in again.

We couldn't see what was coming—what was rushing at us from the horizon.

It was a tidal wave.

It was ten thousand feet high and roaring in fast.

And not easy to keep afloat in.

CHAPTER 15

Allan in Wonderland

Octobers 7, 1962. At 7:30 in the morning the phone next to the bed rang and I picked it up.

"*Grmplsh?*" I said.

It was Frank Crow, one of the writers of *Your Surprise Package*. "Quick, turn on the radio! They're playing 'Sarah Jackman' on the radio! Bob Crane on KNX! It's a funny song, ha ha! *Quick!*"

That was how the tidal wave began.

The only radio in the house was the built-in AM-FM radio-intercom I had designed into the kitchen wall. I jumped out of bed and ran into the kitchen, hurdling over the antiques in the living room. I turned the radio on. *Son of a bitch! Static!*

"Dee! *Dee!*"

She was right on my heels, wondering what all the excitement was. "What's wrong?" she asked.

"How many for-Christ-sake kilocycles is KNX?" I shouted.

"I don't know," she said. "I'll look in the paper."

"Hurry!" I yelled. "Quick, the whole Goddam song is three minutes!" And I furiously wheeled the dials back and forth. *Nothing. Static, whistling, wailing.*

I began to pound with my fists on the magnificent brushed-aluminum face plate of the built-in AM-FM radio-intercom.

"Here it is," Dee called. "Ten-seventy."

"Good," I exclaimed. And I turned the dial knob, but I had broken it with my pounding, so I never did hear the first air play of a song from *My Son, the Folk Singer.*

But other people did.

I heard from people all over the United States about the first time they heard "Sarah Jackman" or "Oh Boy" or "My Zelda."

They would tell me: "I was driving on the freeway and I started laughing so hard I had to pull over to the side." A nurse at Memorial Hospital in New York said: "You owe me thirty-five dollars. Because of you, I had a collision on the New Jersey Turnpike." A woman in Massachusetts laughed so hard she fell and broke her leg.

And wherever they played the record, the switchboard of the radio station lit up with calls from listeners who wanted to find out who was this nut who was singing and where could they get this record?

That's what happened. People heard the record and they liked it and they wanted it. Another phenomenon: They wanted to be the first on their block to have it. They wanted to be the first to play it for their friends, and they wanted to look at their friends' faces when *they* heard it for the first time. No money had been spent to promote or publicize or advertise The Album. Harry Apostolaris, the New York distributor of Warner Brothers Records, originally ordered 100 albums. Sid Schaefer, the New York Sales Manager, talked Apostolaris into buying an extra 100.

That was on Monday. On Wednesday, Apostolaris called in for 30,000 more.

Reggie Tobin, a salesman for Warner Brothers Records, went in to see the record buyer of the White Front Discount House in the San Fernando Valley. He was trying to sell her The Album.

She said, "I never heard of this record and I never heard of Allan Sherman." Tobin gave her the hard sell and begged her to believe him. As they were discussing all this, a woman ran in like crazy and said, "Listen, I just heard something in the car. On the radio. I'm driving along and I hear things about 'Glory glory Harry Lewis and the drapes of Roth.' Have you got this crazy record? I laughed so hard I thought I'd have an accident with the car."

"I never heard of this record," the store lady said. "All right, Mr. Tobin, I'll take two albums of this Allan Sherman album, just to please you, but I'm telling you, I won't sell a copy of it."

Tobin said, "*That's* what I've been telling you—'Glory Glory Harry Lewis.' "

"*What* 'Glory Glory Harry Lewis'?"

"That's from the Allan Sherman album. That's what this woman here wants to buy."

"All right—I'll take ten. Eight mono and two stereo."

Frank Sinatra bought twenty-five records to give his friends. Sammy Davis, Jr., gave one to each of *his* friends, including Frank Sinatra. Irving Berlin bought a copy in New York and was mad for it, and he said such nice things about my abilities as a parodist that I'm too embarrassed to quote them. Ah, the hell with modesty. I'll quote them. He said I was the most ingenious and brilliant parodist in the history of songwriting. Cole Porter, who was very ill, told Carol Channing, who told me, that listening to the album had given him the biggest laughs he had had in two years. Peter O'Toole, whom I met at a party, told me: "You're the greatest man who ever lived." Anthony Newley agreed with him. I tended to agree with both of them.

Joe Smith called from Warner Brothers and said there was trouble in San Francisco. He said the San Francisco distributor had only bought 125 albums. He said none of the San Francisco disc jockeys would play The Album because they were worried about its being too ethnic, which in my case meant Jewish. He said we would have to fly up to San Francisco the next morning and "do a number" for the most important disc jockey in town, Don Sherwood of KSFO.

I asked Joe what does it mean, "do a number"?

And he said, "You know, make nice on Don Sherwood. Let him know you care enough to fly up and have breakfast with him."

So we flew up and I had breakfast with Don Sherwood at the Fairmont. We didn't say much, just hello, and he went right back to his studio and played "Sarah Jackman," and the KSFO switchboard lit up. And then the other San Francisco disc jockeys started to play cuts from The Album, and people started calling the record stores, asking for it, and two days later the San Francisco distributor ordered 6,000 albums.

I had left Los Angeles at seven in the morning and I had breakfast with Don Sherwood at nine. By 9:45 I was upstairs at KSFO, shaking hands with Jazzbo Collins and Del Courtney. And then *they* started to play the record, and then Don Graham, the promotion man, drove me across the Bay Bridge to KEWB in Oakland, a Top 40 station, and I shook hands over there—not only with the disc jockeys but with the Record Librarian and the Manager. And they put "Sarah Jackman" on their play list and made a cartridge tape of it.

And then Don drove me to the San Francisco Chronicle Building and I had an interview with Herb Caen and another interview with Ralph Gleason.

Don Graham pointed out another disc jockey, at another radio station, who was sitting in the usual little glass cage and talking as they usually do, but nobody was listening to him. He was talking into a dead mike. The reason was that this disc jockey had a love affair with one of his listeners and she became pregnant and she called up the station and told all and they asked him to resign and he refused to resign and insisted on playing out his contract. And so for months he had been sitting there every day, in his little glass cage, playing his records for five hours, making clever remarks in between, and not a soul heard a sound of all this. When he saw me through the glass, he came running out and said he was glad to meet me and he loved The Album and he was plugging "Sarah Jackman" three or four times a day. It made me very sad, and I asked Don Graham to take me some place where I could get a Scotch right away.

At first I only used the Scotch to flavor the seltzer. Then I left out the seltzer altogether and only retained the ice cubes with the Scotch. Today, I am proud to say, I have emancipated myself from all such crutches. I drink my Scotch straight.

By now it was three o'clock in the afternoon, and Don took me to meet Bill Gavin. Bill Gavin puts out a weekly four-page mimeographed tip sheet called *Bill Gavin's Record Report,* and all the Top 40 stations and all the record companies buy it for $120 a year. Gavin handicaps records the way they handicap horses in the *Racing Form.* So I expected to meet a sharp character in a raw-silk Italian suit, wearing pointed shoes and a slim tie. A swinger. But I found him to be a tall and dignified man, simple of manner and for all the world like a rugged, square, down-to-earth Iowa farmer, and his wife is a fine, upstanding, respectable woman. All day long they listen to records, making the decisions, "This will be a hit," "This will not be a hit," and this $800 million industry accepts their judgments as infallible.

Mr. and Mrs. Gavin found me to be a clean, wholesome person, which I certainly am, and they listened to The Album and had a chuckle out of it, and then they gave it a nice review and advised deejays to program it even though it was an album, not a single. And they picked "Sarah Jackman" as a "sure winner."

Every rock 'n' roll station in the United States began to play The Album after that.

More disc jockeys and more newspapers, and now they took me to shake hands with the distributor and with some people who own record stores, and they were bringing me Cokes to keep me awake, and at one the next morning they took me to the hungry i and I went on the *Les Crane Show* and answered phone calls.

And a Mexican lady called up and said she thought "Sarah Jackman" was very funny—it reminded her of *her* family. And Enrico Banducci, who owns the hungry i, offered me a contract to play there. And while he was offering it, I got a phone call from the man who owned the Purple Onion, offering me a contract to play *there*.

Lewis Carroll said that in a wonderland you have to run very fast to stay where you are, and so at four that morning I ran very fast to the San Francisco airport and took a jet back to Los Angeles, which is where I was in the first place.

Radio stations began complaining to Warner Brothers: their library copies of The Album were being stolen. It became the most stolen album in history, and Warner Brothers had to give out an extra 5,000 free copies.

The phrase "My Son, the Folk Singer" became a part of the American language. *Time* Magazine did a story on Rose Kennedy called "My Son, the President." El Al Airlines took a full-page ad in *The New York Times* under the headline MY SON, THE PILOT. *Playboy* published a cartoon quoting Whistler's mother: "My Son, the Painter." A Greenwich Village avant-garde magazine called *The Realist* published a drawing of the

Virgin Mary and the Christ Child, with the caption, "My Son, the Saviour."

A graduate student at Harvard wrote his Ph.D. thesis on "The Sociological Implications of the Success of Allan Sherman's *My Son, the Folk Singer*." He said that all over America people were expressing their secret wish to be Jewish. *Won't that be news to the New York Athletic Club?* I thought.

The first week, Warner Brothers sold 65,000 albums. I figured it out. *Without lifting a finger, I had made $23,000 in one week*. And the week before, I had been on the Unemployment line. Lou Busch calls this "pillow money." While you are sleeping with your adorable head nestling on your pillow, someone, somewhere in the world, is buying The Album, and you are making 26 cents.

Sam Goody's record shop in New York put up a sign next to my album. LIMIT: 12 TO A CUSTOMER. Everybody was buying five or ten or twenty. People were sending them to each other in the mail. I heard of a dozen cases where Jones mailed one to Smith and at the same time Smith was mailing one to Jones.

In California, there was such a shortage of album covers that the records were sold in plain sleeves for ten days. The customer received a little ticket entitling him to an album cover when they were in stock again.

Billboard, the record-industry trade paper, carried a picture of me on the cover and said I had saved the recording industry.

The vocal coach of Warner Brothers Pictures offered to give me singing lessons and teach me how to use my voice properly. Mike Maitland, the president of the record company, said, "Don't you dare! If he learns how to sing, it'll ruin his career."

Ed Sullivan called me at home and asked me to go on his show and sing "Sarah Jackman" and I said no. I was too scared. So he hired the comedy team of Norman and Dean, to do a pantomime to the record. Sullivan must have liked it, because he called me again. And I said no again. So he hired Rowan and Martin and had them do a pantomime to "Sir Greenbaum's Madrigal."

Joe Hyams, the columnist, interviewed me at the Polo Lounge. "How does it feel to be a success?"

"When did I become a success?" I asked him. *"Is it definite? Is it permanent? When was it? Was it when the hundred thousandth album was sold? The two hundred thousandth? When did I change into a success? What is different about me?"*

A man named *Allen* Sherman called me from Beverly Hills.

"For God's sake!" he said. "What are you doing to me? I'm getting calls in the middle of the night from people who want me to go sing Jewish songs in Philadelphia. And I'm not Jewish!"

The Jack Paar Show called. I said no.

Joe Smith, the Promotion Manager of Warner Brothers Records, called and said they were erecting a statue of me in Lincoln Park in Chicago.

The Boston promotion man called. "Sales of John O'Hara's books have quadrupled in Boston," he said. He was referring to the lines from "Sarah Jackman":

> Whatcha doing, Sarah?
> Reading John O'Hara.

My friend Marshall Migatz called from Chicago. "Allan! You're a status symbol! Nobody's allowed into the London House for lunch unless they're carrying a copy of your album."

Dee went to Bullock's Westwood to buy some socks for the kids. She gave the lady her charge-a-plate.

"Is your husband *the* Allan Sherman?" the clerk asked.

"I guess so," Dee said.

"You're not sure?" the lady said.

"Well, there is one in Beverly Hills, but he's not Jewish."

"Oh—the one I mean is *definitely* Jewish. Girls! Girls! You know who this lady is? She's the one with the crazy husband who sings about Zelda!"

Record companies have what they call a BPI. It means Buying Power Index. Each city accounts for a certain percentage of the total sales of a record or album. It is not directly related to population. People in San Francisco buy 4.7 percent of all albums made. Houston has a greater population than San Francisco, but Houston people buy only 1.2 percent of all albums. Dallas is just a little over half as big as Houston, but people in Dallas buy three times as many albums.

With *My Son, the Folk Singer,* Warner Brothers figured they would be dealing with a special audience. So they spent $5,000 to have a special survey made—a Jewish BPI. They very carefully determined where the Jews live in the United States so they could concentrate on those places.

Then one day Bob Summers, the Sales Manager, called me. "We just sold 500 records in La Jolla!" he said.

La Jolla, California, is restricted. Jews don't live there.

So they threw out the Jewish BPI.

Jim Backus' wife, Henny, called up. "I just got a letter from my brother. He's a scientist at the Chaim Weizmann Institute in Israel. He just heard your record on a disc-jockey show there."

Jim got on the phone and said, "In your honor, Allan, the people of Israel are planting a tree in Beverly Hills!"

John David Griffin, columnist of the New York *Mirror,* called Bullets Durgom. "I just got back from the Carlyle Hotel. President Kennedy just walked through the lobby singing 'Sarah Jackman.' *Honest!*"

I received a letter from Newton N. Minow, head of the Federal Communications Commission, the man who had dubbed television a "Vast Wasteland." (I had never met him.) It read:

DEAR ALLAN,

I just heard your record. It is hilarious! Do you mind if my whole family starts a fan club?

NEWTON N. MINOW

P.S. Why aren't you in television?

Now he asks me. After I labored in the Wasteland for seventeen years.

Then came a letter from the Wasteland:

DEAR AL,

Your songs are magnificent. You are a genius.

MARK GOODSON

I liked that note. I saved it. Mark Goodson had made nice on me.

Garry Moore called. Would I come on his show in early January?

I said to Garry, "I get too nervous. I'm not a performer."

Garry said, "Don't worry about it. We'll make it easy for you."

I said, "Okay. I'll be delighted." And so Garry Moore made nice on me, too.

Steve Allen had made nice a month before when he wrote the liner notes for The Album.

In four weeks The Album sold 575,000 copies.

One night I was driving the Buick to P.J.'s when I finally heard one of my own records on the radio for the first time. It was "My Zelda," being played on KMPC by Gary Owens, and I laughed and I laughed and I laughed.

Mike Maitland called to ask if I would have lunch with Jack L. Warner and accept a Gold Album on Friday. You don't have to sell a million albums to get a Gold Album—you have to sell one million dollars' worth of albums at the wholesale price.

* * *

The Album was selling like hot cakes everywhere in the United States except Palm Springs, California. They didn't sell a single album in Palm Springs, because Bullets Durgom has a house there and Bullets is a charming, adorable fellow and he got a bunch of free albums from Warner Brothers and went down to Palm Springs and gave everybody who lives in Palm Springs a free album as a personal gift from Bullets Durgom.

A friend called and wanted to borrow money. We had been friends for twelve years and he never asked before. Now I knew I was a big success.

They flew me to Chicago for publicity and promotion. And I was in a state of shock. I was drinking two bottles of Scotch every day. I couldn't sleep. Or eat. Going going going from nine in the morning until six the following morning. "Making the scene," they call it. Interviews. Interviews. The Irv Kupcinet Show. The Jack Eigen Show. The Tony Weitzel Show. The Dan Sorkin Show. The newspapers. Shaking hands with the record dealers. Talking to deejays. Interviews. Autographs. *My Aunt Kate is in the autograph line with a pot of chicken soup.* Making the rounds of the clubs. Tweaking bunny tails in the Playboy Club. I'm a Celebrity. *Wheee!*

I was already writing my next record, *My Son, the Celebrity,* to be released in December and sell hundreds of thousands of copies. But now I got those terrible depressions. And muscle spasms. I was in a whirling madness.

Nothing in my life had prepared me for the insane success in which I suddenly found myself. You look forward to it all your life and when it comes it comes as a shock.

The Album was over one million. It was the fastest-selling album in history.

Hello, Horatio Alger. You were right all the time. I shouldn't have lost faith in you, Horatio-baby. Ragged Dick, Phil the Fiddler, Honest Harry the Newsboy—roll them all up together and put them in a long-playing album of parodies and you've got Allan Sherman in person, now playing with exhaustion, tension, insomnia, pains in the heart, spasms in the stomach.

Look, there is Allan. See him. See the Celebrity. Run, Allan, Run. Say something funny. See the Celebrity drinking Elixir of Alurate. He is drinking it for his nerves. He is having a nervous breakdown. He is a silly Celebrity. Now he is drinking a glass of whiskey from Scotland. Scotland is a nice country. The people there wear kilts. They play bagpipes in the backyard every Sunday. They make whiskey out of malted barley. Horatio, Horatio, you made the pains too long.

I went to Dr. Newman. "Battle fatigue," he said.

He sent me to bed. From bed I ordered a gold Lincoln to prove I was rich and successful. Dr. Newman said I mustn't drive it. I had to stay in bed and have complete rest and peace of mind.

Then came the lawsuits. I learned that being sued is part of the Complete Success Kit.

I had never read a recording contract before. Now I read mine. In the charming, adorable contract that Bullets negotiated for me with Warner Brothers, it says in print too small for even Bullets to read that I "indemnify Warner Brothers against all lawsuits."

Two of the most popular songs from *My Son, the Folk Singer* were "My Zelda"—a parody of "Matilda"—and "Seltzer Boy" —a parody of "Water Boy."

"My Zelda" went:

> *My Zelda! My Zelda!*
> *My Zelda, she took the money and ran with the tailor!*
> *Once again now!*
>
> *My Zelda! My Zelda!*
> *My Zelda, she took the money and ran with the tailor!*

My Zelda, she found her big romance
When I broke the zipper on my pants—
My Zelda, she took the money and ran with the tailor!

It turned out that "Matilda" was in copyright and its composer was living in Jamaica or Trinidad or some place, name of
Lord Something-or-Other, and he was a professional Calypso
composer and he wanted money. I paid.

Now, you would be willing to bet your life that "Water Boy"
was written maybe by a prisoner on a Georgia chain gang,
maybe by a cotton picker working on a Mississippi plantation.
So I figured who would care if I turned it into:

Seltzer boy—where are you hiding?
If you don't come right now,
I'm gonn' tell you' boss on you.
Oi.

Don't bring me water.
I'd rather have seltzer,
'Cause water don't bubble,
And water don't fizz.

Water, I hate it,
'Cause it ain't carbonated.
But a glass of seltzer,
On the other hand, is.

Don't bring me Pepsi,
Don't bring me a Kool-Aid,
Don't bring me a malted,
Don't bring me champagne . . .

I'll tell you what, boy,
Bring me one Scotch and soda,

> *Then you'll take back the Scotch, boy,*
> *And leave the 2 cents plain . . .*

But the music publishers Boosey & Hawkes filed an action in New York Federal Court in which they pointed out that, far from being an anonymous folk song, "Water Boy" had been copyrighted in 1922 by its author, a gentleman named Robinson, and Boosey & Hawkes didn't like I should make a "Water Boy" into a "Seltzer Boy."

When you have lawsuits, you need Lawyers.

I had Lawyers. By the time six weeks had passed, I had a myriad Lawyers and assorted Managers and multitudinous Agents and miscellaneous Advisers and I was a Corporation.

Robbie began to call me "Starfather."

Was he trying to tell me something?

CHAPTER 16

Now He Belongs to the Agents

I N The Old Man and the Sea, Ernest Hemingway wrote about this old man who all his life had wanted to catch a certain marlin, and finally he catches it, but before he can get it home, all the creatures of the sea come and each one takes a bite out of the marlin, and when the Old Man finally gets home with his prize, there is no prize left. Just the bones of a marlin.

I think Ernest Hemingway was trying to tell me something, too.

From the moment I began to Smell Sweet Like Success, I found out I had a new hobby: people-collecting.

First there were Agents. I still had the Frank Cooper Agency to handle me as a producer and writer. (Of course, in show business you get pigeonholed—you get typed—and so, after eighteen years of producing and writing, nobody would have given me a job as a producer or writer because that isn't what I was any more. Now I was a comedian.)

To handle my career as a comedian, Bullets found me a bunch of agents who called themselves UTM (United Talent Management). They had banded together and formed this agency when the Government put MCA out of business. Bullets chose UTM because they agreed to take five percent commission rather than the usual ten percent. The other five percent they agreed to give to Bullets.

The UTM people were nice, but it was a brand-new agency and, to quote Mark Goodson, "disorganized and chaotic."

Before long, UTM merged with GAC (General Artists' Corporation) and I had literally *hundreds* of agents.

Bullets found me a Public Relations Counselor, because a star needs public relations or else nobody will know he's a star except his private relations. He made a deal for me with a company called Arthur Jacobs. It wasn't long before Arthur Jacobs went out of business. Before it did, it sold me. (*Look, Ma, I'm a liquid asset.*) Jacobs sold me to a company named Rogers and Cowan. I paid them $5,000 for six months, plus a large amount of money for expenses. They got me a lot of nice items in the Hollywood trade papers and several interviews with columnists, and while I was with them, there was a magnificent two-part story in *TV Guide* about Bullets Durgom.

My lawyers were Mortimer Becker and Jack London, who were left over from my years of poverty. I stayed with them because I think they're marvelous and also because if I left them I would have to let Bullets find me a lawyer.

Of course Bullets Durgom and his New York partner, Ray Katz, were my Personal Managers. The function of a Personal Manager, as they explained it to me, is to take 15 percent of your gross receipts, and at this point they stopped explaining it to me. (The 20 percent applied only to my recording contract.)

Lou Busch became my Musical Conductor.

Nita Archambeau left the *Steve Allen Show* and became my Secretary, because I now had all kinds of press clippings to be clipped and fan letters to answer.

There is a nice Cupid story coming in the next chapter with Lou and Nita. Oh, hell, I can't wait for the next chapter. Lou and Nita met at my house and fell madly in love and got married and I lost a damn good secretary and Lou gained the best wife he ever had.

I acquired Marvin Tabolsky as my Road Manager. A Road Manager is a person who goes out on the road with you and makes sure that everything is where it is supposed to be, and he is supposed to tell you how great you were after every show, although I insisted that Marvin refrain from being a yes-man, and he never was. Nice, young, good-looking Marvin Tabolsky. Every time he picked up the phone, he would say his name. And then you would hear him spell out, "T-a-b-o-l-s-k-y." Nobody in the world except Marvin knows how to spell Tabolsky. Lou Busch kept urging him to change his name to Merwin Taber, but I thought it would be more high class if Marvin named himself after one of the fancy Los Angeles suburbs, Brentwood. For a while there, we all called him Brentwood Tabolsky. Marvin got sick and tired of spelling his last name to people on the telephone, and one day he announced to me that he was going to change it to his mother's maiden name, BENNETT. He made the change just before I played the Fairmont Hotel in San Francisco.

Opening day at the Fairmont, we decided to rent a car, and Marvin called the Hertz people.

I heard him say: "Hello? This is Marvin Bennett. What? Sure. B-e-n-n—to hell with it. This is Marvin Tabolsky."

It was a completely new Cast of Characters, featuring Record Promotion men and Disc Jockeys and Record Distributors and a Custom Tailor and a Music Librarian and Many Others. The Complete Star Kit.

My lawyers helped me to find a Business Manager. Part of the Complete Star Kit is to have a Business Manager.

There are lots of Business Managers in New York and Hollywood. They handle the money made by performers. Most performers have been very poor at one time, and the lucky ones are suddenly raking in large amounts of money and we don't know what to do with this money. So you get a Business Manager and he puts you on a budget and invests your money wisely.

I went around and scrutinized many Business Managers. I finally picked the one who was the wisest-looking, Colonel Alexander Tucker. He has a wise gray mustache, and I'm positive his bellybutton is indented.

Business Managers have a marvelous language which they use on you. They talk about "tax-shelters," "reversible mortgage debentures," "capital gains," "capital losses" (which turn out to be just as good), "deductible investments," "hard dollars," "soft dollars." *They know you don't know what the hell they're talking about, but you have to nod your head and agree with them so you won't look like a Goddam moron in front of them.*

They all have marvelous theories of how they're going to make you as rich as Rockefeller, and I could never understand any of those theories. Some believe in common stocks, and when Wall Street prices are going up, they're geniuses; if the stock market is going down, they blame it on you. Some of them believe in oil. Some believe in undeveloped real estate. Some in bonds and convertible debentures. Some in hotels and motels and buildings. Some in cattle. Some in precious metals.

I would have liked to own a delicatessen store, where I could drive by with a friend I wished to impress and say proudly, "That's *my* delicatessen. You see that customer buying a corned-beef sandwich? He's giving me two and five-eighths cents profit."

But Colonel Tucker said, "We're going to put you into cattle."

I liked that.

I could picture it. Tex Sherman.

Beautiful.

Maybe my own brand burned on the steers? *The "Big S" Ranch.* Oh, boy, I went for that.

So I pictured those cows and bulls and steers, and I imagined myself producing the nation's meat, milk, leather and shoes.

But that isn't exactly how it works.

How it works is, you buy the cattle, and you borrow money from a bank, and you use this money to feed the cattle, and then the cattle have calves and you have more cattle, and so you borrow more money to feed *them,* and at the end of three or four years you have lots more cattle than you started with, and you sell them.

I asked, "At what point do we milk these cows to slake the thirsty babies of America?"

And Tucker said, "Oh, we don't do that."

So I said, "Well, then, at what point do we skin them and use the leather to help shoe the unshod citizens of this country?"

And Tucker replied, "We don't do that either."

"All right," I went on, "then tell me when we send my cattle to the slaughterhouse so that we may provide nutritious meat for the growing numbers of hungry Americans."

He was silent for a moment. Then he shook his head sadly. "We don't do that *either,*" he said.

"In that case," I asked, "who buys these cattle? And for what?"

"Somebody else who is also in show business buys the cattle. And he breeds those cattle and *he* gets more cattle, and then he sells *them* all to someone else who is in show business."

A cow is supposed to be a cow, but to a Business Manager a cow is nothing but a grazing and mooing tax shelter.

"But wait a minute," I asked my Business Adviser, "what happens when these poor bulls and cows grow old and die?"

He smiled. "Ah, that's fine—then they are *deductible!*"
I still don't understand the whole business.

Sometimes late at night I worry about my cattle. Who's minding them? Are they getting enough to eat? Are they being taken care of properly? Have they been left out in the rain all night?

Is anyone making nice on them?

Nice cow, nice bull. Why don't you two go to a movie? I'll sit with the calves.

CHAPTER 17

I'll Never Forget
What's-His-Name
OR How It Feels to Be a Thrilling
Celebrity

Y ou've got to *run very fast to stay where you are, Lewis Carroll said.*

I wrote the songs for my second album in three weeks. Lou Busch and I drove down to Palm Springs in my gorgeous new gold Lincoln. In the back seat we had a piano, an electric piano Steve Allen had loaned me. We worked and slept at Bullets Durgom's house.

One night I had dinner with my new fans Frank Sinatra and Porfirio Rubirosa. *Together at last—the three Great Lovers of our time.* Frank and Porfirio taught me all about drinking fancy wines (you feel the cork to make sure it's damp), and they had me drinking Chateau La Fitte 1947 (the odd-numbered years are the most amusing), and I drank it like it was water. And that night I was sick all over Bullets Durgom's bedroom, hall and bathroom.

He only charged me $65 for having the rooms painted over. *Of all the money I have paid Bullets, I enjoyed that $65 the most.*

It was clear by now that nobody was going to hire me as a producer or writer, so I said to hell with it, I'll be a comedian, if that's what they want. That was certainly what all my agents and managers wanted.

I made up my mind when Bullets called me and said, "You want to play Carnegie Hall?"

Jesus! I thought.

I mean, my whole career as a performer had been one big ridiculous joke which the whole world had been going along with, and now for me to play Carnegie Hall—that I couldn't resist.

So I said okay. Bullets booked me into Carnegie Hall for December 28, 1962. In two days the performance sold out, so they booked another concert for December 31st, New Year's Eve.

Everybody told me that I needed an act. I needed a choreographer to stage an act for me. Thrilling movements. Fancy lighting. Maybe scenery.

Bullets Durgom took me to Nick Castle, a famous choreographer and routiner of night-club acts. A very fine fellow. He listened to my problems and told me that for $10,000 he'd choreograph me a beautiful act—it would be an honor for Carnegie Hall to feature me there. I said the hell with it. At those prices, I could choreograph my own act. And I did.

The only choreography I have in my act is where I walk about ten feet, from stage right to stage left. Then I say, "You may be wondering why I went from over there to over here.

Well, that was choreography."

I did this at a banquet in honor of President Johnson. Ambassador Adlai Stevenson told me it was the best definition of choreography he had ever heard.

Still, I had to do *something*. I couldn't just stand there in front of an audience like a big fat *shloomp,* and read lyrics from a piece of paper.

So I went to Steve Allen and Jayne Meadows and I said, "Help me with an act. I can't just stand there. I've got to move around and do something."

Steve suggested that I do an impersonation of Judy Garland singing "Over the Rainbow," sitting on the edge of the stage, with my feet dangling over. He even suggested calling the parody "Overweight." So I wrote:

> *Somewhere, overweight people,*
> *Just like me,*
> *Must have someplace where folks don't count*
> *   every calorie. . . .*
>
> *Somewhere, over the rainbow,*
> *Way up tall,*
> *There's a land where they've never heard of*
> *   cholesterol.*
>
> *Where folks can eat just what they want*
> *And still be trim and slim and gaunt,*
> *You'll find me—*
> *Where every little thing I taste*
> *Won't wind up showing on my waist,*
> *Or worse—behind me.*
>
> *Somewhere, overindulging is divine. . . .*
> *If their waistlines aren't bulging,*
> *Why then, oh why does mine?*

> If bluebirds weighed as much as I
> You'd see some big fat bluebirds in the sky.

We put Jackson in the sexy Hollywood kennel, and on December 18th Dee and Robbie and Nancy and Lou Busch and I flew to New York.

It was icy cold and they ran me around to all the disc jockeys and the offices of *Billboard* and *Cashbox*. I went to all their office Christmas parties. *It was icy cold, but I was hot hot hot.*

There were a few frantic days of rehearsing the show with Lou Busch and the musicians and the New Christy Minstrels.

On Wednesday morning a chartered bus pulled up in a sleet storm and twenty-five of us piled into it. Bullets counted the heads and decided that everybody was there, and we drove off for Hartford, Connecticut.

My name was painted in letters two feet high across the side of the bus. I looked out the window and saw people noticing my name and heard them saying, "Who the hell is that?"

On that bus I realized what it means to be a star. To those associated with him, a star is a gold mine, an oil well, a cornucopia, a bird that lays plutonium eggs.

In the bus were Durgom and Katz and my Concert Manager, Felix Gerstman. Felix, in his best continental-impresario manner, would ask me how my throat was feeling. Durgom and Katz would tell me to relax—all the time they told me to relax. This made me nervous; sweat was pouring out of me. Bullets Durgom had a supply of towels, and he was continually drying me as I was sweating. I was smoking a cigarette. Some ashes dropped on my hand. Ray Katz at once sprang up and got another towel and wiped off the ashes.

I figured out it was costing me about $800 a night to get myself wiped.

* * *

273

Wednesday, December 26, 1962.

Eight-thirty of a freezing evening in Hartford, Connecticut.

There was a music stand on the stage of Bushnell Auditorium with all my lyrics on it, because I was afraid I'd forget them. I was shaking all over. And everybody kept telling me not to worry, which made me shake twice as hard.

The stage was dark except for a pin spotlight which focused on a small white modern table on which there stood a lone seltzer bottle. There was a tympani drum roll.

And then, from a tape recording, the voice of Jack Benny: "Ladies and Gentlemen, I've been asked to introduce a young man who *was* a good friend of mine until a couple of months ago, when he ventured into the recording business and became an overnight sensation and made a lot of money. Well, if he prefers success and money to my friendship—you can have him. And here he is, Allan Sherman."

I walked onto the stage and cleared my throat, and for the first fifteen minutes I couldn't hear what I was saying, I was in such a state of sheer terror.

I opened my act with these words:

"Hello. Before I begin, I'd better explain why I look different tonight from the way I really look. You see, in real life I am six foot two and a quarter. And I look exactly like Cary Grant. That's what's causing all the confusion—not just for him but for me. He's got all these girls following him around Hollywood thinking that he's me. Oh Boy—that's a joke on them. Anyway, with the kind of material I do, looking like Cary Grant is not the proper image. So I hired these publicity people—they work on your image—and they decided I ought to look short and fat and wear glasses. So I'm trying it out for the month of December, and if it works I'll keep it in the act."

A few weeks later in San Francisco the jazz pianist and composer George Shearing came to my concert. Shearing is blind.

Afterward he came backstage. He ran his fingers over my face and stomach.

"You don't look like Cary Grant," he said.

"How do you know?" I asked.

"I felt Cary Grant last week," he said.

That first night in Hartford I also did "Somewhere Overweight People," sitting on the edge of the stage. When I finished, I discovered I couldn't climb back. I was simply too fat. So I jumped down and ran along the first row of the orchestra and entered the backstage through a side door. This got such screams that I kept it in the act. I'd purposely run through the theatre as the band played "Stars and Stripes Forever." (*In Cincinnati, when I got to the side door, it was locked. So I ran up the aisle and went outside and tried to get in through the stage door, and the stage doorman didn't recognize me and wouldn't let me in to play my own show.*)

Thank God eleven o'clock finally came and it was over—that first time was over—and we piled in the bus and Bullets counted us and we drove north through the snow to Boston.

Thursday, December 27th. Symphony Hall in Boston.

I was standing backstage, waiting to go on, when I heard three thousand people give out with as big a laugh as I've ever encountered. I didn't know what had caused it till after the show was over, when Lou Busch told me. The tympani player had raised his arm in readiness and, on Lou's downbeat, had brought the drumstick down so hard that it went right through the skin of the drum, and the momentum and shock caused the drummer to fall into the tympani after it.

Friday, December 28th. Carnegie Hall.

Carnegie Hall is a beautiful and elegant place, and when you walk out on that stage, no matter how much of a smart alec you may be, you are awed. You look out at those chandeliers and red velvet seats and that New York audience, and you say to yourself, *This must be the place, this is it, this is Carnegie Hall.*

There was a newspaper strike going on in New York, so I opened the Carnegie Hall show with a parody on "Just In Time":

> *Just the* Times . . .
> *I miss* The New York Times . . .
> *You just can't get the* Times *around my block* . . .
> *No one knows*
> *If Taubman liked the shows*
> *Or what James Reston thinks of Arthur Krock* . . .

Mark Goodson was in a center-aisle seat in the front row, ten feet away from me.

I better not forget my words. I better not do anything disorganized. Jesus!

That week in New York, on the *Garry Moore Show*, I sang "Sarah Jackman" and a medley of little rags and tags from songs (which I call "Shticks of One and a Half-Dozen of the Other") and for about six minutes of singing I got $7,500. *Wheee!*

I developed throat trouble. I do not sing as a real singer sings. Also, I was under such psychological tension from all this stardom that I developed a terrible laryngitis between December 28th and New Year's Eve.

Felix Gerstman sent me to a Dr. Burkhart, who takes care of opera singers and cures the sick throats of Carnegie Hall. Dr. Burkhart told me there was some kind of inflammation of my vocal cords. He rubbed me on the outside and he sprayed me on the inside. He massaged my throat with an ultrasonic device. He gave me a massive injection of Vitamin B_{12} for my nerves.

He prescribed a nasal spray. He said not to drink alcohol during my concert tour. (*Fool!*) He said to suck on a tablet called Vocalzone if I felt trouble in my throat. (*I did. They make your tongue turn navy blue.*)

Dr. Burkhart advised me to "sing like you eat." He told me to chew my notes, and he gave me a chewing musical exercise which called for me to sing *"yumyumyum"* over and over while making chewing motions with my mouth. I practiced it all the time. I began doing it so much it became second nature to make *yumyumyumyumyumyumyumyumyumyum* wherever I was and whatever I was doing. I was sitting in the Stage Delicatessen late one night, and the joint was crowded with customers eating corned beef and sipping Dr. Brown's Celery Tonic. Unconsciously I started doing the *yumyumyumyum* and making the chewing motions, and Max Asnas, the proprietor of the Stage, came over and slapped me on the back and said I was the most enthusiastic customer the place had ever had.

I haven't been allowed to pay for anything at the Stage Delicatessen since. I am the perpetual free-loading guest of Max and his brother Hymie.

So I dedicated to them this quatrain from "Shticks":

> *Do not make a stingy sandwich;*
> *Pile the cold cuts high!*
> *Customers should see salami*
> *Comin' thru the rye.*

When I got to Cleveland, I was the subject of the most indepth radio interview I've ever heard of. As I walked into the theatre, the interviewer told his audience, "Here comes Allan Sherman, walking through the stage door." Then I said, "Hello." He explained, "Folks, that was Allan Sherman saying hello." Then he asked me all of the usual questions about my early life and career, and I thought we were finished. But he remained in the dressing room, and when I told him I had to start getting dressed, he said to his audience, "Now Allan Sherman is going to get dressed." He gave them a blow-by-blow report of how I took off my slacks and put on the trousers of my tuxedo, how I tied my bow tie, what kind of cologne I put on, and even my going to the bathroom. Thousands of Clevelanders will remember hearing the toilet flushing.

Another "shtick" in my medley was based on the old folk song "Mary Ann":

> *All day, all night—Cary Grant.*
> *That's all I hear from my wife—Cary Grant.*
> *What can he do that I can't?*
> *Big deal! Big star!—Cary Grant!*

After the first week of the tour, Bullets went back to Palm Springs. You can't blame him. It was 15 below zero in Buffalo, 22 below in Toronto, 18 below in Montreal. There was no chance of my sweating in that weather.

There are certain basic problems that face all performers on the road—be they Jascha Heifetz, Vladimir Horowitz or me.

Laundry, for example. The first thing you do when you get into a hotel is attend to your laundry. I checked into the Sheraton-Rochester Hotel and was being interviewed by two reporters and a TV cameraman when a bellhop came up to get the laundry.

I stopped everything and told the bellman, "I must have this back tomorrow because I'm leaving town."

"Yes, sir!" said the bellhop, taking the laundry bag.

The next day came and I sent Marvin Tabolsky to get the laundry and pack it in my suitcases. When Marvin returned, he handed me the *same bag of dirty laundry*. When I had said, "*I must have this back by tomorrow*, the bellhop had taken it *literally*. The hotel figured I gave it to them for safekeeping, so they kept my dirty laundry and returned it safely.

When I played Chicago, Marshall Migatz, my old fraternity brother, booked me a suite in the Ambassador East Hotel. It was named the George Raft Suite. I checked in there in the late afternoon, tired because we had been riding all day and I hadn't slept for several nights. I took off my clothes and lay down to sleep.

Suddenly I heard a terrible crackling noise like a machine gun. I called Migatz and told him that even if I was in the George Raft Suite, I didn't need machine-gun fire. He called the manager, who said it was a drilling machine remodeling a nearby room. "How did we know Mr. Sherman goes to sleep at four o'clock in the afternoon?" the manager said. But he agreed to change my suite.

Being too tired to get dressed again, I threw a bathrobe over my weary carcass and trudged down the hall, into an elevator and off on another floor, where I entered the Jean Harlow Suite. This was also a beautiful suite, decorated entirely in white. Gorgeous. Over the bed was a modernistic Bronx Renaissance chandelier hanging from the ceiling by a fixed brass pipe. I lay down, and before I closed my eyes I looked at the lamp. It was a few inches above my nose. I realized that if I awoke with a start (and lately I had been awakening with a start) I would bang my head on this light. I was so worried about this that I couldn't sleep.

"Marshall," I said, "I hate to do this—but you've got to get me another suite."

So we went on safari again—Migatz, my naked self, eight pieces of luggage and the bearers. When we got into the crowded elevator, I could hear people whispering, "*Must be some kind of maharajah.*" We went to another floor, and finally they put me in the Greta Garbo Suite, all soft blues and grays and quiet, and without any dangerous light fixtures over the bed.

Later the manager said to Migatz, "I've taken care of many

stars in my career, but your client is the most temperamental. Three suites in one day—well, I must say, really. . . ."

After Dee and the kids returned to California, I called home every night. One night I called and a man answered. O *faithless wife! O infidel of infidels!* Then I realized what had happened. While I was away, Robbie's voice had changed.

After two months, when I finally got home, I rushed to Colonel Tucker's office to find out how rich I was.

"Let's see," he said, "on this tour you grossed a total of $321,419.55."

"Splendid!" I said. "Call my stockbroker and my tailor and the Rolls-Royce factory—"

"For commissions you disbursed a total of $89,962. The bus cost you 65 cents a mile times 12,906 miles. The posters and handbills cost you $100 per concert. The orchestra was $3,354 a week. The singers were $2,500. Hotels, meals, gratuities, laundry and cleaning, telephone and telegrams—"

"Never mind the insignificant details, Alex," I said, lighting a dollar cigar from his humidor. "I realize I am rich, but how rich am I?"

"As of this morning," he said, "and remember we haven't paid any State or Federal Income Tax yet—you have a grand total of $281.42."

When I got home, Bullets Durgom had called, all excited. He had talked Dave Zeitlin of *Life* Magazine into doing a "Life Goes to a Party" feature at my house. All I had to do was give a party and sing my songs. They would take pictures and write nice things about me, and millions of Americans would read about me the next Tuesday and for God knows how long after that in barbershops and dentists' reception rooms.

"Strangely enough," I said, "my brother-in-law Alex and his

wife Shirlee are coming to visit from St. Louis next week, and we're having a little party so they can meet some of our friends. How about next Friday?"

Bullets asked, "How many are coming?"

"Fourteen," I said.

"*Is that all?*"

"I love big parties, Bullets, but since this is Dee's family, I felt I would bow to her wishes and make it a small, intimate party—just seven couples."

"You're thinking small, Allan-baby. For *Life* to go to a party, it has to be a party—a real party, with real Hollywood movie celebrities. You're in the big time, Allan-boy. Let Rogers and Cowan handle the whole party. Let them arrange for the catering and the champagne and the Scotch, and let them invite the guests."

So from a simple dinner for Alex and Shirlee, it suddenly became a high-class sit-down banquet for ninety-eight people, including all kinds of stars like Keeley Smith and Carol Lynley and Stella Stevens. The photographers from *Life* took hundreds of pictures—thousands, maybe—and the floors were soon covered with empty boxes which when full had held film and flash bulbs.

When *Life* goes to a party, it doesn't clean up the mess—at least it didn't clean up this one. That party cost me $1,600, and to date only one of those photographs has appeared in *Life*. I'm not in it. It's a picture of Robbie—*with Bullets Durgom.*

While I was playing at the Sands Hotel in Las Vegas in January, 1963, I got a call from the National Press Club of Washington, D.C. The man said, "We like your album and we'd like you to do a show for us on the night of February fifteenth when we inaugurate our new President, Bryson Rash of NBC News."

I said I would be happy to do the show.

I guess the man had some second thoughts. Two days later he called me up again, this time with a note of apprehension in his voice. "Mr. Sherman," he said, "I don't quite know how to say this, but—well—you see, we were a bit concerned because your material is rather—uh—er—uh—"

"Ethnic?"

"Yes, *that's* it," he jubilated. "I just wanted to prepare you, Mr. Sherman, for the fact that the audience will only be about ten percent Jewish."

"What percent Jewish?" I asked.

"Ten," he repeated. "Stretching a point, maybe eleven."

So I did the National Press Club show, and the guest of honor in the front row of the audience was Chief Justice Earl Warren. I opened the show with these words:

"Thank you very much. I am very proud and grateful to be in your elegant city, and among such distinguished Americans.

"I was warned before coming here that the audience tonight would only be ten percent Jewish. Perhaps they thought I would be disappointed. On the contrary, I am delighted.

"Mr. Chief Justice, I am delighted to hear that you are even ten percent Jewish. I didn't know you were Jewish at all."

Three weeks later, on March 3rd, I was asked back to Washington to appear at the 50th Anniversary Dinner of the Department of Labor at the Sheraton-Park Hotel. There were so many people, the dinner had to be held on two different floors. President Kennedy spoke on one floor while the performers (Victor Borge, Leslie Uggams and I) entertained on the other. Between shows the Secret Service men guarded the escalator so the entertainers could meet President Kennedy.

As he shook my hand the President said, "I've got your record and I like it very much."

* * *

I was home for a few days in April. Nancy was—how am I going to say this? Well, Nancy was beginning to have a shape. I mean, she was no Jayne Mansfield or anything like that—she was only eleven. But she was starting to wear one of those learner's brassieres. Nothing fazes Nancy. She's always laughing and singing and happy. She's popular and well adjusted and gets straight A's in school.

Where did we go wrong?
Why isn't she crazy like the rest of the family?

One morning the phone rang, and Dee picked it up.

"Allan," she called, "it's for you."

"Who is it?" I asked her.

She held her hand over the mouthpiece and laughed. "You'll never believe this," she said.

"By now I'll believe anything," I said. "Who is it?"

Then she started to cry, suddenly. As she handed me the phone, she sobbed, "It's Mr. Zanuck."

Mr. Zanuck sent me a script of a movie to read, and while I was in town Frank Cooper took me out to Universal Pictures to talk about another movie. The producer asked me if I could act.

"I don't know," I said. "I never tried."

So they gave the part of Corporal Laibowitz in *Captain Newman, M.D.* to Tony Curtis.

I went on the *Steve Allen Show,* not once but six times. The first time was my favorite.

After the show George Wonderful took me aside. "They thought you were great," he said.

"Thank you," I replied. "And please tell They that I am in excellent health, and hoping They are the same."

* * *

Robbie got all excited because he found a paragraph about me in the *Encyclopaedia Britannica's* "Book of the Year." *That makes two of us, Jackson B. Sherman and me, who are immortalized in* Encyclopaedia Britannica.

Goodson-Todman made more nice on me. I appeared on *What's My Line* as the Mystery Guest. But what really shook me up was being the Celebrity Guest on *I've Got a Secret.* Garry Moore made still more nice; he asked me to replace him as host of his one-hour variety show for the summer.

I was writing the third album, and I said to Lou Busch, "Someday I'd like to do an album with a whole symphony orchestra."

"You are stark, staring, raving mad," Lou Busch said in reply.

"That may well be," I said, *"but nothing is impossible."*

Lou was noodling at the piano, playing "Dance of the Hours," from the opera *La Gioconda* by Ponchielli. Dee walked through the living room. "I'll be back in time to give you lunch," she said. "I'm going over to Bullock's and buy Nancy some clothes for camp."

Good God! My little Nancy, my baby, going away alone to some strange wilderness for the whole summer? I won't have it.

The whole song came to me almost at one moment:

> *Hello, Muddah; hello, Fadduh,*
> *Here I am at Camp Granada.*
> *Camp is very entertaining,*
> *And they say we'll have some fun if it stops raining. . . .*
>
> *I went hiking with Joe Spivey.*
> *He developed poison ivy.*
> *You remember Leonard Skinner?*
> *He got ptomaine poisoning last night after dinner.*
>
> *All the couns'lors hate the waiters,*
> *And the lake has alligators,*

> *And the head coach wants no sissies,*
> *So he reads to us from something called* Ulysses.
>
> *Now I don't want this should scare ya*
> *But my bunk mate has malaria.*
> *You remember Jeffrey Hardy?*
> *They're about to organize a searching party.*
>
> *Take me home,*
> *O Muddah, Fadduh,*
> *Take me home,*
> *I hate Granada.*
> *Don't leave me out in the forest where*
> *I might get eaten by a bear.*
>
> *Take me home.*
> *I promise I will not make noise*
> *Or mess the house with other boys.*
> *O please don't make me stay;*
> *I've been here one whole day.*
>
> *Dearest Fadduh, darling Muddah,*
> *How's my precious little bruddah?*
> *Let me come home if you miss me,*
> *I would even let Aunt Bertha hug and kiss me.*
> *Wait a minute! It's stopped hailing!*
> *Guys are swimming! Guys are sailing!*
> *Playing baseball! Gee, that's better!*
> *Muddah, Fadduh, kindly disregard this letter!*

The single record was Number One in the United States. It sold over a million copies before Labor Day. All right. At least that's *possible.* But it was Number One in Hong Kong, where there are no children's camps; and in Australia and New Zealand and Johannesburg. *What's going on in the world? Is everybody getting disorganized and crazy?*

A Houston disc jockey played "Hello, Muddah, Hello, Fadduh." A lady listener phoned him.

"That song you just played," she said. "They play it too much. I'm sick and tired of it."

"*What?*" he shrieked.

"I said I'm sick and tired of it."

"Madam," he said, "how dare you not like 'Hello, Muddah'? I am outraged," he said.

To punish her, he played "Hello, Muddah, Hello, Fadduh" over and over again for one solid hour.

July 19, 1963. Two weeks after "Hello, Muddah" came out, I did a concert at the Hollywood Bowl. It was the largest Friday-night audience in the forty-two years since the Bowl was built—more than eighteen thousand people. And it swung—all those people together—like one giant thing. I've never seen anything like it before or since.

August 1963. I flew to New York to replace Johnny Carson for a week on the *Tonight* show.

Monday night. At the beginning of the show I challenged Cary Grant to come on the show and once and for all let the audience decide which of us was the more adorable.

Tuesday night. I opened the show by saying that I had not heard from Cary Grant and that was, of course, an admission of defeat on his part.

Wednesday night. I read the audience this authentic telegram:

YOU WIN YOU TALENTED MAN I ADMIT IT YOU'RE MORE ADOR-
ABLE. CARY GRANT

Thursday night. Cary Grant called me person-to-person from Universal City and said he was sorry he hadn't been able to surprise me and come on the show.

I knew he would come around eventually.

Friday night. Toward the end of my last show I read the audience this statement:

"I want to thank NBC and Johnny Carson and everybody on the Tonight show and everybody in the audience for letting me be Cary Grant for a week.

"I know I'm not really Cary Grant.

"But neither is Cary Grant. Mr. Grant and I and everybody else who presumes to step in front of the public—all of us—we are what you made us. All of us are human beings, and the only thing we have that is really special is your trust and your warmth and your precious time. And the best of us are the ones who live up to that responsibility.

"I want to thank the New York Post Office for delivering to me hundreds of letters that were addressed: 'Cary Grant, New York City.' I want to thank the beautiful girl with the hatbox— she must have been a model—who stopped me on Fifth Avenue this morning and said, 'You look much younger in person, Mr. Grant.'

"I want to thank the hundreds of people who this week have asked me for Cary Grant's autograph. I proudly signed his name for every single one of them.

"The thing is, I believe that we all have a right to be Cary Grant once in a while. Not all the time. But once in a while it feels good to be able to melt someone of the opposite sex with that look.

"And so I've done more kissing in these last five days than I usually do in six months. For me, that's a big deal. But for Cary Grant it's nothing.

"This whole week has been wonderful and crazy and much better than the usual type of thing that has been happening to me all my life. Thank you.

"I'd better stop talking now, because if I talk any more I'll start crying, and if I start crying I'll be Jack Paar, and I'd rather be Cary Grant."

* * *

That long hot summer of 1963 I was hot hot hot.

From the *Tonight* show I went to Chicago to play a theatre-in-the-round. Everywhere I went, little bands of kids followed me around and pointed at me because I was the "Hello, Muddah" man. I made an appearance at the Northfield Shopping Center. When I got out of the car, I was mobbed by more than three thousand children and their parents, and they don't care if they smother you. *You're not a person, you're a thing—a Celebrity, whatever that is.* And the owners of the store where I was supposed to sign the autographs wouldn't let me in the store because they were afraid of the mob. And so the mob pushed in against me until my back was against a plate-glass window and I felt like I was suffocating, and I was very glad when the three squad cars of police came and made them line up. And I sat there for four hours signing autographs.

I signed whatever they put in front of me—a piece of paper, a shirt tail, half a plucked chicken, blank checks. Whatever they put in front of me, I signed. And every time I signed anything, I said "Thank you" and smiled, because a lot of those kids had learned very bad manners somewhere and I didn't want to make them any worse.

I played the Steel Pier in Atlantic City, and I broke the attendance record at Freedomland in the Bronx, and I played Grossinger's and the Concord in the Catskill Mountains and they gave me tremendous ovations, but they were laughing in the wrong places all the way through and I realized I'm at my worst in front of all-Jewish audiences because they seem to want something from me that I can't give them. They want me to fit into a mold that I never made but they did. They want me to be a professional Jew, an inside Jew, and they want to sit there and laugh their version of the hipsters' laugh—"*I dig you, but the Goys don't.*" And I can't give them that—that's too much Jewish.

I don't know why those same people go every summer to the

Catskill Mountains. I don't know why they want to be in a ghetto, even one that's full of mink and thick carpets and championship golf courses and costs as much as a trip to Europe or California or Hong Kong or Israel, for that matter. What are they afraid of?

Don't be afraid, please, you people up there. Don't be afraid any more. Jump in, the water's fine in the human race.

Saturday, September 28, 1963. The University of Illinois made nice on Dee and me.

How many times had she dreamed secretly of erasing that terrible hurt of getting kicked out of school?

She was sitting beside me, and when the Mayor gave me the key to the city, I turned and gave it to her.

She was sitting beside me at the football game that Saturday afternoon, and we sat in the private box of the President of the University, and I remembered the exact moment when I had fallen in love with her.

She was sitting beside me at the football game on that Saturday in 1943, and Buddy Young got the ball and ran eighty-four yards and made a touchdown. And then seventy thousand people stood up and yelled and cheered. And I looked at her and she was still sitting. And while everybody else was cheering, she was crying. There were tears rolling down her cheeks because she had never in her life seen anybody cheer a Negro before and now she was seeing seventy thousand white people cheering all at once, and it was too beautiful and too big for her to adjust to.

And she was still sitting beside me that September Saturday in 1963, and of course Illinois won the game. They beat California 10–0, and, of course, they went on that year to win the Rose Bowl game.

She was with me when we met the Governor, and she was with me when we walked into her sorority house for the first time since that nightmare night. And they gave her a plaque, and

it said we were welcome there always. But what meant so much
to Dee and me was that we were welcome there now.

We stood together and shook hands with Dean Turner. And
that night at the concert in that unbelievable new Assembly
Hall that covers the once-forbidden land we used to call South
Campus—that night she sat in the front row. She sat among
8,236 students and townspeople and professors who said Welcome Home by just being there. They said the crime is over and
the punishment is over, too. Welcome Home.

And I stood on that vast stage, and there wasn't one minute
of that day that I didn't feel like crying. But I was there because
I could make them laugh, and so I made them laugh:

> *Hello, Muddah, Hello, Faddah,*
> *Here I am at Alma Mater.*
> *Where I once got educated—*
> *Eighteen years ago I almost graduated.*
>
> *Everyone remembers me here,*
> *'Cause I averaged two-point-three here.*
> *Met Dean Turner at the station.*
> *He's deciding if he'll take me off probation.*
>
> *The athletics ain't the same here.*
> *Gosh—today they won a game here.*
> *And the coeds are so purty,*
> *That on week nights they get locked up at ten-thirty!*
>
> *Getting beer is very hard now*
> *'Cause they ask you for a card now.*
> *And this hall is quite a haven.*
> *I sincerely hope the ceiling doesn't cave in.*
>
> *Take me back, Old Alma Mater, take me back.*
> *I promise I will not cut class,*

> *This time I won't cut class,*
> *At least, I'll go enough to pass.*
>
> *Reinstate me, please, I want to graduate.*
> *I want to wear a cap and gown*
> *(That is if there is one*
> *That's large enough in town.)*
>
> *I'm the father of a boy now,*
> *Making plans for Illinois now.*
> *He's a scholar—he's a learner,*
> *And I'll send along an apple for Dean Turner.*
>
> *I look forward with elation*
> *To his day of graduation.*
> *I'll go home and get his trunks out—*
> *Boy, will I be disappointed if he flunks out!*

And the last song I sang, I sang to her. I had written it on the plane from Denver that morning:

> *Every year in the middle of September,*
> *No matter where I may be,*
> *I can hear happy voices I remember,*
> *Calling, calling me!*
>
> *I hear their distant laughter,*
> *I hear each word they say—*
> *It can't be twenty years ago . . .*
> *It's only yesterday!*
>
> *Just this morning we noticed on the Broadwalk*
> *Young couples walked hand in hand.*
> *We walked there once when you were little babies;*
> *My wife and I understand.*

This campus is a part of us.
It's so much in the heart of us—
In fact, it was the start of us.

We're sorry that we stayed away so long—
Will you join me as I sing our favorite song?

We're loyal to you, Illinois!
We're Orange and Blue, Illinois!

It was a new verse to the Illinois Loyalty Song. Our verse. Dee's and mine. And it was a shameless theatrical trick, because when I started singing it, *they all had to stand up.* I made them all stand up for her because I love her.

My Press Agents booked me into Macy's Thanksgiving Day Parade in 1963. When they made this arrangement, I was sitting in a warm room in a warm climate in my house in Bel Air, and I didn't stop to think that it might be chilly outdoors in New York late in November. All I knew was my Press Agents strongly advised me to do this because it would give me valuable "exposure"—both NBC and CBS cover the Macy's Parade. (I forgot that there were several meanings to the word "exposure.") I was going to play the Copacabana anyway on November 14th, so I figured, *What the hell—I'll sit on a float and be seen by millions of televiewers, and they'll buy my latest records or they'll come to the Copacabana, and it will make little children happy.*

November came and I was ensconced in the Plaza Hotel, sipping a little J&B, when the phone rang.

"This is Mitzi from R. H. Macy's," said a dulcet voice.

"Howdy, Mitzi," I said.

"Could you please give me all your sizes?"

"Why?"

"We have to have your sizes for the parade."

"I don't see the connection, Mitzi."

"You will wear a Cub Scout outfit as your costume."

"This is news to me, Mitzi-baby," I said. "I am thirty-nine years old, you know."

"Well, you see—we have this toyland sort of float for you, and there'll be Girl Scouts on it and Boy Scouts, and there'll be a loudspeaker playing 'Hello, Muddah, Hello, Faddah,' and you'll be a Cub Scout at camp."

"I think you will have some trouble finding a Cub Scout outfit in my size. There is no Cub Scout in the world who is my size."

"Don't worry," she said, "Mitzi of Macy's will be on the job."

So I gave her my sizes—hat, shirt, trousers, jacket.

That night I did my shows at the Copa. The last show breaks about 2:30 A.M. By the time you finish unwinding and talking to your friends and setting up business deals and reading the morning papers, it's five A.M., but that's show biz, and I was living the life of a show-biz star. *Wheee!*

It was about nine o'clock and I was just beginning to sleep when the phone rang. It was Mitzi from Macy's.

"About your underwear," she said.

"About *your* underwear," I shot back. "What kind of remark is that to make to a stranger? *Your underwear,* indeed!"

"Now, Mr. Sherman. It's going to be very cold out there on Thanksgiving Day, and you'll be exposed to the elements, and you should wear arctic underwear."

"Thanks a lot," I said.

At six o'clock, on the morning of the parade, there arrived a messenger with the Cub Scout uniform and the arctic underwear.

I tried to get into the shirt, but it was so tight with the heavy underwear underneath that I couldn't breathe. But I'm a good sport. I got into the whole insane regalia. I was suffocating. At 7:30 A.M. came a call to remind me to be all dressed and ready to march (or float) at eight A.M. I was still foggy with sleep, stumbling around the room, trying to button up the Goddam Cub Scout uniform. The buttons kept opening up on me until finally I said to hell with the arctic underwear. So I took it off, and then the uniform was merely tight—not impossible.

Downstairs in the lobby were Mitzi from Macy's and somebody from Warner Brothers Records. They were waiting for Troy Donahue, who was also in the Macy's Parade and also staying at the Plaza.

To have a fat man stumbling around half asleep in an unbuttoned Cub Scout uniform with a Cub Scout hat and a neckerchief is not exactly what the Plaza people had in mind when they built their elegant lobby.

I tromped into the Edwardian Room—one of the fanciest dining rooms in the world. It was filled with a merry, bustling throng of richly attired wealthy families enjoying their Thanksgiving morning breakfasts. Into this elegant assemblage, I stalked, an overgrown, fat Cub Scout with the hair on my chest sticking out of the too-small shirt, and my bellybutton showing. (But not protruding.) Feeling silly, I nevertheless determined to make my way inside and get a little juice. I got as far as the *maitre d'hôtel.*

He froze me with, "Ah, Monsieur Sherman, and what is it that you wish?"

I knew he thought that if I were allowed to sit down in the Edwardian Room it would be the end of the great tradition of this room, and he wasn't going to let it happen if he could help it.

I said, "I would like a large glass of orange juice, freshly squeezed, please."

He snapped his fingers. Several waiters appeared. "One orange juice, large," he said, *"and quickly."* He didn't add "For God's sake," but it was there in his tone.

An orange juice was brought. With one hand, he handed it to

me. With the other, he gently but firmly pushed me out of the door and into the lobby. I swallowed my pride and swallowed the orange juice in the lobby.

Troy Donahue finally showed. He informed me that I looked mighty silly. I glowered at him. We drove over to 79th Street and Broadway, where the parade would start. I stood there, waiting for my float to arrive so I could board it. Troy's float came. He leaped up on it, as agile as a mountain goat. My float came. It was very large and very tall, and the first step was four feet up. I wanted to emulate Troy and debonairly leap aboard. I couldn't. Then I tried to flip myself up onto it. No. I also saw that the chair I would have to sit on was on the top of the float, which was about thirty feet high.

By now I was in no mood for the whole Macy Parade. It was cold. I was freezing. My shirt was wide open. I refused to sit on that tottering throne. The float was full of children, the off-spring of Macy's employees. They were happy and grinning and greeting me with cries of "Hello, Muddah, Hello, Faddah" and "There he is in person" and "Sarah Jackman, Sarah Jackman, how's by you?"

Somebody finally hoisted me up on the float with an improvised block and tackle. I took a position in front of the float, and I stood there like a manatee on the prow of a clipper ship, and I sent one of the kids up to sit on the throne. Two other kids I took in my arms to keep my bosom warm.

Our float finally began moving into the parade. (Remember, the reason I'm going through this agony is for the publicity on television.) The CBS cameras were on 72nd Street, and as we came near I waved and laughed and cheered and sang. But the cameras were capped. By the time my part of the parade got there, *their* part of the telecast was over. Oh, well—there were still the NBC cameras at 34th Street. Two frozen hours later my float got there. Just as I came into camera range *they cut away to a station break*. The next time I march in a Macy

Thanksgiving Day Parade—which I doubt—I want to be in the front. And it better be in June.

By the time we got to 34th Street, I was frozen blue. At Macy's, I was rushed right up to the Hospitality Room of the big store, and there all the celebrities who had marched were present, along with the Macy executives. My lips were frozen. It was not until a very fine human being, Lorne Greene of *Bonanza,* gave me a quadruple belt of Scotch that I was able to say hello to the President of Macy's.

I opened at the Copacabana on East 60th Street in New York on Thursday, November 14, 1963. Frank Farrell's headline in the *World-Telegram* read: MY SON, THE COPACABANA SMASH, and the review was even nicer than the headline. The first weekend we did terrific business. (The night-club business is a weekend business nowadays, since television.)

Everybody was saying the second weekend would be a record-breaker, with those great reviews and the word-of-mouth.

But there wasn't going to be a second weekend. Not for anybody in the United States.

At noon on Friday, November 22, 1963, Lee Harvey Oswald killed President John F. Kennedy in Dallas.

Nobody knew what to do. We sat by the television set and blamed the Right-Wingers and the Communists and Ourselves and The Way We Live, but nobody knew who to blame and nobody knew what to do.

On Saturday night I had to do three shows.

The Copa was packed, and you couldn't blame people. After they had sat by their television sets all day Friday and all through Friday night and Saturday morning and afternoon you couldn't blame them—you couldn't blame anybody—for wanting to get away, to get out, to be with somebody, anybody, just to prove that life goes on.

But nobody wanted to laugh.

And, God knows, nobody wanted to try to make people laugh.

So I went on and I said, "*Ladies and Gentlemen. There's no sense pretending that we don't all know what happened yesterday. We know. But one of these days—today or Tuesday or a week from Tuesday—one of these days we're all going to have to go back to work, and we're all going to have to remember that we're still alive.*

"*Tonight is the night I had to go back to work. If you were in the business of making people laugh, like I am, you'd probably feel the way I do: you'd probably want to wait a month or a year before you tried it again.*

"*But I'm here and you're here tonight.*

"*Once, I was lucky enough to be asked to do a show for President Kennedy. He had a warm and beautiful sense of humor.*

"*I'd like to do for you exactly the same show I did for him.*

"*You don't have to laugh. I don't expect you to.*"

I did the show I had done at the Sheraton-Park Hotel the night I met the President between floors and he shook my hand.

Then I got my overcoat and walked in the snow back to the Plaza.

May 26, 1964. Dee and I went to Washington, D.C., and I appeared at the National Guard Armory in the Gala for President Lyndon B. Johnson. I wrote this song and I yelled out the words so the audience could sing it with me:

> *Once in love with Lyndon,*
> *Always in love with Lyndon.*
> *And on the Tuesday of the big Election,*
> *Guess who my selection will be!*
>
> *November third, it's Lyndon—*
> *It's Ladybird and Lyndon.*

And on the morning of Inauguration,
What a happy nation you'll see!

You might be quite the fickle-hearted rover
Who throws votes away,
But once you've looked the opposition over,
It's L-B-J!

Once in love with Lyndon,
Always in love with Lyndon.
Love him and love him till our hearts are aching.
And why are we making this fuss?
Cause Lyndon's always been in love with us!

The audience of dignitaries went crazy, and the next day the television newsreels showed me singing my song.

Two days later we did the same show at Madison Square Garden.

After the show President Johnson got up and in front of twenty thousand people he said, ". . . *and I could not leave without saying that I love the way Allan Sherman sings.*"

The day after the Madison Square Garden Gala the phone rang in our suite at the Hampshire House. It was Ben Snyder, the manager of the Syracuse Symphony Orchestra. He asked if I would go to Syracuse on June 15th and read *Peter and the Wolf* at a benefit for the orchestra.

I don't know why, but I said, "I think the music of *Peter and the Wolf* is wonderful, but the story is the dullest story I ever heard. If you'll let me rewrite the story, I'll come and do it."

"Be my guest," Ben Snyder said. "I'll see you June fifteenth."

I had to fly to Vancouver from New York. In the plane, ideas kept popping into my head. Ideas for all kinds of crazy things I could do with a symphony orchestra.

For example: I thought up twenty-six well-known melodies, both classical and popular, that all began with the same four notes as "How Dry I Am." Also, I had wanted to write something I called "The End of a Symphony," because all of the great symphonies sound to me as though they have the same ending—or at least you could interchange the ending of any one for the ending of another and nobody would know the difference. Beethoven's Fifth, which is certainly a very nice symphony, ends with *forty-one bars of the same chord!* Beethoven was deaf. What's Mozart's excuse? Or Brahms'?

By the time we arrived in Vancouver, "Variations on How Dry I Am" and "The End of a Symphony" were finished.

But I can't write music.

So I called Ben Snyder in Syracuse, and he sent a brilliant young music graduate of Syracuse University to meet me and make the orchestrations. Calvin Custer. At night I would play two shows at a night club called The Cave. Through the night and into the morning and into the next day Cal Custer and Marvin Tabolsky and I worked in my hotel suite. There weren't enough professional music copyists in Vancouver to do the enormous job, so we hired students from the music school. And piano teachers. And housewives who played instruments. Around the clock, there were always at least half a dozen of those little elves in my hotel suite, copying music. There were, all told, nine thousand pages of music copied in those six days. I kept running around, encouraging them: *"Nothing is impossible! We'll make it! Have faith! Carry on!"*

Nine of us—Cal, Marvin, six of the elves and I—met in my hotel suite after the last show at 1:30 in the morning and we packed the music. When we came to a sheet we didn't need—there were thousands of them—we crumpled it up and threw it on the floor. We finished at five A.M. and I called the bellhop. When he opened the door, he didn't believe what he saw.

We drove to Seattle and took a nine-o'clock plane. After three or four more planes, we were in Syracuse. On each plane they served us lunch, so we had five lunches. I slept three hours, and two boys from Syracuse came and woke me up and got me dressed and took me over to the Armory, and we did the concert and the audience went crazy.

Then the Baltimore Symphony Orchestra called and asked me to do this material on June 30th, and I said yes, gladly. And I called Becker and London and asked them to get in touch with all the record companies in New York and see if they would send somebody down to Baltimore to hear my Great Classical Masterworks in which I had composed such immortal tunes as Beethoven's Fifth Symphony, Tchaikovsky's *Swan Lake* ballet, and Mozart's Overture to *The Marriage of Figaro.*

On the first page of the orchestration of "Variations on How Dry I Am," the arranger had written a note to me: *"Be sure and get three toilet plungers for the trombones to use as mutes.*

Jazz and show musicians have their own toilet plungers, but I figured the Baltimore Symphony trombone section wouldn't have them, because Beethoven and Brahms never wrote for toilet plunger.

I went to a little hardware store.

The man said, "Can I help you?"

"Yes," I said. "I'd like three toilet plungers."

Pause.

Then the man said, *"Three?* They're reusable, you know."

"I know. But I need three."

"Okay, three," said the man, and he started toward the back of the store.

"By the way," I yelled after him, "I don't need the sticks."

He walked back and looked me straight in the eye. "Oh, yes, you do," he said. "Toilet-plunging is not a hand thing."

"No, really. I don't need the sticks."

"Look," he said sympathetically, "if you're worried about the price, I can give you three used plungers free."

"No, thanks," I said, "I definitely need three new plungers without sticks."

He gave them to me in a bag, and I paid him and started to leave.

"Excuse me, sir," the man called after me. "But I am curious. Just what are you going to use those toilet plungers for?"

I looked him straight in the eye, for the truth was on my side.

"For the trombone section of the Baltimore Symphony Orchestra," I said.

"*Sure* you are," he said as I walked out.

Nothing is impossible.

There were five thousand people at the Baltimore concert, including one from each of the big record companies.

The next morning I flew back to New York, and Morty Becker, my lawyer, called. He said, "I just got a call from the Tanglewood Music Festival. They'd like you to come up and do your classical masterpieces with Arthur Fiedler and the Boston Pops Orchestra on July twenty-second. And they want to record the concert live and put it out on RCA Victor Red Seal records."

Nothing is impossible nothing is impossible nothing is impossible.

Red Seal. Toscanini's label. There had never been a comedy album on Red Seal records before.

I had all the arrangements rewritten again, and I rewrote the words again, and Marvin and I flew to Boston and I spent three days with Arthur Fiedler, who is certainly the nicest man in the world. One day we were in a delicatessen having lunch and Mr. Fiedler volunteered to do the solo hiccup in "Variations on How Dry I Am" and his secretary said, "Mr. Fiedler, think of your image!" And Mr. Fiedler said, "Nuts to my image!"

And for that remark I will always love him dearly.

We rehearsed four hours at Tanglewood on the afternoon of

the 22nd. There were ninety-six members of the symphony, plus five great jazz men from New York.

Mr. Fiedler kept trying to teach me how to conduct, but it was no use. And when I got up to conduct "Variations on How Dry I Am" in rehearsal, I began by saying: "Gentlemen, I am a musical ignoramus and I don't know how to conduct. But I love music, and if you will indulge me, we'll get through this somehow."

A viola player shouted, loud, so the other hundred men could hear, "I don't have to do this! I don't have to sit here and be conducted by a moron!"

That punctured me like a balloon. He had taken all the fun out of it. I got scared.

I'm doing something I shouldn't be doing. All these people are grownups. They know what they're doing. I don't. I can't do anything.

I went back to the hotel and had four double Scotches, real fast, and showered and got dressed and went back to the Shed at Tanglewood. People were starting to come in. It had been raining all day, and the Shed was sold out; it holds six thousand, but there's room for that many more on the Lawn.

People bring their dinner and thermos jugs of hot coffee, and they sit on the Lawn and listen there among those lovely, rolling green Berkshire Mountains. It stopped raining, and more people came, and more and more, and when they were all there, it was the biggest crowd in the history of Tanglewood—13,327 people —and on a Wednesday night.

They cheered and they screamed and they applauded. And William Steinberg, the Conductor of the Pittsburgh Symphony, was laughing. And Eugene Ormandy of the Philadelphia Orchestra was having a good time. And when I finished conducting, I guess they could all tell that I loved music. When I walked off, those one hundred musicians were standing there applauding, and I looked at the viola player. He was applauding the way a viola player does—tapping his bow against his music stand, and louder than all the others.

August, 1964. I made the fifth album for Warner Brothers. "Shine On, Harvey Bloom," "Grow, Mrs. Goldfarb, Fatter, Fatter." "Casey Jones" I called "J. C. Cohen." Mike Maitland and all the other gentiles at Warner Brothers were delighted with the Jewish-type album.

Then my Jewish agent called and said some of the executives at NBC would be interested in my doing a one-hour special, as long as I wasn't too Jewish.

I remember a story about a producer who asks an actor, "Are you Jewish?" The actor, who needs a job, says, "Not necessarily."

The State Fair in Great Falls, Montana. I followed the Horse-Pulling Contest. George Gobel and I drank Scotch together.

The Hollywood Bowl again. Not so thrilling this time—only ten thousand people. *Am I slipping? Muscle spasm.*

Campaign dinner for Pierre Salinger for Senator. *Booze.*

My acting debut: a one-minute cameo role on *Mr. Novak*. It took from 7:00 A.M. till 7:30 P.M. to shoot this one minute. The show is fifty-two minutes long. *At this rate they can only shoot seven shows a year if they work weekends. How do they do it?*

October. More campaign shows for Salinger and President Johnson and Hubert Humphrey. Two weeks at the Fairmont Hotel in San Francisco.

The Venetian Room at the Fairmont is elegant and romantic and up to its chandeliers in candelabras. Opening night, I felt an uncontrollable urge to sing passionate love songs. I seized the microphone and arabesqued out into the audience in my most dashing Continental fashion. I came to rest beside a beautiful woman. I arched my eyebrow sexily and sang to her:

> *There's a small hotel,*
> *Come on, what the hell—*

Tingling with passion, I tangoed over to another table and another lovely woman. Softly into her ear I purred:

> *You are too beautiful for one man alone,*
> *So I got a group together. . . .*

At one table there was a teen-age couple holding hands in delirious ecstasy. To them I sang:

> *Hello, young lovers,*
> *You're under arrest . . .*

Then my hot eyes caught a glimpse of the most beautiful girl in the room. I flew to her side. I dismissed her handsome escort with a sexier-than-thou sneer. Then to her I crooned:

> *You do something to me,*
> *And then I'll do something to you*

My new Sex Image was an immediate hit. Richard Burton hasn't spoken to me since. Or before either, for that matter.

November, 1964.

New York. Rehearsals for the NBC *Follies*, starring Steve Lawrence. *Muscle spasms. Big ones. And I can't breathe, either. Loud or quiet, I can't breathe.*

Doctors Hospital. "You are the best candidate for a heart attack I ever saw," the doctor said. "You have to lose weight."

The NBC *Follies* in Living Color. *On-the-air muscle spasms.*

The *Tonight* show. During the commercial Johnny Carson said, "I could see you were having some kind of pain, and the audience could too. You'd better explain after the commercial." On-the-air explanation of on-the-air muscle spasm.

Mrs. Abel from the White House called to say President Johnson wanted me to do a show in Austin, Texas, on Election Eve. *I can't. I don't feel good. I'm sick.*

Somebody stole my credit cards and charged $800 on American Express and $400 on The Diners' Club. *Gee, it's great to be a Celebrity.*

Jackson B. Sherman was gored by some wild animal in the hills in back of the house. Dee couldn't bear to look at him with his skin opened up and his insides showing, but Robbie picked Jackson up in his arms, with all that blood pouring out—Robbie, who's supposed to be so disorganized and afraid and unwilling to face reality. Robbie picked him up, and located a veterinarian who would treat him on Sunday, and took him to the doctor, and saved his life. *Who am I? I'm Robbie's father.*

CHAPTER 18

A Gift of Laughter

OF ALL THE CRAZY and wonderful and hectic and nerve-racking and glorious and ugly and beautiful things that have happened to me since I became an entertainer, the thing that moved me the most deeply happened in the Pasadena Civic Auditorium on the night of January 19, 1963.

I will never forget that moment, and neither will the three thousand other people who came to the theatre that night to see Harpo Marx and me do a concert together.

I have already told you what Harpo Marx's encouragement and laughter meant to me when we first moved to Los Angeles and I found myself his next-door neighbor. I have told you about the angel music in our bedroom every morning when he practiced the harp, and his wild, pixie sense of humor that bedeviled the ladies of the California State Unemployment Service.

But maybe I didn't make it clear enough what Harpo was to me beyond a person who was a friend and a neighbor and an all-around decent human being.

When I was a small boy, growing up in the wreckage of a broken marriage in Los Angeles, when I was cutting school and paying a dime to sit all day and most of the night in the movie houses, when I was being formed, being made into whatever I am today, when most of the things that happened in my house were things to be afraid of and to cry at and to turn away from, when reality was something that couldn't be faced—that was when Harpo Marx came into my life *really*. That was when he gave me, for the first time, a gift of laughter.

They were insane and wild and breathtakingly funny, the Marx Brothers. The whole world was poor then, and there was something going on called the Depression, something a child couldn't understand, but I knew it was bad. And in the middle of all the badness there were those movies for a dime, and some of the movies were full of songs, lovely hopeful songs—"Who's Afraid of the Big Bad Wolf?" And then there were the Marx Brothers pictures, and they made you scream and jump with laughter, and the world wasn't so poor then—it was rich with the sound of people laughing till their insides hurt and they forgot the real hurt of being out of a job and humiliated. And what was *really* real, what was the beautiful fact of life, was that you were smiling, and as long as you could smile, you knew things were going to get better.

I saw them all—*A Day at the Races, A Night at the Opera, Monkey Business, Horse Feathers, Duck Soup, Animal Crackers* —I saw them all, not once but over and over again until I could do the jokes by heart. I could do Chico's nutty Italian dialect: "*Tootsie Frootsie Ice-a Crimms! Get-a you' Tootsie Frootsie Ice-a Crimms!*" I could go flapping around with my knees bent low like Groucho, with a pencil in my mouth like a cigar, leering and making my eyebrows go up and down, saying, "*I shot*

*an elephant in my pajamas. How he got in my pajamas I'll never
know.*" I could sing the songs. "Hooray for Captain Spalding,
the African Explorer, Did someone call me schnorrer? Hooray,
hooray, hooray!"

I was never too good at imitating Harpo, though. I could
make big eyes and roll them around, all right; I could flub my
lips. But there was always something about Harpo I couldn't
imitate. Later on I knew what it was. After meeting Harpo, I
knew it was the simplicity of the man—the beauty inside, the
thing that God gives to maybe one in every fifty million of us.
To see, and to laugh, and to give joy to others in a way so special
that you *can't* imitate it—it's a gift from God to one person
alone at a time.

Harpo was a child who never grew up. He was the best part
of a human being—the innocent part that can see things with
Wonder. He was beautiful, like a naked child dancing around
free-form because of joy, because the world is music to dance to,
because other people are delights to laugh with and play with.
And Harpo had in him that wonderful vision that made him
see in others the Beauty Part, the Good Part, the Happy Part.

He knew very well that there were Sad Things and Bad
Things, and he knew that these are things we call by the name
of Reality. But Harpo could see more clearly than that. He
could see deeper, where the *real* reality is, inside all of us where
there is a warm place bubbling with fancy and laughter and music and playfulness and love. Harpo could *feel* all those things
inside himself and inside every human being. He knew we were
all born like that, but most of us get so scared to go around
dancing free-form or singing out loud in public or laughing at
the madness around us—most of us get so scared, so *civilized*,
that we teach ourselves how to be ashamed and embarrassed,
and we invent a disguise for ourselves, and we walk around looking serious and acting very somber and self-important. And
we call it grown-up.

So here we all are in our Grown-Up suits, busy doing our Grown-Up jobs, rushing our children to get Grown-Up as fast as possible. And where has all the fun gone to? And why does the music sound so far away? And we Keep Off The Grass, we put everything in Little Orderly Piles, we Get Things Organized. And if Grown-Ups had made the world instead of God, then the world would be Organized in Neat Orderly Piles, and every tree would be exactly like every other tree, and there would be a snowflake factory so they could all be exactly the same, and people would be standardized and factory-packed in Models X, Y and Z, and bananas would have zippers, and eggs would be cube-shaped to save shipping expenses.

But if children had made the world, it would be very much the same as God made it, only there would be more laughter and simpler music, and funny games to play, and more inventions and more pictures and more imagination and more simplicity and more honesty. And there would be less fear and less crime and less war and less status-seeking and less embarrassment and humiliation and shame. And prejudice and genocide just simply wouldn't exist at all.

I believe we all secretly know this. I believe we all walk around acting Grown-Up, and we secretly know that inside us is this child who wants things to be wonderful again, and simple, and wants things to be really true that are supposed to be true. But we hide the child inside—we push it down and squelch it until some of us burst wide open. And the others, the ones who *don't* go mad—they go along all their adult life acting Grown-Up, and finally they die of being too Grown-Up, and in the few moments they allow themselves for the living of their lives, they wander—like the Prophet said—they wander in a seasonless world where you laugh, but not all of your laughter, and you weep, but not all of your tears.

Harpo Marx had the good sense and the great gift never to Grow Up. And that was the soul of his Comedy.

309

Children loved him and old people loved him because they saw themselves in those beautiful big rolling eyes. They saw themselves moving and dancing free and unembarrassed and not a bit worried about being Grown-Up. And Harpo made eyes at pretty girls, the way we all wish we had the nerve to do, and he invented harps out of broken pianos, and piccolos out of strands of spaghetti. And wherever he was, there was music for everyone, and laughter. And when he was sad, he was *so* sad, so very very terribly sad that we could see that there is even something funny about being sad, and so we laughed and forgot some of the things that made *us* sad.

Harpo *was* Comedy.

Comedy is gentle and sweet and good and intelligent and honest, and that is what Harpo Marx was.

Comedy makes you *feel good*, and that is what Harpo Marx did.

And when I met him, I found out the best thing of all: that the man, the person, was even more beautiful than the image. And we had this thing, this feeling for each other, and it was there five minutes after we met and ever after. And I will treasure it as long as I live. I was able to sit at his feet in the crazy shade of the second largest rubber tree in the Western Hemisphere that summer, and later in other places, and I would hear him tell his stories. One day that summer Howard Merrill was visiting in our backyard with his little boy Scotty, who was in a wheelchair, and who do you think came creeping around the fence in full costume, with the curly wig and the flapping trench coat, flubbing his lips and honking that nutty klaxon horn and whistling that shrill whistle with two fingers in his mouth? And who do you think laughed the loudest at my songs? And who gave the parties so everybody in Hollywood could hear me sing my songs? And who wrote on my album liner: "Don't have a party without Allan Sherman or this album"? And who bought dozens of my albums and sent them to everybody in show business? And who took more delight than even I did when it became such a big hit overnight? And who headlined *his own son's* album "Harpo Marx Presents My Son, the Folk Swinger"?

Harpo Marx, that's who.

One day, after all the big hullabaloo of the first album, I was down in Palm Springs writing the second album, and I called Harpo to say hello, and he invited Lou Busch and me to come over to lunch at his lovely house on the Tamarisk Golf Course.

Susan, his wife, was busy making picture frames in the garage, and Harpo had been painting his marvelous pictures. Mostly Harpo gave those paintings away—many to the Mount Sinai Hospital in Los Angeles. There was one real goofy one that I noticed, a picture of several women (*I guess they're women*) sitting nude on a beach, but facing away from you, so you can't be sure if they're women or not. I admired it, and Harpo gave it to me. Like that. "You like it? It's yours."

There were a lot of flies around that day, and I told Harpo about a new way of getting rid of flies I had heard about. You suck them up into a vacuum cleaner, right out of the air, *poof!* Well, Harpo had one of those tremendous factory-type vacuum cleaners, and he thought this was a marvelous fly-removal method, and he turned the damn thing on, and it made a sound like a hundred jet planes all at once, and it was certainly the most beautiful and insane scene I have ever seen in my life—this lovely little baldheaded seventy-five-year-old man who had had five heart attacks, running around and leaping up and down like a kid with a wild new toy, trying to suck up flies in that vacuum cleaner. And he never got *one. Not one.* And he was glad, and so was I. Because, what the hell, Harpo never wanted to kill a fly anyway.

Then Harpo showed us around the house, and he took us into one little room that was full of pictures and theatrical posters, and it was all there, his whole beautiful life, with Groucho and Chico and Zeppo and Gummo, and his mother, Minnie, and his uncle Al Shean, of Gallagher and Shean. And there was Harpo with President Coolidge, and, by God, Coolidge was almost smiling. And Harpo with President Franklin D. Roosevelt, who was laughing. And Harpo with Alexander Woollcott and H. L. Mencken and George Gershwin and the Prince of Wales —and here and there a king or two. Harpo with all those important, serious Grown-Ups from all over the world, because his Comedy had no language barrier. They laughed and they are still laughing in Russia and France and China and Africa— wherever there is still a child inside a man.

Another thing.

From the first moment I met Harpo Marx, I called him Harpo. It wasn't rude, and it wasn't lack of respect. The thing is, he *was* Harpo, and that's what everybody called him. That's what you would call him, Harpo, like a kid on the block—the one it's fun to be with. Not "Mister" Anybody. Not that far away from you. Not that Grown-Up.

Hiya, Harpo. Whaddya doin? Wanna have some fun? Wanna catch flies in a vacuum cleaner? See ya later, Harpo.

We went into the house and Susan served us lunch, and Harpo asked me a lot of questions about how it felt to be a Big Fancy Recording Star, and was I going to go out on the road and do personal appearances? I had never performed professionally at that time. I told him I was booked into Carnegie Hall and the Sands Hotel and I was scared as hell. And he said not to worry, it would be all right.

And Lou Busch said there was one great thing about show business: Eleven o'clock always comes, and it's over, no matter how murderous or horrible it was. Eleven o'clock always comes. And Harpo laughed, because it was true.

And we were sitting there, and I said—joking because I knew it could never really happen—"Hey, Harpo, wouldn't it be great if we could do a concert together?"

And Harpo said, "Yeah—that sure would be great." And that was the end of it, and I forgot about it.

When we finished lunch, Harpo and Susan walked us out to the driveway, and he was mighty impressed with my De Luxe Fancy Solid-Gold Lincoln, and pleased that I hadn't bought a Rolls-Royce. And he knew—or at least I hope he knew—that it was a toy and I hadn't really gone nuts. Then we drove away.

About two weeks later, just before I was about to leave for New York for the Carnegie Hall tour, my phone rang.

"Allan?"

"Yes?"

"Harpo."

"Hiya, Harp. How you feeling?"

"Wonderful. Say—remember you were talking about you and me doing a concert together?"

"Sure. But I was only—"

"Why not?"

"Are you kidding? Harpo, you *mean* it?"

"Sure, kid," he said. "I'd love to. We'll have some fun."

So we scheduled two concerts: on Friday, January 18th, at Santa Monica Civic Auditorium, and on Saturday, January 19th, at Pasadena Civic Auditorium.

Both concerts sold out within a few days of the announcement. The one in Santa Monica was a charity affair at $50 a seat. The promoters were so happy about the sellout that they wanted a second concert each night. I called Harpo and asked if this would be too much for him, and he said, "No, go ahead, it's great, we're a big hit, kid." So I said okay to the promoters, and they scheduled the second show each night.

All this was right in the middle of my appearance at the Sands in Las Vegas, and Jack Entratter gave me the two nights off to fly into L.A. and do the concerts with Harpo.

313

I finished my last show at the Sands about 1:30 Friday morning, and then I sat down at a blackjack table for a few minutes. No matter what I did, I kept winning. I couldn't lose, and it wasn't just a few minutes, it was all night. And when I got up to take the plane to L.A., it was ten in the morning and I was ahead $5,800.

So I got into Los Angeles without having been to sleep all night, and I was all excited and up and turned on from winning all that money and being such a big hit, and I didn't need sleep.

I went straight from the airport to my house, and there wasn't time to sleep if I had wanted to. There were a half-dozen people there, agents and Bullets Durgom and lawyers and business managers, and they had papers for me to sign.

You sign each one in about four places, and then you initial the riders, and then you sign and initial about eight carbon copies, and each piece of paper is somebody who is giving you a bunch of money to go some place and sing your silly songs. And the agents and managers get a percentage of this money, so they hold the papers out nice and flat for you, and hand you a pen, and then point with their index fingers at the line where you do the signing or initialing. It's all very Grown-Up and Official.

Before I knew it, it was two in the afternoon and I still hadn't had any sleep, but I had to go over to Santa Monica Civic Auditorium to rehearse.

When I got there, Harpo was rehearsing on the stage, and I stood in the wings and watched. I had never seen Harpo perform *live* before.

What a beautiful act it was.

It began with no Harpo at all. It began with a lovely, shapely young soprano in a chic black formal gown, and she walked out on the stage, very haughty, and she began to sing, very semi-classical:

"*I was born in Vienna. . . .*"

Her voice was sweet and pure, and her face was pretty, and everything was going along swell—she was making those big, graceful, semiclassical, sweeping gestures, smiling and singing away. My grandma would have loved it.

And then, from the wings, in wandered Harpo. A wild child he was, and when he saw the beautiful soprano, his eyes told you exactly what he had in mind. *Sex. Mad passion. Lust.* He looked at the girl, then at the audience. He didn't have to speak, those eyes said it: "*To hell with semiclassical music. I must get this girl naked immediately.*

Then there came over Harpo's face an awful look of shame that he should ever have had such a thought. So he walked over and stood beside the soprano, facing the audience, and he busied himself with nonlustful activities. He looked out at the audience and sized them up. *Ooops!* He thought he recognized someone out there. Better make sure. So, from his enormous coat pocket, he took a telescope, and he put it to his eye, and he extended it to its full length, and he looked out at the audience.

But passion was not to be denied. As Harpo stood there, innocently looking out at the audience with his telescope, something began to happen. Slowly—at first too slowly to notice—the telescope began to bend around toward the beautiful soprano. Harpo didn't move a muscle. It was the telescope that moved; it bent and curled and curved of its own volition, like a snake. And when it was finished, Harpo's eye was still looking straight out at the audience, but the end of the telescope was resting comfortably on the soprano's bosom.

Now he took from the wonderful pocket a chalk dress-marker, the kind they use for marking the hem of a dress. And he began marking the soprano's beautiful black gown, squirting chalk powder from the syringe. Now this dress-marker is supposed to rest on the floor—that way, the chalk mark is always at the same height. But Harpo didn't rest it on the floor. No sirree. He held it

315

in his hand, so as he walked around the soprano the chalk mark spiraled up and up around her beautiful gown, and the chalk line never met itself. Every once in a while Harpo would stop and look at the chalk line, very disappointed, scratching his head, wondering why the line didn't meet itself. Then he would go on chalking, ever upward—ever upward—until the chalk line was up to the soprano's neckline.

And all through this she sang, beautifully:

"I was born in Vienna. . . ."

Now, from the pocket, Harpo took the biggest pair of scissors I have ever seen. And he shrugged his shoulders—what the heck, I might as well get on with it—and then he began to cut along his chalk line. Up and around the gown he cut, until there was almost nothing covering the beautiful soprano. And still she sang bravely:

"Life is gay in Vienna. . . ."

Then from the shreds of the soprano's clothing Harpo took many wonderful things, and the last of these was a brassiere. Harpo looked at it with amazement, and then he held it out for all to see. It had three pockets. *Three.* Harpo held up three fingers and looked at the girl quizzically but adoringly, and she screamed and ran off the stage.

Harpo shrugged. It was sad that she was gone. He sighed once, longingly, and then he went over and sat down at his harp.

This was the moment. This was Harpo's shining, shimmering, lovely moment of truth when everything was pure and beautiful and serene and right.

There was something in the way he touched that harp—it was an act of love, almost too private for us to watch. There was something you could see then of the almost unbearable beauty of this man and his love for music. And you could feel his love for every other creature on earth in the way he touched his harp and in the way he played the music.

Harpo played many songs, but the one I remember best was "Swanee River."

Was there ever a more corny song than "Way Down Upon the Swanee River"? Was there ever a song more hackneyed, played too much, more made fun of, more parodied, more sung by drunks in barrooms, more arranged and rearranged and tricked up? Was there ever a song you were more sick of hearing? Was there ever a song you wanted less to hear than "Swanee River"?

I can still hear Harpo playing "Swanee River."

There were no tricks, and he had no fancy arrangement.

A man of beauty and simplicity was sitting at a harp, and with love in his eyes and his hands and his soul he was playing a melody of beauty and simplicity. "Swanee River."

Perfect is the word. *Perfect.*

As Harpo finished rehearsing, his son Bill walked over to me and said, "Say—is there anything you can do about Dad's billing?"

I hadn't seen the marquee on my way into the auditorium, so I walked over to Harpo and asked, "Is there something wrong with your billing?"

Harpo smiled and said, "Well—it *is* the smallest billing I've had in a long time."

I went outside and looked at the sign.

Harpo's name was not on it at all.

Just my name, real big. No Harpo.

I know this is a Tough Commercial World we live in. I know I was what they call "hot" then. For a few weeks there, I was like the Beatles. My name was magic and I was a Brand-New Wonder Of The World and I was a "Hot Ticket."

I know that life is real and earnest and hard, but I wonder sometimes if there is any end to the hardness and cruelty of people who have set out in this world to make money, and to make money only. I know these so-called Grown-Ups, these Sophisticates, this Elite. I have met them and seen them up close and lived with them and done business with them, and let me tell you this about them: They are *scared*. Plain scared.

I suddenly thought of Dave Number Two. What made him the way he was? He must have spent his life thinking, *I am nothing, I am rotten, so therefore it must be that everyone else is rotten, too, and that is how I will treat them.*

These people live in terror of being found out, in their private hells, and they go out in the world and act tough, as though they Don't Give A Damn. What a stupid waste, because it's so much tougher to Give a Damn, to Care, to Get Involved.

So the promoters of the concert just simply didn't put up Harpo Marx's name at all because it costs extra labor and, what the hell, they were sold out without it.

By now I had learned what to do. I am ashamed of this, but I have learned it, and when it is necessary I do it. You can get what you want by acting like a baby. You say to them, "If I don't get what I want, there will be no show. I won't go on." And that is exactly what I did. I said to them, "Either you put Harpo's name up, as big as mine, or there will be no show." They understand this, they sense it in their pocketbooks, and they do what you say.

I swear to you that I have never done this to gain anything for myself. But I have done it several times, and I am ashamed that I ever did it at all.

So they put Harpo's name up.

I had been up all night, and in the couple of hours before the show, Harpo, who was seventy-five years old, kept saying to *me:* "You ought to lie down and rest."

But the Santa Monica Civic Auditorium—that glorious multi-million-dollar structure—doesn't have a sofa or even a cot in any of its dressing rooms.

*I've found this in many of the beautiful theatres and audi-
toriums all over the country. Performers are still strolling players,
itinerants, with higher insurance rates, undependable, not like
other people, not quite as good. And they'll be gone tomorrow,
anyway, so why provide a place for them to lie down?*

So Harpo and I stood, or sat in chairs, for the two hours before the shows.

The house filled up with people, and just before we were
about to go on, Harpo offered me a drink of bourbon.

"Not now," I said. "After the shows I'll get smashed, but not
now."

"Just a minute," he said. "You're not going out there *alone*,
are you?"

By God, he was right. I took a large shot of the bourbon, and
I didn't go out there alone.

We were a smash. Harpo did his act, and I did mine, and, besides, he taught me a few things we could do together, and we
were great. The second show we were a little more tired, but we
still had the momentum and excitement of the first show going
for us, and we were a smash again.

After the two shows we were both too pooped to go out and
celebrate anywhere. It was about one A.M., so we just shook
hands and thanked and congratulated each other.

Susan Marx came over to me and said, "Harpo was watching
you, and he says you're not just a flash in the pan. He says you
can stay in this business as long as you want."

What a beautiful thing to hear. I can hear it now, again,
whenever I want it—or, more important, whenever I *need* it.

The next night, Saturday, January 19th, I drove out to Pasadena Civic Auditorium, and I got there late, and the house was
already filling up with people. Some were milling around out

front. I went in the stage entrance and straight to my dressing room.

In the middle of the floor was a folding cot, brand new, opened out.

On top of the cot was a gift bottle of cognac.

There was a brown paper bag which had been torn apart and flattened out to make a piece of writing paper, and written on it were these words:

DEAR ALLAN,

Tonight, as I retire from show business, I pass on to you Bernard Baruch's advice to me when I was starting. Baruch said, "If you want to succeed you must always remember three things. . . ."

I would gladly tell them to you, Allan, but unfortunately I've forgotten all three.

With great affection,
HARPO

I ran into Harpo's dressing room and thanked him for the presents and then I asked him what he had meant in the note about retiring from show business.

Susan said, "This is Harpo's last performance."

My eyes began to fill up.

Harpo said, "We were driving home last night, and I suddenly thought, Gee, we could be home now. What are we doing here? What am I trying to prove?"

I had to go out of the room. I felt this bad thing in my stomach—this hurt.

Later, when I got control of myself, I went in again and asked Harpo if it was all right if I told the audience it was his final performance in show business.

"Sure, if you want to," he said, "but, for heaven's sake, not before I go on. After."

*   *   *

So we went on. First I did my twenty minutes. Steve Allen and Jayne Meadows were in the audience, and I got Steve to come up and play piano for me, and I got Jayne to sing "Sarah Jackman" with me. And then I introduced Harpo, and he did that beautiful funny act, and then he played the harp, and then he shuffled off, after his bows.

And then I walked back on the stage and took the microphone and said:

"Ladies and gentlemen, you have just seen Harpo Marx. Since the world began, there has only been one Harpo Marx, and I don't see how there is ever going to be another. Harpo has been delighting everybody in the world for fifty-six years. And what you have just seen, ladies and gentlemen—these beautiful minutes we have just spent with Harpo—this was the last . . . it was Harpo's final . . ."

By now I was blubbering so badly I couldn't talk. There were three thousand people sitting there in Pasadena Civic Auditorium, and what they were watching was a short, fat man with glasses crying like a baby. And I couldn't get myself together, and I couldn't leave the stage either, so I just stood there and bawled. And that was the show they were watching. I don't know how long I stood there like that.

The audience began to mumble—they didn't quite know what the hell was going on. Whatever it was, it sure wasn't very professional.

And then, from the wings at stage right, Harpo wandered out, and the audience began to applaud, and Harpo waved his hand to stop them. And then he took the microphone from my hand, and for the first time in fifty-six years this lovely little man that so many people had thought was a deaf-mute spoke, on a stage, in his costume. I think he made the decision to speak at that moment, watching me blubber there, because the first word he said—so help me God—his first word was "*Allan* . . ."

"Allan," he said, "you're too emotional."

Well, Jesus Christ, now I *really* fell apart.

But Harpo was an old pro. He knew you don't just stand on a stage like an idiot and cry. He knew you owe the audience something. So now he turned to the audience and he said:

"Now! As I was about to say in 1907 . . ."

They roared. They screamed and yelled and laughed and applauded.

Harpo went on talking, and almost every word got a tremendous laugh as the audience realized with delight how articulate this deaf-mute really was.

Harpo said, "Say, I *like* this talking business. I think I found a whole new career."

They cheered and applauded.

He said a lot of nice things about me, and he told them he was leaving show business, and there were yells of *"No! No!"* and there were many people in the audience weeping, and over in the wings at stage right Steve Allen and Jayne Madows were bawling, and the orchestra was crying, and the chorus, and the beautiful soprano was blubbering, and there was Susan Marx and Bill Marx and the other kids—all of us crying.

Then Harpo said, "Thank you. Thank you—but, you see, I am going on seventy-five years of age, and I want to play golf and relax and travel. But thank you."

And he handed me the microphone and began to amble off the stage, but they wouldn't let him.

The standing ovation lasted six or seven minutes. I never expect to see anything like it again. It wasn't a mob, like the Beatles get, or a politician. This was an outpouring of love from children and Grown-Ups—love gathered over the years for this man who had given them his Gift of Laughter.

Somehow I finished the show. I took a lesson from Harpo, and I remembered that *eleven o'clock always comes,* and I finished the show.

*   *   *

This morning the phone rang and woke me up in my bedroom at the Fairmont Hotel in San Francisco, where I was working. It was Dee.

"Allan?"

"What time is it?"

"Eight-thirty. Did you hear about Harpo?"

"No. What?"

'He died last night, at Mount Sinai Hospital."

So eleven o'clock came for Harpo Marx.

I called Alex Tucker to find out where Harpo's funeral was going to be. He told me there wasn't going to be any funeral, Harpo was going to be cremated.

Beautiful, funny Harpo. I wonder if he wasn't smiling when he planned this, knowing he was cheating Georgie Jessel out of a chance to make a speech. And I knew why Harpo had wanted it this way: because he didn't want to make sadness for the people he loved.

I picked up the manuscript of this book and began going through it, changing the tenses of the verbs wherever I had mentioned Harpo. Every "is" I made into "was." I don't know why I did it. It was just something to do. It was a way of spending a few more minutes with this beautiful, funny man.

And I thought, *Life is fantastic and good and exciting and full of treasures and happiness and sadness and miracles, and I will be sorry as hell when I have to die. Because there isn't a minute of it—even the rottenest parts, even the shame and humiliation, even the loneliness, the physical pain, everything—there isn't a split second of it that hasn't been beautiful and filled with God's wonder and, all around us, angel music—angel music called laughter.*

And I thought about you who are reading this book. I thought about why I wrote it—because I wanted to make contact with you. *Hello out there*. I wanted you to laugh at the things I've laughed at, to feel what I have felt, to hurt with me when I've hurt, to touch everything I've ever touched and kiss every girl I've ever kissed, and hate the things I've hated. And when you've finished reading this book, I wanted you to say, "I feel good. I am a little less alone. I have been with someone else. I have touched another human being—not an Image or a Celebrity, but a real human being who was right sometimes and wrong sometimes and decent sometimes and cheap sometimes. But that doesn't matter because I understand him, and he is, after all, simple—he is another human being, like me."

I wanted to call this book *A Gift of Laughter* because in these last three wonderful and crazy years you have given me the gift of *your* laughter. And it feels good and warm and loving and full of the delightful news that somebody wants me.

But when I thought of calling it *A Gift of Laughter*, I didn't realize that those words were from a famous quotation.

When I mentioned my title to my friend Maurice Zolotow, he said, "That's from *Scaramouche*."

I said, "The hell it is. I made it up myself."

"So did Rafael Sabatini," Maurice said, "in 1927, when he wrote *Scaramouche*."

You can't trust Maurice, so I looked it up. Maurice was right, as he always is.

The full quotation is:

"He was born with the gift of laughter, and a sense that the world is mad."

I don't know why Mr. Sabatini stole my title. All I know is, the world *is* mad. I kind of like it that way.

Index

Index

Abbott, George, 117
Ace, Goodman, 140
Alger, Horatio, 47, 48, 51, 260–261
Alice in Wonderland, 13, 255, 270
Allbritton, Louise, 128
Allen, Gracie, 207–8
Allen, Steve, 110, 209, 210, 238–239, 249, 259, 272, 322; Steve Allen Show, 224–26, 230, 234–36
Allen, Mrs. Steve, *see* Meadows, Jayne
Allison, Fran, 109
American Broadcasting System, 233
Andy Williams Show, 12
Apostolaris, Harry, 251–52
Archambeau, Nita, 235, 238, 266
Arquette, Cliff, 188
Arthur Jacobs Company, 265
Asnas, Max, 277
Astaire, Fred, 48
Aubrey, Jim, 189
Axelrod, George, 115

Backus, Henny, 258
Backus, Jim, 208, 258

"Ballad of Harry Lewis, The," 11, 172–73, 252
Banducci, Enrico, 255
Bannister, Roger, 133
"Barry Is the Baby's Name," 174
Bean, Orson, 128
Becker, Mortimer, 265
Becker, Dr. Oscar, 55–56
Benchley, Robert, 67, 157
Bennett, Linda, 246
Bennett, Tony, 186, 187
Benny, Jack, 5, 207–8, 249, 274
Benson, Hugh, 216–17
Berle, Milton, 12, 116, 207
Berlin, Irving, 11, 252
Bernie, Al, 115
Bevens, Bill, 135
Bidwell's, 64–65, 68, 75, 76, 79
Bikel, Theodore, 11
Bill Gavin's Record Report, 254–55
Borge, Victor, 181, 233
Bower, Roger, 104
Brewer, Teresa, 186, 187
Brown, Joe E., 219
Brown, Oscar, Jr., 22
Buick automobiles, 100–101
Burns, George, 5, 207
Burrows, Abe, 121, 165
Busch, Lou, 211, 212, 256, 266, 284, 311, 312; conductor of

Busch, Lou (*continued*)
  My Son, the Folk Singer,
  10, 11, 245–47; conductor
  for Sherman, 265, 270, 273
Bushkin, Joe, 83
Bushnell Auditorium, Hartford,
  274–75
Burton, Richard, 200, 304
Burtson, Bud, 113–14

Caen, Herb, 253
Camp Wolters, Texas, 71–72
Cantor, Eddie, 5
Capitol Records, 211–12
Carlisle, Kitty, 83
Carnegie Hall, New York, 13,
  271, 275–76
Carroll, Lewis, 13, 255, 270
Carroll, Pat, 11
Carson, Johnny, 110, 286–87,
  304
Castle, Nick, 271
Cavalcade of Stars, 109–10
Cerf, Bennett, 124
Chackes, Alex, 174–75, 280–81
Chackes, Dee *see* Sherman, Dee
  Chackes
Chackes, Shirley, 281
Channing, Carol, 252
Charles, Ray, 186, 187
Clooney, Rosemary, 202
Cole, Nat King, 212
Collins, Jazzbo, 253
Columbia Broadcasting System,
  123, 126, 151, 233; buys
  I've Got a Secret, 127; *Your*

Surprise Package, 189, 194;
  Hollywood offices, 192–93
Como, Perry, 186
Conkling, Jim, 212–13
Connolly, Cyril, 167
Cooper, Frank, 239–40, 283
Cooper, Melville, 128
Copacabana, 121
Copelon, Percy, 18–19, 38–40,
  68–71
Courtney, Del, 253
Crane, Bob, 250
Crow, Frank, 250
Curtis, Tony, 283
Custer, Calvin, 299

Daly, John, 124, 125
Darrow, Clarence, 34
Davis, Sammy, Jr., 252
Delmar, Kenny, 116, 117
Dick-Read, Dr. Grantly, 114
Donahue, Troy, 294–95
Dougherty, Bill, 246
Dumbrowski, Homer, 23
Dumont, Margaret, 58
Dumont Network, 109, 116, 118
Durgom, Bullets, 210–13, 245,
  248, 265; personal manager,
  260–61, 270–71, 273, 275,
  278; in *TV Guide*, 265; in
  Life, 281

Ed Wolf Associates, 184–85
Elman, Mischa, 34
Emerson, Faye, 128, 142, 164

Famous Music Corporation, 85–86
Fast, Howard, 210
Faye, Alice, 58
Feldman, Chester, 150
Fenneman, George, 194
Feuer, Cy, 121
Fiedler, Arthur, 301–2
5100 Club, Chicago, 77–78, 79
Foch, Nina, 128
Frank Cooper Agency, 224, 238, 264

Gable, Clark, 22, 55
Garland, Judy, 272
Garry Moore Show, 276
Gavin, Bill, 254–55
Gehman, Dick, 11, 246, 249
General Artists Corporation, 265
Gershwin, George, 181
Gerstman, Felix, 276
Gibby's, Chicago, 82–83, 87
Gleason, Jackie, 96, 144, 188–189, 211
Glenn, Capt. John, 133
Glickman, Will, 116–17
"Glory, Glory, Harry Lewis," *see* "Ballad of Harry Lewis, The"
Gobel, George, 303
Godfrey, Arthur, 86
Goodson, Mark, 126–27, 134, 140–45, 182, 259, 265, 276
Goodson-Todman Productions, 126–27, 134–52, 162–63, 181–84

Grable, Betty, 58
Graham, Don, 253–54
Grant, Cary, 48, 274–75, 286–287
Greene, Lorne, 296
Greene, Shecky, 210
Griffin, John David, 258

Hackett, Buddy, 116, 117
Hardwicke, Sir Cedric, 210
Heifetz, Jascha, 31, 278
"Hello, Muddah, Hello, Fadduh," 284–86
Hemingway, Ernest, 264
"Here's to the Crabgrass," 177–179
Hibbard, Bob, 224
Hillary, Sir Edmund, 132
Hilliard, Jimmy, 244–45
Hobson, Laura Z., 128
Hoffman, Helen, 95
Hoffman, Ruth, 95
Hollywood Reporter, The, 241, 242
Hope, Bob, 59, 116
Horowitz, Vladimir, 278
"How Are Things with Uncle Morris?" 170
Hyams, Joe, 257

Illini Daily, 66, 69–70, 75
I've Got a Secret, 123–33, 138, 181–82, 185
"I've Got the Customers to Face," 172

Jack Eigen Show, 260
James, Harry, 68
Jessel, George, 5, 323
Jewish Daily Forward, 34
Johnson, President Lyndon B.,
    101, 272, 297–98, 304
"Jump Down, Spin Around, Pick
    a Dress o' Cotton," 11
"Just the *Times*," 276

Kane, Stella, 75
Karloff, Boris, 134
Katz, Ray, 265, 273
Keesely, Nick, 184
Keller, Sheldon, 64, 76–78
Kennedy, President John F., 13,
    136, 282, 296–97
Kim, Ken, 249
Kreisler, Fritz, 34
Kukla, Fran and Ollie, 109–10

Lancaster, Burt, 219
Lawrence, Steve, 304
Lazar, Irving, 82, 83
Leacock, Stephen, 67
Leff, Perry, 238
Lehman, Ernest, 208–9
Leon, Sol, 184
Leonard, Jack E., 96
Le Roy Hospital, 114–15
Lester, Jerry, 109–10
Levy, Lou, 12–13
Lewis, Jerry, 249
Liberace, 203
Lincoln Hotel, 89, 92, 95

Literary Digest, The, 45–46
Livingstone, Mary, 207–8
Loeb, Johnny, 86–87
Loesser, Frank, 120, 121
London, Jack, 265
Lynley, Carol, 281

Maitland, Mike, 244–45, 259
Mansfield, Jayne, 203, 283
Martin, Ernie, 121
Marx, Bill, 317, 322
Marx, Harpo, 11, 28; and Un-
    employment Bureau, 4–9;
    friendship with Allan Sher-
    man, 206–8, 310–11; and
    My Son, the Folk Singer,
    249, 310; character, 308–
    310; final performance,
    312–22; death, 323
Marx, Susan, 311, 319, 320, 322
Marx Brothers, 10, 45, 58, 207;
    movies, 306–7
Meadows, Jayne, 209, 225–26,
    235–39, 272, 322
Menuhin, Yehudi, 34
Mercer, Johnny, 10
Merrill, Howard, 100–101, 104,
    123–26, 128, 203, 310
"Merry Christmas," 86
Migatz, Marshall, 76, 257, 279
Miles, Jackie, 96
Millay, Edna St. Vincent, 97–
    98
Miller, Glenn, 68
Minow, Newton N., 258–59
Monroe, Marilyn, 58

Montalban, Ricardo, 49
Moore, Garry, 128, 134, 141, 168, 182, 259, 284
Morgan, Henry, 139, 168–69, 182
Mumford, Lewis, 145
Music Corporation of America, 120
My Son, the Celebrity, 260
My Son, the Folk Singer, 244– 246; recording of, 4, 10–12, 246–47; popularity of, 12– 13, 247–60; sales, 13, 259; legal difficulties, 261–63
"My Zelda," 261–63

Nash, Ogden, 48–49
National Broadcasting Company, 151, 233
Nelson, Christine, 11–12, 208
New Christy Minstrels, 273
New York *Mirror*, 258
New York Times, The, 255
Newhart, Bob, 248
Newley, Anthony, 253
Norman and Dean, 256

Oakie, Jack, 210
O'Brien, Edmond, 83
"Oddball," 73–74
"Oh, Boy!" 11
O'Hara, John, 257
Old Man and the Sea, The, 264
"Once in Love with Lyndon," 297–98

Ormandy, Eugene, 302
O'Toole, Peter, 252–53
"Overweight," 272–73
Owens, Gary, 259

P. J.'s, Los Angeles, 194–95
Paar, Jack, 110, 257
Parker, Dorothy, 67
Parker, Lew, 87–88, 95
"Party's Over, The," 173–74
Pasternak, Joe, 248
Peter and the Commissar, 144– 145, 298–300
Peterson, Roger, 147
"A Piece of Rye Bread Isn't Very Tasty," 171
Playboy, 151, 197, 255
Plaza Hotel, New York, 294–95
Polonsky, Eddie, 23
Porter, Cole, 252
Prado, Gino, 137
Pulaski, Jack, 82, 85–86, 94, 96

Quinn, Louis, 11, 70–71, 208, 244
Quinn, Mrs. Louis, *see* Nelson Christine

Rash, Bryson, 281
Realist, The, 255–56
Reiner, Carl, 180
Reznick, Sidney, 116–18
Robin, Leo, 10
Robinson, Elsie, 48–49

Robinson, Hubbell, 164
Rodgers, Richard, 10, 85
Rogers, Ginger, 58
Rogers and Cowan, 265
Roosevelt, Eleanor, 83
Roosevelt, Franklin D., 50, 83
"Rosen's Designing for Picardy,"
    175
Rubirosa, Porfirio, 270
Ruby, Harry, 10

Sabatini, Rafael, 324
Salinger, Pierre, 303
Sam Goody's Record Shop, 256
Sands Hotel, Las Vegas, 13
"Sarah Jackman," 245–46; re-
    cording of, 11–12; popu-
    larity, 12–13, 255; and
    President Kennedy, 258
Satenstein, Frank, 143–44
Scaramouche, 324
Schaefer, Sid, 251
Schneider, Romy, 58
Schwartz, Maurice, 26
"Seltzer Boy," 11, 262–63
"Seventy-six Sol Cohens," 157
Shearing, George, 274–75
Sherman, Allan: the gift of
    laughter, 3–4, 324; unem-
    ployment, 4–5, 9; success,
    13–15; on being Jewish,
    20–21, 172, 288–89; love
    of show business, 25, 45,
    76; on the Yiddish theatre,
    25–26

Childhood and Adolescence:
    and Esther Sherman, 23–
    25; and Leon Sherman, 25,
    35; on eating, 30; and par-
    ents' separation, 39–40; on
    childhood, 40; at grammar
    school, 40–41; unhappiness
    at home, 45; first job, 45–
    46; love of music, 46; and
    Horatio Alger, 47; on re-
    ality and fantasy, 47–48,
    52, 241–42; plagiarizes Og-
    den Nash, 47–48; high-
    school activities, 48–50; pa-
    triotism, 50; on sex, 50–51;
    the electric trains, 52–53;
    on fears, 53; and Natalie,
    54–55; and Shmoozie, 56–
    58; and Conchita, 58–59;
    illness, mumps, 58–59; and
    Miss Giggle, 59–61; on re-
    jecting people, 60; and
    Eleanor, 61–62; on ado-
    lescence, 61
College Years: public speak-
    ing, 63–64; Sigma Alpha
    Mu, 65–67; army career,
    71–72; illness, asthma, 72;
    and Dee Chackes, 73–75;
    Keller and Sherman, 76–
    78; expelled from college,
    79–80
Marriage and New York: Chi-
    cago, 1945, 82–83; pub-
    lishes first song, 84–87;
    marries Dee Chackes, 89–
    92; married life, 92–98,

Sherman, Allan (*continued*)
102–7; on the Buick, 100–101; automobile buying, 107–9; on television, 109–110; writer for *Cavalcade of Stars*, 109–10; writer for *Broadway Open House*, 110–11; out of work, 112; first child, 112; writer for *The 54th Street Revue*, 115–16; writer for *Schoolhouse*, 116–17; on overeating, 119–20; audition for *Guys and Dolls*, 120–21; out of work, 122; writer and producer of *I've Got a Secret*, 123–35; and Goodson-Todman Productions, 139–40, 145–50, 152, 158; second child, 152; hobbies, 154–57; psychiatric help, 159–67; on having roots, 168–70; house in Bronxville, 176; on home-owning, 176–79; house in Rye, 183–84; parties, 183–84, 206, 208–10, 281; produces *Masquerade Party*, 184; produces *Perry Presents*, 187; as television doctor, 188

In California, 189; on swingers, 196; parodies, 207–8; producer of *Your Surprise Package*, 209–13; house in Bel Air, 214–15; the Cast of Characters, 215–16, 224; fire and flood, 216–20; out of work, 223; producer of *The Steve Allen Show*, 225–36; on adjustment, 227; illness, muscle spasms, 234–35; out of work, 235–37

My Son, the Folk Singer: writing of, 245; recording, 4, 10–12, 246–47; publicity and promotion, 253–54, 260; on being a celebrity, 260–61, 264–68; legal difficulties, 261–63

Public Appearances and Concerts: at Carnegie Hall, 271, 276; banquets for President Johnson, 272, 297–98; in Hartford, 274–75; in Boston, 275–76; on *Garry Moore Show*, 276; illness, throat trouble, 276–277; in Cleveland, 277–78; in Rochester, 278; in Chicago, 279–80, 288; in Washington, 281–83; on *Steve Allen Show*, 283; on *What's My Line*, 284; on *I've Got a Secret*, 284; at Hollywood Bowl, 286; on *Tonight* show, 286–87; in the Catskills, 288-89; at University of Illinois, 289–92; Macy's Parade, 292–93; at the Copacabana, 293–96; at Madison Square Garden, 298; with Syra-

Sherman, Allan (*continued*)
cuse Symphony, 298–99;
with Baltimore Symphony,
298–99; with Baltimore
Symphony, 298–99; at
Tanglewood, 301–3; per-
formance with Harpo Marx,
313–22; on life and laughter, 323

Songs, *see individual song
titles*

Sherman, Dee Chackes, 15, 142,
157, 174; description, 72–
74; pinned to Allan Sher-
man, 74–76; leaves college,
79–80; marriage, 89–92; in
New York City, 92–98; first
child, 112–14; second child,
152; and dog, 200–201; and
My Son, the Folk Singer,
250–51, 257–58; return to
University of Illinois, 289

Sherman, Edith (aunt), 42–44

Sherman, Esther (grand-
mother), 23–25, 27–29,
41–42, 73, 89–90

Sherman, Jackson B., 15, 199–
200, 284, 305

Sherman, Leon (grandfather),
22, 25, 27–28, 32–35, 42–
43

Sherman, Maury (uncle), 30,
41–44, 72, 91–92, 158,
179–80

Sherman, Nancy (daughter),
174, 200, 283, 284

Sherman, Robbie (son), 114,
115, 154–55, 157–58, 174,
175, 183, 200, 249, 263,
280, 284, 305

Sherman, Rose (mother), 19–
21, 39–40, 44, 46, 68, 71,
77–78, 80, 89, 158

Sherman Family, 16–17; Aunt
Kate, 17–18, 30; Uncle
Dave, 17–18; Cousin Ken-
neth, 17–18; Aunt Annie,
22; Aunt Fannie, 22, 23;
Great-Uncle Leon, 22;
Uncle Shaya, 22; Uncle
Max, 24–25, 31–36; Aunt
Dora, 35; Stepfather Dave
Number Two, 90–92, 318

Sherwood, Don, 253

Shriner, Herb, 188

"Shticks of One and a Half-
Dozen of the Other," 276–
278

Shuman, Nick, 75

Sigma Alpha Mu Fraternity, 65–
67, 74

Silvers, Phil, 181–82

Simms, Ginny, 82–84

Sinatra, Frank, 252, 270

Singer, Allie, 189, 191–93, 197

$64,000 *Question*, 137–38

Slate, Henry, 87–88

Sloane, Everett, 208, 248

Smith, Joe, 244–45, 253, 257

Smith, Judy, 235–36

Smith, Keeley, 281

Snyder, Benn, 299

Sorkin, Dan, 248, 260

Spier, Larry, 85

Stang, Arnold, 219
Stein, Gertrude, 102
Stein, Joe, 116–17
Steinberg, William, 302
Stevens, Stella, 281
Stevenson, Adlai, 173, 272
"Streets of Miami, The," 11
Streger, David, 131–32
Sullivan, Ed, 12, 256
Summers, Bob, 248, 258
Susskind, David, 120, 121
Symphony Hall, Boston, 275

Tabolsky, Marvin, 266, 278
Taylor, Elizabeth, 18, 58
Thomas, Danny, 76–79, 202
Three Stooges, The, 8
Thurber, James, 67, 157
Tillstrom, Burr, 109–10
Time, 255
Tobin, Reggie, 252
Todd, Michael, 17–18
Todman, Bill, 126–27, 140–41
Todman, Howard, 150–51
Tony Weitzel Show, 260
Tucker, Col. Alexander, 267–69, 280, 323
Twain, Mark, 67

Unemployment Clubs, 197–98
United Talent Management, 265
University of Illinois, 63–80, 289–292

Van Doren, Charles, 137–38
Variety, 82, 85, 94, 120
Vern, David, 193–94, 203

Warner, Jack L., 259
Warner Brothers, 10, 35–36, 216, 244–45, 255–56
Warren, Chief Justice Earl, 282
Warren, Harry, 10
Wayne, John, 21
"We Have Often Walked West End Avenue," 171
Weber, Willie, 96
Weinstein, Jerry, 72, 102
"We'll Call Him Barry," 174
Westinghouse Broadcasting Corporation, 225–41
What's My Line, 124–25
"When I Was a Lad, I Went to Yale," 186–87
Wildberg, Joe, 113
Wilk, Max, 115
William Morris Agency, 184, 224, 245
Willson, Meredith, 210
Wilson, Earl, 210
Winston, Jackie, 96
Woolley, Monty, 139

Young, Buddy, 289

Zanuck, Darryl, 113, 122
Zolotow, Maurice, 324

Allan Sherman

Born in Chicago, Illinois, in 1924, Allan Sherman was a writer, producer and director for radio and television before achieving international fame as a songwriter and performer. He has won two *Look* Awards for the television show *I've Got a Secret*, of which he was producer and co-creator; gold records for the phenomenal sales of his first two record albums; and four *Radio and TV Mirror* Awards. Two of his best-known song lyrics, *Hello Muddah, Hello Fadduh* and *I Can't Dance*, have been published as books for children, and his third book, *Instant Status*, is a collection of self-improvement letters. Mr. Sherman lives in Los Angeles, California, with his wife and two children.